The AMERICAN HERITAGE
HERITAGE
History of
*A*ntiques
from the Civil War to World War I

By the Editors of
AMERICAN HERITAGE
The Magazine of History

Author and Editor in Charge
Marshall B. Davidson

Published by
American Heritage Publishing Co., Inc.
American Heritage
Book Division

The AMERICAN HERITAGE
HERITAGE
History of
Antiques
from the Civil War to World War I

American Heritage
Book Division

EDITORIAL DIRECTOR
Richard M. Ketchum

GENERAL EDITOR
Alvin M. Josephy, Jr.

Staff for this Book

EDITOR
Marshall B. Davidson

MANAGING EDITOR
Beverley Hilowitz

ART DIRECTORS
Marcia van Dam
Constance T. Doyle

ASSOCIATE EDITOR
Mary B. Durant

PICTURE EDITOR
Robert Bishop

ASSISTANT EDITOR
Audrey N. Catuzzi

ASSISTANT COPY EDITORS
Helen C. Dunn
Eleanor Pearson

ASSISTANT PICTURE EDITOR
Anne Palmbaum

American Heritage
Publishing Co., Inc.

PRESIDENT
James Parton

CHAIRMAN, EDITORIAL COMMITTEE
Joseph J. Thorndike

EDITOR, AMERICAN HERITAGE MAGAZINE
Oliver Jensen

SENIOR ART DIRECTOR
Irwin Glusker

PUBLISHER, AMERICAN HERITAGE MAGAZINE
Darby Perry

Contents

Preface

In the scant half century between the end of the Civil War and the outbreak of World War I the United States underwent even greater changes than it had during the preceding hundred years. The Civil War had radically altered the very character of the Union itself. With the conclusion of that conflict the territorial unity of the nation was established as a fact that, it seemed certain, would never again be contested. But the government that emerged bore small resemblance to the federal republic of Thomas Jefferson and Andrew Jackson; this was a national government whose sovereign power increased with the passing years. As a further assurance of unity, almost immediately following the peace, railroads reached across the continent to the farthest West, and before the end of the century tracks had been laid over the entire country in a stout and binding web of steel. By then a gigantic industrial machine of rapidly and constantly increasing potential had been reared to appropriate and develop the raw resources that flowed into it from every quarter of the land. The American people prospered—most of them—as no people had ever prospered before. And there were ever more Americans. Quite aside from the natural increase of the population, between the two wars more than twenty million immigrants entered the country from all parts of the earth—from Russia and Sweden, from Japan and China, from France, Germany, and Italy, as well as from the British Isles and a score of other lands. That influx was in itself more than ten times the size of the entire American population at the close of the Revolution.

As in all the long years since the beginnings of settlement, there were among the later immigrants craftsmen who brought with them the traditions of their different homelands and who adapted their skills to the requirements of the American market. Increasingly that meant adaptation to the mechanical processes that in this country more generally than anywhere else were replacing the age-old handicraft methods. Indeed, it began to seem that most Americans had little interest in anything that could not be mass produced.

Whether the machine could ever be expected to serve the cause of good design and sound construction as well as the individual craftsman had done was a question hotly debated over the second half of the last century. Most early manufacturers went to great pains and expense to turn out machine-made goods that resembled in design and ornament traditional handmade products. Looking backward rather than forward for inspiration, they appropriated the styles of the more or less distant past—often indiscriminately and with little care or understanding—to lend prestige to their mechanically contrived articles. The spate of historical revivals that resulted presents a bewildering mixture of forms and motifs of which the labels that were given them—Gothic, Renaissance, Louis XVI, and the rest—provided only a vague explanation.

In revolt against such practices, and against the shoddy performance of which the machine was all too capable, thoughtful designers and theorists looked for more acceptable solutions. They, too, turned to the past for help, not for models to copy but for sound, basic principles to emulate. Such English reformers as

William Morris and Charles Eastlake, and their American followers, found in medieval craftsmanship an ideal of sound construction and straightforward design, lovingly achieved, which they hoped to recapture in terms of their own time and its needs, with or without benefit of the machine. In a way that seems strange to us, their efforts were charged with moral overtones. To those earnest men the "sincerity" and "honesty" with which a piece of furniture was designed and constructed was the test of its merit and the essence of its "style."

There were those who despaired of the machine, and who advocated a return to craft methods, not only to ensure attractive and durable merchandise, but to sustain the integrity of the workman. "No machine yet contrived, or hereafter contrivable," wrote the great English reformer John Ruskin with almost Biblical authority, "will ever equal the fine machinery of the human fingers"—a sentiment that Morris heavily endorsed. Ruskin's works enjoyed wide popularity in this country. As one consequence, in the last two decades of the nineteenth century, following English precedents, more than thirty organizations devoted to the revival of the arts and crafts were established in American towns and cities, from Portland, Maine, to Portland, Oregon, and from Minneapolis to New Orleans.

However, there were others who saw in the machine a deliverance from needless toil, and a source of more abundant material blessings than the world had ever known. With its help, indeed, want might be eliminated as a familiar factor in the human condition. In addition, it was confidently hoped that, properly developed and controlled, the machine could expand the province of art—and could ultimately produce a new, modern art of the people.

Nearing the turn of the century insurgent designers in various lands led a quest for styles that would be completely independent of the past, totally modern in character. Out of this search emerged the luxuriant, passing fashion of Art Nouveau, on the one hand, and, on the other, the more strictly functional designs that led into the mainstream of twentieth-century developments. In either case the results were worlds apart from the artifacts and fabrications of the post-Civil War period. No half century in history produced such a variety of styles and designs, or such a profusion of objects of every description, as appeared in America during the fifty years preceding World War I. With the rapid changes of outlook and ways of living, the interest and merit of much that was made in that period were quickly forgotten or lost sight of—interest and merit that we are only beginning to recall in what has survived from those years and that are presented for consideration in this book.

In 1966 a tariff act was passed that redefined antiques as objects "made prior to 100 years before their date of entry" into this country. (Earlier, only objects made before 1830 were so qualified.) By that legal definition most of the objects illustrated in the following pages are not antiques. However, among those interested—those who collect and study such material—it is common practice to take an increasingly broader view of the matter. It is a view, significantly, that is shared in the market places of the world.   MARSHALL B. DAVIDSON

An Abundance of Styles

The Post-Bellum Years (1865–1876)

Late on a sweltering July night in 1868 two distinguished New Englanders, Charles Francis Adams and John Lothrop Motley, arrived off New York aboard the Cunard Line transatlantic steamer *China.* Adams, grandson of the second President of the United States and son of the sixth, and Motley, a renowned historian, were returning from their long services as ministers of their country to Great Britain and Austria respectively. In the black darkness and in the midst of a tropical shower the two eminent passengers, with their families, clambered down the side of the vessel and stepped precariously into a government revenue cutter that had been sent to take them ashore. Some confusion attended their landing, and after awkward delays they found their way with difficulty to the Brevoort House, a relatively new hotel on lower Fifth Avenue, where they all took shelter for the night before proceeding to their homes. For such important personages it was a distinctly unceremonious arrival.

Both men had been away from their native land throughout the years of the Civil War and its immediate aftermath. Although they were not then fully aware of it, they had returned to a different America from the one they had left to undertake their diplomatic missions. "Had they been Tyrian traders of the year B.C. 1000, landing from a galley fresh from Gibraltar," wrote Henry Adams some years later, "they could hardly have been stranger on the shore of a world so changed from what it had been ten years before." (This younger Adams had served overseas as his father's secretary and was with the party that returned to America that sultry night.)

For one thing, in the course of those years there had been substantial changes in the American political parties and their leaders. So different was the outlook that for the first time in three generations there seemed to be, for the while at least, no opportunity for an Adams in the public service of his country. For three generations the White House itself had been a second home for the Adams family. But politicians, bankers, and businessmen were now in greater demand as leaders of the nation's destiny than statesmen of the Adams breed. The Civil War had accelerated developments that were revolutionizing not only the practical aspects of government but the nature of the American economy and the very structure of American society. As Henry Adams clearly saw in retrospect, those ten years "had given to the great mechanical energies—coal, iron, steam—a distinct superiority in power over the old industrial elements—agriculture, handwork,

Opposite and above: details from The Hatch Family, *painted in 1871 by Eastman Johnson*

9

Grain elevators at Chicago's depot grounds, 1866

The ruins of the Catholic cathedral in Charleston

and learning." To apply those new, growing sources of power profitably on an adequate scale, as he remarked, required a sweeping reorganization of business and industry, great armies of clerks, mechanics, and laborers, and a steady remodeling of social and political habits, ideas, and institutions to suit the changing conditions. In short, he concluded, the postwar generation of Americans would have to create a new world of its own.

More than a score of years before the bombardment of Fort Sumter, in 1861, one perceptive French visitor had predicted that if, as seemed possible even that early, America were to suffer a civil war, the nation would actually gain strength and purpose from such a trial. And so it had happened. Even while it was engaged in the bloodiest war in history, the North exported huge quantities of wheat and other foodstuffs, harvested and processed by modern machinery and hauled to seaports by a growing network of railroads that was constantly binding large sections of the nation ever closer together. During the war years the popular English novelist Anthony Trollope visited the grain elevators at Chicago and commented on the incessant "rivers of wheat and rivers of maize," which he saw there, pouring into the huge bins in almost suffocating abundance. "And then I believed, understood, and brought it home to myself as a fact," he concluded, "that here in the corn lands of Michigan, and amidst the bluffs of Wisconsin, and on the high table plains of Minnesota, and the prairies of Illinois, had God prepared the food for the increasing millions of the Eastern world, as also for the coming millions of the Western."

Even while it supplied the needs of a war machine of unprecedented size, the industry of the North was able to supply manufactured products in mounting quantities for its civilian population as well as for export. "Nothing struck me more," Trollope recounted, "than their persistence in the ordinary pursuits of life in spite of the war which was around them. Neither industry nor amusement seemed to meet with any check." In the midst of the conflict scores of thousands of sewing machines were shipped abroad; sugar mills and steam engines were supplied to Mexican industries by California foundries; boots, shoes, clothing, locomotives, and steamships were made for export to various parts of the world. Under the circumstances, it was a display of material resourcefulness unparalleled in the history of the world.

At the close of hostilities, in 1865, the titanic vitality and enterprise that had been generated during the war was entirely diverted to peacetime channels. (Both armies were demobilized almost instantaneously.) The nation's industry surged forward to further accomplishments, such accomplishments as were undreamed of in ante-bellum years. One chronicler of the times observed that to recall what had been achieved before the war in contrast to developments that immediately followed was like reviewing "ancient history." All industrial records were shattered during those postwar years. Never before had there been such a profusion of consumer goods, so much construction, so many different kinds of manufactories established to produce such a variety of products. Most significant in terms of future developments was undoubtedly the introduction of the Bessemer process for the manufacture of steel. In 1864 steel was a rare and costly material in America, largely restricted in its use to cutlery, hand tools, and other small objects. Over the next score of years it became a basic commodity that was used on a colossal scale to undergird the national economy.

The first reporters who visited the defeated South saw there a different prospect, a grim spectacle of prostration. Richmond, Charleston, Atlanta, New Orleans, and other proud communities were deeply scarred with the blackened ruins, crumbling remnants of walls, and other signs of devastation that only war can bring. Yet, in spite of that desolation and the searing trials of the Reconstruction period, the South was restored with phenomenal speed. "As ruin was never before so overwhelming," wrote one prominent southerner, "never was restoration swifter. The soldier stepped from the trenches into the furrow; horses that had charged Federal guns marched before the plow, and fields that ran red with human blood in April, were green with the harvest in June." Some aspects of the southern economy did not recover for generations, to be sure. But less than fifteen years after hostilities ceased, the cotton crop was larger than it ever had been. By that time also, the tobacco crop of the Upper South had gained an important role in the region's economy. Through skillful advertising such fragrant blends as Bull Durham and Duke's Mixture became known throughout the world. James Russell Lowell introduced Alfred, Lord Tennyson to Bull Durham, a smoke also enjoyed by Thomas Carlyle.

During those years immediately following Appomattox, the nation became truly aware for the first time of the vast, unexploited, and largely unexplored resources of the continent at large. It was in a sense a rediscovery of America. A small army of reporters toured the farther West and were awed by their first sight of the nation's enormous natural heritage. Almost to a man they returned, as one of them wrote, "with fuller measure of the American Republic and larger faith in its destiny." To the reunited nation all things seemed possible. In 1869, in relatively short order and just twenty-one years after *The New York Herald* had pronounced such a project "ridiculous and absurd," the transcontinental railroad was completed. (Eighteen miles of track was laid in the final twenty-four hours alone.) To Robert Louis Stevenson this was the "one typical achievement of the age"; in romance, heroism, and colorful contrasts, this actual performance, he believed, surpassed anything described in the storied legend of ancient Troy. *The Nation* reported that the newly completed railroad provided not only a guarantee of national unity but, as well, an expressway toward the Orient. The exultant claim, often repeated in the literature of the day, that the wealth of the Indies was now at last close to hand, sounded strangely like the triumphant boasts of navigators in the age of exploration three centuries earlier.

Untold and untouched riches were spread across the continent itself, and in the 1860's and 1870's the nation mounted a gigantic treasure hunt to find and unearth whatever the land would yield. During the 1860's more than eight million acres of new land were brought under cultivation in Illinois alone, and great trains of mass-produced agricultural machinery were pushing inexorably farther westward across the prairies. During the Civil War, Lincoln had referred to the fertile basin of the Mississippi as "the Egypt of the West." As the century waned, the grain and meat that were grown and harvested in that inland empire drastically modified the economy not only of America but of a large part of Europe. The immense quantities of American produce that were shipped abroad in fact upset the habits of Europe as radically as the exportation of American gold and silver had done during the days of the conquistadors. But instead of precious metals funneled through the royal courts, it was now American bread, cheese, pork, and corned beef that found its way directly to the tables of the European workman and artisan.

Those harvests were merely from the surface of the land. Beyond reach of the plow, the threshing machine, and the cattleman's roundup, buried in the hills

A poster for the Union Pacific Railroad

11

Above: threshing grain with steam power

Below: steamers to the mining districts

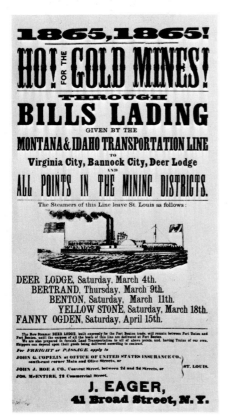

and mountains from Pennsylvania to California, an incalculable wealth of minerals lay waiting to be tapped—a large share of the world's coal, seas of oil, some of the greatest deposits of iron ore on the earth's crust, silver, copper, and lead, all in quantities beyond dreams of avarice. And during the decades following the war, large-scale, consolidated assaults were made upon those hidden holdings of nature. It was in the late 1860's that the famous Comstock Lode at Virginia City, Nevada, one of the richest veins of silver on the globe, started to yield its great bounty. Organized capital on a very large scale and prodigious engineering talent were required to exploit this deep, apparently inexhaustible Golconda. Over the years it paid off handsomely to stockholders across the land, a point made ostentatiously clear by a superintendent of one of the mines, who filled his water tank with champagne to satisfy the thirst of his guests at a wedding. Other rich strikes of silver and gold scattered about the mountains of the West kept that large area in a ferment for years to come.

Few people had heard of petroleum before the war. Until its more practical properties were determined, the oil was principally known as a natural remedy, good for various types of aches and pains. (Through its instrumentality, one advertisement maintained, the lame were made to walk and the blind to see.) Five years after the war the precious oil was being pumped from the earth at the rate of five million barrels a year and in the form of various derivatives, such as kerosene and gasoline, it was quickly put to an increasing number of domestic and industrial uses. The early history of the Pennsylvania oil fields typifies the development of those large extractive operations—a first lucky "strike," then a frenzied scramble for quick wealth by speculators of every stripe, the intensive plundering of likely fields, and, finally, the emergence of a relatively few powerful and heavily financed controlling interests which soon dominated the industry. As an enduring example of that last phase, the Standard Oil Company (of Ohio) was formed in 1870 with a capital of one million dollars and a position of massive strength in the mushrooming industry.

It was one sidelight on this booming prosperity, with its unbridled speculations, its attendant corruption, and its extravagant display of new wealth, that Mark Twain and Charles Dudley Warner referred to those years as the "gilded age" in their novel of that name published in 1873. The boom burst that same year and the nation was temporarily reduced to financial panic and general depression. But even before that collapse, and after the nation had recovered from it, all was not gilt by any means. Paupers seemed to multiply as rapidly as millionaires. Many of the "new poor" were immigrants who surged across the Atlantic to help man the American industrial machine; immigrants who all too often got trapped in the growing slums of cities and for whom the railroad was not the highroad to the open West but a social barrier that hemmed them in on the wrong side of the tracks. Ironically, in the year that ushered in the panic, almost a half million newcomers, more than in any previous year, arrived to look for their fortune in the New World.

Nevertheless, the per capita wealth of the North, at least, had doubled over the decade ending in 1870, and save for the depression years it continued to mount. There was no visible limit to the output of American industry and agriculture and no apparent saturation point of consumer demands, constantly stimulated as those were by increasingly ingenious advertising. In 1875 *The Nation* decried the "almost diabolical cast" recent advertisements had taken, leading to a distortion of values. One pioneering promoter had even installed an illuminated sign on the roof of a building on Broadway in New York. Elsewhere, legislation was passed to discourage the practice of disfiguring mountainsides and boulders with announcements of "certain pertinacious bitters and rare ointments."

The ancient belief that the want of material goods was a natural condition of life for substantial numbers of the population was apparently now reduced to a quaint superstition. Almost anything that could be made would find a market. In the last year of the war, it was reported, "furniture dealers saw their customers selecting Tables and Chairs, Book Cases, Bedsteads and Sofas, not because of their intrinsic beauty, but because they cost round sums. High prices were an inducement and prices were much higher than ever before." Even the poverty that marred the social scene might have its eventual rewards for, as Andrew Carnegie later pointed out, it provided a stern but efficient school from which many millionaires were "graduated" early in their careers, as he had been.

The clutter of furnishings of all sorts that we tend to associate with the Victorian domestic scene was in part a consequence of the rising productivity and spreading affluence of the period. In addition, articles fabricated or ornamented by machinery could be less expensively produced than handmade objects. Even before the Civil War, the machine had in good measure replaced the craftsman who had provided for the wants of people, rich and poor alike, for time out of mind. But now as never before it became economically feasible for families of ordinary means to cram their homes with goods turned out in abundance and at relatively low prices by factories across the land. For many such families furnishing a home on the scale now made possible involved problems that they had not been prepared to meet by their earlier experience. As Edwin Lawrence Godkin, founder and editor of *The Nation*, wrote in 1866, plenty of Americans knew how to get money, but not many knew what best to do with it. In any event, a spate of books, magazine articles, and newspaper reports issued from the presses to guide the homemaker in matters of taste and economy in architecture, furnishing, and interior decoration. One prominent author observed that the problem was not made easier by the fact that America was "the only land known

A caricature of the rush for petroleum

to geographers where the greater part of the population lives to please its neighbors, and to earn their approval by coming up to their social standard"; "keeping up with the Joneses," or trying to surpass them, all too often led to unfortunate domestic consequences, as William Dean Howells told in his novel *A Hazard of New Fortunes.*

Years earlier Alexis de Tocqueville, a very keen French reporter of our then infant democracy, had remarked that the American's persistent faith in progress and improvement kept the country in a state of impatience with the achievements of the present. He asked an American sailor why his ship was built to last so short a time and was told that the arts of shipbuilding and navigation were making such rapid daily progress that the finest vessel he could build would be obsolete in a few years. "In these words," wrote Tocqueville, "which fell accidentally, and on a particular subject, from an uninstructed man, I recognize the general and systematic idea upon which a great people direct all their concerns." But built-in obsolescence might be a concession to endlessly changing whims and fashions as well as a tribute to improving technology. As one critic of the 1870's protested, too many modish people of those years shied from soundly made and expensive furniture because they had no wish to spend money on things that would "last a life-time!" Once upon a time furniture was commonly expected to serve successive generations, but that was no longer necessarily so. "What is life," rhetorically asked one lady of the times, "without new furniture?"

The new furniture of the postwar years, like that of the 1850's, represented not so much a style as a medley of different styles; styles that paraded under an assortment of names confusing even to those who bestowed them. "It would be extremely difficult, and in some cases impossible," reported one responsible contemporary periodical, "to give a name to the principles and precedents of art recognized by most of the American manufacturers." Indeed, so much had lately been written about styles and designs of furniture with so many disparate opinions, concluded one author in 1877, that the whole subject was in a state of "hopeless confusion." The relative ease with which new machinery could manipulate materials encouraged manufacturers to simulate by mechanical means the designs and decorations that earlier had been so laboriously worked out by handcraftsmen. This led to revivals of historical styles, or rather to free adaptations and combinations of the forms and ornaments of earlier days. As the same periodical quoted above pointed out, "the vast accumulation of historical precedents, and the convenient publication of them in books, prints, and photographs, so that they are accessible to every student," had created a spirit of eclecticism peculiar to the age. With an interesting allusion to Charles Darwin's *The Origin of Species,* published in 1859, the author observed "the law of the 'survival of the fittest' has placed at the disposition of the designer all the best works of past ages."

That analogy to the "great natural law" Darwin had so recently expounded was hardly sound, but it carried conviction at the time and helped to rationalize the current pillage of the past and of distant, exotic places, in whatever shape the evidence remained, for inspiration and for models. More than one critic of the times lamented the wholesale revivalism that was being practiced. "The things we see for sale in the shops," wrote Clarence Cook, one of the sternest of those critics, "are all either good or bad or indifferent copies of old-fashioned things, or of Oriental things of today. Hardly anything with the stamp of our own time and country is to be had." As another contemporary author tried to explain to her public, among the designs that were to be considered before a home could be

Design for a hall stand made by Frank Rhoner and Company of New York City

properly and fashionably furnished were those in the Gothic, Renaissance, Elizabethan, Jacobean, Louis XVI, Pompeian, Moorish, Eastlake, Queen Anne, Oriental, and modern styles. Often enough the terms were interchangeable, according to the fancy or ignorance of the supplier. "Renaissance," ventured one
reporter, was "a style sufficiently comprehensive to cover much variety in design
and treatment." It was elastic enough, wrote another authority, to apply also to
the revival of Elizabethan designs, as well as to those related to the period of
Louis XIV and Louis XV "and others." However, neither the American cabinetmakers nor their customers, he confessed, could really distinguish the separate
French styles from one another.

Looking back, we can see that Clarence Cook was not altogether accurate in
his pronouncement. However much or little the furniture of the 1860's and
1870's owed to the period styles of the past, these were interpreted and modified
in a manner that often clearly bore the stamp of its own time and of its own country. The mixtures of motifs and elements and their translation into "modern"
concepts created period styles in their own right. "The world has seen so many
mutations of style of furniture," one American architect concluded, "that it is
almost impossible to construct a new character without combining a number of
those in use before"; a character, he might have added, that was shared to a degree by contemporary architecture. It was in such a spirit that Samuel Colt, between 1855 and 1862, built Armsmear—a "long, grand, impressive, contradicting,
beautiful, strange thing...," according to *The Art Journal*. It was somewhat like
an Italian villa ("yet not carrying out any decided principles of architecture"),
but with Turkish domes and pinnacles, among other Oriental features, and yet,
with its substantial homelike and comfortable aspects, English in feeling. It was,
in short, a "characteristic type of the unique."

But no period in history is ever uniform in its appearance. The past lingers,
and dies slowly; the future is born in the present. Some of those styles that were
popular in the 1860's and 1870's had made their debuts in the decades before
the war; some of these and others remained in fashion throughout the rest of
the nineteenth century, undergoing gradual changes of spirit as the years passed
and competing with still other styles that were subsequently introduced; competing also with stylish European imports, largely from England and France
and, at times, from the Orient. An American visitor to the Paris Universal Exposition of 1867 came upon one display of French furniture of "extra-sublime"
quality that had been made specially for the American market. The exhibitor
explained that he could hardly produce goods splendid enough for the Americans,
who would pay any price for what they wanted. "As wealth and European travel
have increased," it was reported in 1876, "a taste for the skilled handiwork of
foreign craftsmen has been rapidly developed among our [American] people,
and the desire to become the possessors of elegant objects to make home attractive has amounted almost to a passion." Even moderately rich Americans, the
account added, were looking abroad for furnishings to accomplish this end. In his
novel *The American* Henry James dramatized the sorry plight of the wealthy
American who fled to Europe to acquire the culture he felt could not be found
in the raw, commercial atmosphere of post-bellum United States. On the other
hand, to the delight of a large audience, Mark Twain pointed out in *The Innocents
Abroad* that much of European culture was pretense and fraud and alien to solid
American virtues that might better be cultivated and appreciated.

James himself, with similar doubts about the trend of America's industrial

Above: advertisement for an armchair

Below: a drawing for a center table

15

Armsmear, Samuel Colt's house in Hartford

civilization, quit his native land to live abroad as an expatriate. There were others with more sanguine views about the future prospects of the nation. If European art was an index of cultural refinement, as some maintained, it was a simple matter to come abreast of the older nations. "What is fine in the buildings of the old countries," observed the editor of *Harper's Magazine* in 1859, "we can borrow; their statues and their pictures we will be able in good time to buy." It was a prophetic statement. Not many years later, Richard Morris Hunt, enriched by his years of study and travel in France, particularly, and the Near East, began the series of Gothic and Renaissance "palaces" he designed for the Vanderbilts and others of his wealthiest American clients. (As a young student in Paris, Hunt had helped to design one of the pavilions of the Louvre.) According to one French visitor, those elaborate structures, recalling the châteaux of the Loire Valley and other contemporary French monuments, were not "weak imitations, pretentious and futile attempts, such as in every country bring ridicule upon braggarts and upstarts. No. In detail and finish they reveal conscientious study, technical care. Evidently the best artist has been chosen and he has had both freedom and money." And he added with emphasis, "Especially money!"

Even before Hunt undertook those resplendent show places, money in growing abundance had started to siphon art treasures, not only from Europe but from around the world, into the Metropolitan Museum of Art in New York and Boston's Museum of Fine Arts, both established in 1870, just as *Harper's* had predicted it would happen. In 1873 George Templeton Strong, after a visit to the Metropolitan Museum, reported in his diary: "Art treasures (so-called) are evidently accumulating in New York, being picked up in Europe by our millionaires and brought home. This collection promises very well, indeed. Twenty years hence it will probably have grown into a really instructive museum."

The affluent American society continued to attract to its midst trained craftsmen from abroad, who brought with them an understanding of the fashions prevailing overseas and who adapted their skills, where necessary, to the special demands of American patrons. From the beginnings of our history many of the most talented and eminent artisans to practice here were, quite naturally, immigrants who sought fresh opportunities for development in the New World, and whose workmanship presented a wholesome challenge to native-born craftsmen. As Benjamin Franklin had remarked in the colonial period, if he had any useful art, the newcomer to America was always welcome. In the 1870's a French correspondent advised his countrymen that Americans were, as well, continually borrowing the methods and skilled processes of European craftsmen and were producing furniture, metalwork, and other forms of applied art that had "the veritable stamp of solidity and good taste." A few years later, the French were further advised by another of their observers that the Americans had their own techniques that saved time and labor. Their workshops were equipped with elevators that moved materials quickly and easily from floor to floor. And, he added, "Everything, or nearly everything, is done by steam, even the carving." In any event, these shops produced merchandise that was cutting heavily into the French markets in South America as well as the United States. "We know of one instance," reported the editors of *The Decorator and Furnisher*, where a New York manufacturer sent a shipment of his wares "*even* to Paris," the capital of high style and fine craftsmanship. To meet the contingencies of the market some firms had workshops and outlets both in France and America. One such, L. Marcotte & Company, of New York and of Paris, displayed an elaborate, American-made, ebony cabinet at the Paris Universal Exposition of 1878; a piece which, according to an illustrated catalogue of the exhibition, competed favorably with the work of the "long-established ebenistes of Paris" and which richly merited "the admiration it excited and the honour [a gold medal] it received." Although such impressive pieces amply demonstrated the virtuosity of our native—or immigrant—craftsmen, they remained far beyond the reach of the average American household. They were made to order for wealthy customers or for a special occasion, such as a trade fair. A sideboard of comparable pretension by another New York firm, shown at the Centennial International Exhibition at Philadelphia in 1876, was priced at eight thousand dollars. That was more than was required at the time to build a comfortable country house.

The Centennial Exhibition, celebrating the one-hundredth anniversary of the Declaration of Independence, was the largest of the world fairs yet to be held. According to those who planned the exhibition, it was a tribute to "the unparalled advancement in science and art, and all the various appliances of human ingenuity for the refinement and comfort of man" in the century that had passed since the birth of the American republic. Although the disturbances caused by the financial panic of 1873 had not altogether subsided, and although the political corruption of the times belied every principle to which the nation had been pledged at its birth, America found reason to admire itself in the centennial mirror. What other people could reflect such astonishing progress in the material benefits of life? James Russell Lowell observed with cutting sarcasm that neither could any other people match the examples of malpractice provided by Boss Tweed, the Grant administration, and Jay Cooke. But interest centered in other things. It was time to stress the positive and worthy accomplishments of the nation and to measure them against the progress of other countries. America was in a mood for self-congratulation and edification. And, as ever, America was also looking ahead. Optimism and progress were the watchwords of the day. The nation foresaw a future which would outshine even its glorious past, as orators and poets assured the opening-day crowds.

Engraving of cabinet by L. Marcotte & Co.

An Epidemic of Splendor

In 1863 a report to the Cincinnati Chamber of Commerce claimed that "the whole people in the Loyal States" were rich above their expectations; "they feel it, and are extravagant beyond precedence." According to *Harper's New Monthly Magazine*, everyone seemed to be speculating in stocks that year, including ladies who pledged their diamonds as margin and clergymen who staked their salaries with a hope of quick gains. Men with business sagacity and men who were rightly placed amassed fortunes. By the end of the Civil War the leading capitalists of the country had acquired new and lofty perspectives. Men who once talked of thousands now talked confidently of millions of dollars. And among the wealthy, again according to *Harper's*, the passion for building large, showy houses was reaching far beyond the bounds of prudence. "There is," pronounced another contemporary periodical, "an epidemic of splendour" in the land, an epidemic that was spreading to the farthest West.

In 1865, when *Harper's* made that observation, LeGrand Lockwood of Norwalk, Connecticut, a successful Wall Street broker and railroad magnate, was constructing what was to be one of the most elaborate and costly mansions in America at the time. Lockwood spared no pains or expense in completing this structure. Egyptian porphyry and Florentine marble carved to his order in Italy were imported to embellish the interiors. The best of exotic and native woods—dark oak, black walnut, brazilwood, rosewood, satinwood, boxwood, ebony, and cedar of Lebanon—all carved, gilded, and inlaid (1,a, b), were used for the architectural trim and for the furniture. Murals (1), wood sculptures, and marble statues added to the princely setting of the other furnishings. With its fourteen bathrooms, two billiard rooms, bowling alley, theatre, library, art gallery, and other accommodations, it was equipped "with every convenience that ingenuity can suggest or the most generous expenditure procure."

1, a, b. Details of the inlaid, carved, gilded, and painted decorations of LeGrand Lockwood's mansion

2,a, b. Elaborate cabinet made of various woods with carved, inlaid, gilded, and painted details and gilt-bronze mounts

Lockwood's great mansion was designed by Detlef Lienau, a German immigrant who had studied architecture in Paris. The interior woodwork and at least some of the original furnishings have been attributed to the firm of Léon Marcotte, a friend and former business associate of Lienau's, who had also been trained in Paris—that same Marcotte whose American-made products won an award when they were shown in Paris. Such men were representative of a sizable number of naturalized foreign craftsmen whose skills both served and excited the demand for luxurious furnishings in America. The cabinet illustrated here (2), with its carved and gilded ornament, its ormolu (gilt-bronze) mounts (2b), and its complicated inlays (2a), shows the influence of the massive styles in furniture, recalling earlier days of France's grandeur, that were fashionable during the Second Empire in France and that were quickly translated into their American equivalents.

During the colonial period and for some years thereafter American silversmiths had to rely upon imported precious metals to practice their craft; metals that often came in the form of miscellaneous foreign coins gathered in the course of trade throughout the Atlantic world. With the discovery of gold in California and the subsequent rich strikes of silver and gold in Nevada, Montana, and other western areas, the nation became almost overnight a leading producer of both metals. In 1873 more than thirty-five million dollars worth of silver alone was mined in this country. There was almost no limit to the amount of that metal available for commercial purposes.

It was in 1873 that Henry Jewett Furber, a New Englander who had amassed a fortune in New York and the Midwest, commissioned The Gorham Company to design and produce for him a princely silver service—with gold decoration, and enough elements to serve a Lucullan, fifteen-course banquet for twenty-four persons. The candelabras (3) were three feet tall and, like the other ceremonial and decorative elements of the service, extravagantly and expertly wrought.

3. A massive candelabrum from the Furber service with chased, engraved, cast, and repoussé *ornamentation*

4. *Intricately wrought punch bowl owned by Furber*

5. *Detail of a fruit dish from the Furber dinner service*

6. OVERLEAF: *Mrs. Astor (seated on the sofa) with her family in the ballroom of their Fifth Avenue mansion*

23

In the decades following the Civil War Mrs. William Astor came to reign as the uncrowned queen of American society. According to legend, the ballroom of her palatial Fifth Avenue home (shown on the preceding two pages) comfortably held only four hundred persons, thus setting the numerical limits to what Samuel Ward McAllister, accepted by the "right" people as an arbiter in such matters, decreed might properly be considered "society." The resplendent jewelry Mrs. Astor wore with formal dress was in itself almost legendary, for it was rarely seen by the general public. However, as *The New York Times* solemnly assured its readers, she did in fact always wear diamonds "with the most effective prodigality." The diamond necklaces and sunbursts worn by other ladies with substantial capital, it was later recalled, were the chief subject of interest at the costly dinners given by the acquisitive cabinet officers of the Grant administration. It was in that period, about 1873, that the brilliant architect and elegant gentleman Bruce Price designed a cabinet (8) to house the jewels his mother-in-law purchased for his wife when they were all on a grand tour in Europe—a cabinet of highly eclectic design.

7. Opposite: a gold brooch and earrings, made in America—possibly in New York—about 1860

8. Right: cabinet designed by Bruce Price to contain the European jewelry owned by his wife

27

9. *Top: this pagodalike bird cage is fancifully ornamented with rococo flourishes and with scrollwork.*

10. *Above: classical motifs, such as egg-and-dart molding and the architectural design of the headboard, were used on a child's crib made of walnut.*

28

A Medley of Borrowed Styles

Although the nation had entered a brash, lavish post-bellum era of prosperity and industrial triumph, innovations in furniture design—as in all the arts—were limited. Newly rich Americans, like their counterparts in Europe, clung to middle-class conventions. Ultraconservative and imitative in their tastes, they preferred stock patterns in their furnishings—the symbols of establishment. The borrowing of past styles and motifs and the mingling of these time-honored ingredients into the eclectic designs of the day was the epitome of artistic conservatism. One critic, Harriet Prescott Spofford, was moved to remark in *Art Decoration Applied to Furniture*, published in 1878: "The nineteenth century is, without doubt, a great one in many ways, . . . and it is not a little singular that in the more personal service of architecture and the kindred art of furniture design it should do nothing but revive that which has been done before." This historical revival, fostered by a naïve and romantic concept of the past, had begun in the 1840's and would reach its zenith during the years directly following the Civil War.

11. An armchair carved in the extravagant naturalistic motifs of the Rococo Revival, with animal heads on the arms, a recurrent pattern dating from pre-Christian furniture

12. Above: walnut side chair, one of a set of six, patterned in the balloon-back form that is popularly associated with furniture forms of the Victorian era

13. Top: "Parlor Suit," from Harper's Weekly, *1876*

14. Opposite: étagère, *or aggrandized "whatnot"*

Parlor furniture was widely produced *en suite* from the 1850's on. One favorite design, which endured for close to thirty years, is pictured here (13)—the medallion-back settee with its complement of matching chairs. The side chair (12) with the splat of paired scrolls is a variation of the standard pattern. These curvilinear forms with cabriole legs are a substyle of the rococo designs of Louis XV's reign, revived in France in the 1830's during Louis Philippe's rule as a nostalgic royal rebuttal to the Empire furniture of Napoleon's regime. The pieces shown here represent, in effect, the bare bones of rococo forms stripped of profligate carvings and decorations. In *Homestead Architecture*, 1861, Samuel Sloan described a comparable parlor set: "This style of heavy mouldings (with just sufficient carved ornament to relieve the joints of the sections) is now very fashionable for persons not wishing very expensive furniture."

The *étagère* was the Victorian version of the open arrangement of shelves designed to display bric-a-brac and treasured trifles. This architectural elaboration (14), complete with mirrored panels and over seven feet tall, is a thoroughgoing compendium of eclecticism with its Gothic and rococo elements, for example, in the framework, and such classical motifs as the patera over the center mirror and the urn-shaped bracket below.

In 1841, apropos of the medieval motifs of the Gothic Revival that had lately been introduced from Europe, one prominent American tastemaker commented: "our people are foolishly frightened at a few crockets & finials." Americans, however, took to the Gothic Revival with a zest that lasted most of the century. Cusps, crockets, trefoils, pointed arches and windows, and the gingerbread trim of "carpenter Gothic" appeared on houses from Maine to California. As for furniture, Mrs. Spofford pronounced Gothic the most picturesque of all. "Its religious meaning," she concluded, "does not unfit it for the uses and companionship of home." This lamp (15), made in 1875, has Gothic arches on the font and trefoils on the globe. The chair (18) and the table (16) were designed in the medieval manner by the architect Alexander Jackson Davis, around 1865, for Lyndhurst (17). Davis, a devotee of the Gothic Revival, originally designed this country seat for General William Paulding in 1838. The mansion was enlarged between 1864 and 1867 for its new owner, George Merritt, when Davis created a baronial castle with the addition of a tower and a dining wing.

15. Top: a bronze lamp with a frosted-glass globe

16. Above: octagonal table designed for Lyndhurst

17. *Above: a drawing and plan for Lyndhurst, near Tarrytown, N.Y.*

18. *Below: armchair, part of a dining-room set made for Lyndhurst*

33

34

The Louis XVI style, both in the original and in the Victorian revival, substituted straight lines for the curved, rococo forms of Louis XV furniture, smoother surfaces for elaborate carvings, and classical motifs for naturalistic vines, flowers, and fruits. Here, an ebonized cabinet (21) reproduces the simplified lines, ormolu trim, and medallion with a mythological scene which typified the fastidious elegance of Louis XVI furniture. The little, straight-legged gilt chair (20), finished with a fleur-de-lis at the juncture between the seat and the back legs, is also typically Louis XVI in feeling. The random eclectic mixture of motifs, so indicative of the nineteenth century, is evidenced on the armchair (19). Its sturdy form, incised carving, and walnut paneling are representative of the so-called Renaissance Revival, but it also bears such classical touches as gilt paterae, a neo-Greek medallion on the crest, and the curule, or "Grecian Cross," legs. The silver kettle (22), by Ball, Black, and Co., of New York City, further combines Renaissance ornamentation with feet, for example, in the Greek key form.

19. *Opposite, below: an armchair, 1860–70*

20. *Opposite, above: side chair believed to be part of the original furniture used in the Lockwood mansion, illustrated on page 19*

21. *Left: cabinet attributed to Léon Marcotte*

22. *Above: silver hot-water kettle, about 1870*

The profusion of marquetry on furniture of French inspiration during the eighteenth century was revived in the nineteenth century. Flowers, stars, and a panel of anthemia are inlaid on the top of this table (23) made in the Louis XV manner. The mahogany settee (24) and its matching chairs (25, 26)—all in the Louis XVI pattern—are inlaid with butterfly medallions and with mother-of-pearl stars set into bands of amboina, a curly-grained wood from southeastern Asia. Louis XVI furniture was approved by Mrs. Spofford as "far more refined" than previous French styles, although she added, rather tersely, that it was "well suited to the frivolities of the life too frequently led nowadays by the extraordinarily wealthy." But such furniture, after all, had first been designed for Marie Antoinette's luxurious and frivolous tastes. The Louis XVI Revival was sparked by Empress Eugénie, Napoleon III's consort. Eugénie set the fashions of the day, not only with her hoop skirts and millinery and her auburn hair (which provoked a flurry of bleaching and dyeing among women everywhere), but in furniture as well, when she restored the royal apartments in the rich, neoclassic style that Marie Antoinette had so extravagantly admired.

23. *Opposite, above: table with inlaid top*

24. *Opposite, below: a settee, Louis XVI style*

25. *Right: a side chair matching this settee*

26. *Above: view of the James L. Morgan house, Brooklyn, N.Y., showing the table illustrated opposite and an armchair that also matches the settee and the side chair*

"Rich carving in the solid . . . ," wrote Mrs. Spofford, "always remains a fit manner of decoration when its model is satisfactory." Mrs. Spofford's concept of satisfactory models would certainly have included the examples shown here. A neoclassic medallion, surmounted with beribboned boughs, decorates the cresting of this settee (27), part of a set of furniture purchased by Jay Gould for Lyndhurst, when he became owner of that Hudson River mansion. The Egyptian masks that top the claw-foot legs of the same settee not only illustrate the persistence of unabashed eclecticism but also typify a continuing interest in Egyptian designs. (The Egyptian Revival, particularly in architecture, had been in vogue earlier in the century.) The ornamentation on the walnut cabinet (28) is pure Renaissance Revival: the incised carving, the pattern of the corner pillars, and the youthful head encircled with a wreath of fruits and vines—a device similar to the Della Robbia ceramic medallions made in Florence some four hundred years earlier.

27a, b. *Opposite: two details from settee (center)*

27. *Left: settee with Greek and Egyptian motifs*

28. *Above: walnut cabinet in Renaissance style*

29. *Two views of a walnut side chair bearing the trademark: "Hunzinger N.Y.* PAT *March 30 1869"*

In the midst of the eclectic revival of traditional forms, there were, of course, quests for innovation. Folding and convertible furniture, for example, fired the imagination of designers and manufacturers. George Hunzinger, who first appeared in New York directories during the 1860's, produced a wide variety of such innovative furniture and advertised himself as the "Manufacturer of Fancy Chairs, Folding and Reclining Chairs, and Ornamental Furniture." His prices varied from seventy-two dollars for a carved walnut and gilt reclining chair upholstered in satin, with a silk fringe in front, to the modest sum of eight dollars for a maple or walnut rocker, with "braided wire seat and back." The two chairs shown on these pages, though not folding chairs per se, reflect the general feeling of lightness, movability, and collapsibility that typified Hunzinger's wares, particularly in the long, delicate line of the leg brace on the chair shown opposite. If an eclectic label were to be pinned on these samples of Hunzinger's work, they could generally be termed Renaissance. The acorn motifs (31) were particularly popular during the Victorian Renaissance Revival.

30. *Above: Hunzinger chair advertisement, 1876*
31. *Right: another chair with Hunzinger's patent*

Persia
on the Hudson

In 1870, when Frederick Edwin Church (1826–1900) was at the peak of his success as a landscape painter, construction began on Olana, the "Persianized" mansion that was to be Church's personal expression of exotic eclecticism. The family took residence in 1872, but for many years thereafter Church devoted himself to the continued ornamentation of his country house. A world-wide traveler, he drew inspiration particularly from the Near East and acted as his own architect and decorator. "I can say," he remarked, "as the good woman did about her mock turtle soup, 'I made it out of my own head.'" Olana, a dramatic composite of Western and Near Eastern architecture, crowns a hilltop overlooking the Hudson River and the Catskill Mountains beyond—the sort of panoramic vista that Church painted in his six- and seven-foot-long canvases. Within, Oriental, Islamic, and European cultures were enthusiastically combined in the grandiose Victorian manner. To Frederick Church, Olana was "the Center of the World." And, he added, "I own it."

32a. Below: tower wing of Church's "Persianized" mansion
32b. Right: interior view, the central hall and staircase

33a, b. Enameled, gilded, and engraved teapot and creamer by Tiffany

34. Teapot by Gorham; classical and floral ornament

Some Sterling Forms
of an Eclectic Age

From almost the earliest colonial days American silversmiths maintained an uninterrupted tradition of excellent craftsmanship. Throughout the colonial period, and for some years later, the silversmith was more often than not a man of consequence in his community, a trusted "banker" of sorts, as well as a craftsman. By the 1860's such individual silversmiths had largely been replaced by manufacturing companies that increasingly relied upon mechanical and power-driven aids to production. However, old standards of excellence survived that transition. The eclectic spirit of those later years brought forth an unprecedented variety of novel designs. At the Centennial Exhibition the Gorham Manufacturing Company was commended, among other things, "for great diversity of patterns and originality of designs"; Tiffany & Company for "genuine excellence . . . variety of treatment, with novel niello work and inlaid decorations, chased designs, and repoussé execution."

45

36. *A water jug and tray made about 1879*

Where the craftsman once shaped his material by hand into traditional forms, a company's professional designer now more commonly created patterns to be worked up in the factory. Styles and shapes no longer followed an orderly progression as they had in centuries past, but rather branched out in all directions—as the examples on these pages suggest. A water jug and tray (36), made by Samuel Kirk & Son of Baltimore, with its grotesque, dolphin-head handle, its torso of a faun, and its animated pattern of leaves, flowers, and tendrils, revives late Renaissance designs in its fashion. The tureen (37), made by Tiffany & Company about 1870, follows precedents of the classical revival in its outlines. Somewhat earlier, Gorham produced a coffeepot (38) which in its tall, gracefully curved shape, if not in its matted bands of naturalistic floral decoration, vaguely suggests the metalwork of the Near East.

37, a. Below: a silver tureen, made about
1870 by Tiffany, and detail (left) from handle

38. Bottom: a coffeepot produced by Gorham

PRESENTED
TO
Richard Lathers Es
BY THE GREAT WESTERN INSURANCE
INGRATEFUL RECOGNITION OF HIS FAITH
and prosperous conduct of its affair
FROM ITS FOUNDATION

47

No. 08.

RIP VAN WINKLE.

Silver Finish, each, ... $3.00.

Silver Finish with gold lined Ring, each, 3.25.

Gold Finish, each, . . . 3.75.

Gilt and Oxydized Finish, each, . 4.50.

This can also be used as a parlor ornament by leaving off the Napkin Ring.

39. *Above: a plated napkin ring; an illustration from a catalogue of 1878*

40. *Surrounding: a selection of napkin rings by different manufacturers*

A Silver Coating
for Every Purpose

Although coating base metals with silver by electrolysis had been practiced in America since the 1840's, it was in the years just before and after the war that the process became the basis for large commercial enterprises. With this development, explained one author in 1868, anything made of sterling silver (even the treasures made for royalty) could now be duplicated "at prices accessible by all." Nevertheless, since coating of varying thicknesses could be deposited on a piece, some assurance of a substantial plating job, either in the form of a reliable brand name or whatever, was looked for by the wary. Thus, the exotic and elaborate centerpiece below (41) is marked by the maker, the Meriden Britannia Company (by the 1860's the biggest company in the business), as being quadruple plated. On a less impressive scale napkin rings, such as those shown opposite, became widely popular novelties starting with the 1870's.

41. A silver-plated centerpiece made by the Meriden Britannia Co.

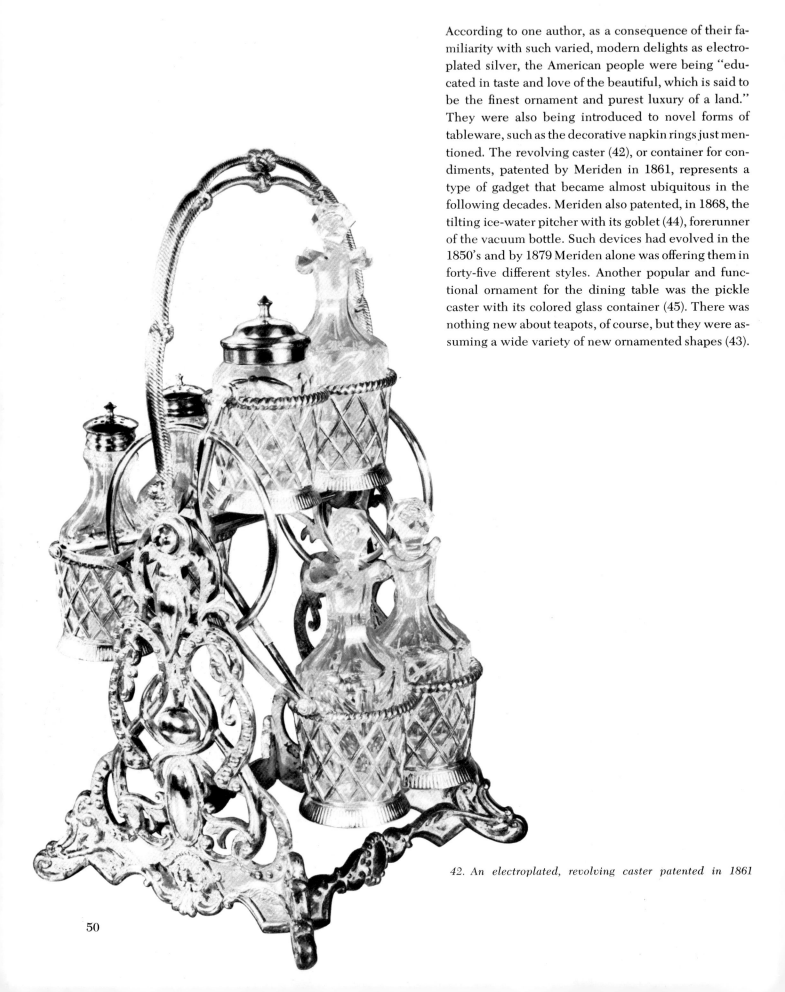

According to one author, as a consequence of their familiarity with such varied, modern delights as electroplated silver, the American people were being "educated in taste and love of the beautiful, which is said to be the finest ornament and purest luxury of a land." They were also being introduced to novel forms of tableware, such as the decorative napkin rings just mentioned. The revolving caster (42), or container for condiments, patented by Meriden in 1861, represents a type of gadget that became almost ubiquitous in the following decades. Meriden also patented, in 1868, the tilting ice-water pitcher with its goblet (44), forerunner of the vacuum bottle. Such devices had evolved in the 1850's and by 1879 Meriden alone was offering them in forty-five different styles. Another popular and functional ornament for the dining table was the pickle caster with its colored glass container (45). There was nothing new about teapots, of course, but they were assuming a wide variety of new ornamented shapes (43).

42. An electroplated, revolving caster patented in 1861

43. Top: a silver-plated teapot made by Rogers, Smith & Company, 1878
44. Above: a tilting ice-water pitcher and goblet, patented in 1868
45. Left: a pickle caster made by Rogers, Smith & Company, 1862–77

Craftsmen
from Abroad

With vast fortunes being lavished by "pioneer millionaires" on the epicurean delights of opulent mansions and opulent furnishings, the influx of European architects, decorators, designers, and craftsmen was inevitable. For artists and artisans alike, affluent America was indeed the land of opportunity. The European domination of the American furniture industry—a domination that had begun before the Civil War—continued on every level during the postwar era.

In factories immigrant craftsmen were in the majority. One survey, for example, published in 1886 by the Berkey & Gay Furniture Company of Grand Rapids, Michigan, revealed that among two hundred fifty-five employees, only eighty-two were native born. The factory personnel was an international roll call of skilled workers from Holland, Germany, Sweden, England, Ireland, Norway, Denmark, Russia, and Belgium. In New York in 1898 the German-language newspaper *Staats-Zeitung* published a review of American industrial art since the Civil War and stated: "Germans make up the bulk of craftsmen in such American trades as furniture manufacture, lithography, and fresco painting. . . ." Berkey & Gay, meanwhile, had personally recruited and imported carvers from Italy. And the *Detroit Free Press*, in 1877, extolled Scottish carvers employed in Grand Rapids—Glasgow men who had learned their trade on the Clyde, "carving figureheads, stem and stern adornments and cabin decorations for the mercantile, naval, racing, and pleasure craft of the world."

In the world of wealth and high fashion, where Europe was viewed as the wellspring of all that was culturally and artistically top drawer, newly rich Americans relied heavily on immigrant decorators and designers. One such pacesetter was Roux & Company, founded about 1837 by the French-born cabinetmaker Alexander Roux. A leading New York City firm until 1898, the Messrs Roux of Fifth Avenue graciously refuted a suggestion that Americans knew nothing about styles in furniture or wallpaper. It was a touchy subject. After all, the comment had been made that among European manufacturers "whatever is so wanting in good taste as to ruin it for the home market, will do for the United

States." Roux & Company disagreed. "It is not true of the class of people *we* deal with," they told the press in 1882.

Another French company in New York was the house of Pottier & Stymus, commended at the Centennial Exhibition for "skillful use of materials, happy blending of colors, and ornamentation of the highest order of art." Among their clients, with spanking new Fifth Avenue houses, were such Standard Oil chieftains as Jabez A. Bostwick and William Rockefeller. In San Francisco, they also furnished the Nob Hill brownstone mansion built by James L. Flood, "the Bonanza king," of the Comstock Lode.

Yet another French firm, famed for showy furniture rich with marquetry, was L. Marcotte & Company, near Union Square in New York, founded about 1854 by Léon Marcotte, who had arrived in America in 1848. The company not only designed and manufactured locally, but was particularly known for its import trade as well. A delicate controversy raged during the 1870's and into the 1880's on the durability of European furniture in overheated American houses. Clarence Cook, for one, had unequivocally stated in *The House Beautiful* that imports could not withstand central heating. "No sooner does winter come than the French furniture—and the English too—begins to gape and yawn and stretch out its arms for home." Not so, Marcotte & Company asserted: "The talk about imported furniture not being good is nonsense. . . ."

Two successful English firms trans-

planted to New York were Cottier & Company, and Robert Ellin & Company. Clarence Cook singled out Cottier's time and time again in *The House Beautiful* for its "carefully thought out" designs and for having "done us the greatest service, in showing us how to unite usefulness and beauty." Robert Ellin, a stone carver by profession, was particularly praised at the Centennial for such carved entries as an oak sideboard and an ecclesiastical reading desk. With carving in both stone and wood a speciality of the house, the firm filled such posh commissions as a marble and Caen-stone reredos, or altar screen, donated by the Astor family to Trinity Church.

Among New York's immigrant designers, "one of the finest and most talented" was Christian A. Herter, "a man who was never idle, always had a pencil in hand, and whether entertaining a customer or reading his paper his thoughts would be busy with new ideas; . . . his remarkable skill and fertility attracted clients and he was very soon in the very swim of a fashionable and lucrative trade." Born in Stuttgart, Germany, in 1840, the son of an accomplished cabinetmaker, Herter studied at the Stuttgart Polytechnic and at the Ecole des Beaux Arts in Paris. In 1860 he came to New York and joined his elder half brother, Gustave, previously a silver designer at Tiffany's, who had established his own decorating firm. In 1864 Christian married Mary Miles, daughter of Dr. Archibald Miles of Cleveland, and in 1868, at his brother's instigation, he went back to Paris for further study and the development of his artistic talents. Upon Christian's return to New York in 1870, he bought out Gustave's interest in Herter Brothers and launched himself as master of his own decorating company. His ideas were "original and entirely novel to the community whose patronage he sought. Out of a chaos of appalling colors, defective drawing, wretched conceptions, and blind ignorance . . . arose the beautiful creations of Christian Herter."

A highly cultivated man of great personal charm, Herter was fluent in German, English, French, and Italian, and was widely read in the literature of these languages. Emerson, whom he counted among his friends, was said to be his favorite author. Herter's interests further

included philosophy, science, and music; he himself was accomplished on the zither. In a later memoir, a colleague recalled the dark-eyed, dark-haired Christian Herter as "a man of extraordinary physical beauty; many, who knew him, thought him the handsomest man in New York. . . . He also was an excellent rider, and one could meet him every morning . . . in Central Park."

In a scant ten years, between 1870 and 1880, Herter's designing skills and business acumen gained him immediate fame and fortune. He was able to retire from the professional world at the age of forty and happily returned to Paris to concentrate on painting, his first artistic love. But during the year abroad Herter contracted tuberculosis; he died in New York at the age of forty-three.

Herter's clients, in his brief decade as a designer, included such California na-

bobs as banker Darius Ogden Mills, Senator Milton Slocum Latham, and railroad tycoon Mark Hopkins. Hotel de Hopkins, as Mark Hopkins himself termed the mansion, was his young wife's extravagant whimsey. She could not bear to be outdone by other San Francisco millionaire families, who were building palaces to left and right. Herter's interiors surely must have fulfilled Mary Hopkins' wildest dreams of glory. The master bedroom, for example, was designed with a Venetian *décor:* the walls of ebony inlaid with precious stones and ivory marquetry, the doors padded with blue velvet, and a ceiling painted with amorous cupids at play. Mark Hopkins, however, did not live to enjoy these delights. He died, in the thirty-five-dollar-a-month cottage that so fully suited his frugal tastes, before Hotel de Hopkins was finished.

In New York, where "The Vanderbilts have come nobly forward and

shown the world how millionaires ought to live," Herter's last commission was executed for William Henry Vanderbilt. As both architect and interior designer, Herter built the block-long brownstone edifice on Fifth Avenue with sixty foreign sculptors and carvers and from six to seven hundred American laborers on the payroll for two years. It was a rush job. Mr. Vanderbilt, possibly aware of Mark Hopkins' fate, was "haunted by the fear that he might die before the house stood complete." The mansion, built at an estimated cost of $1,750,000, was described as "a box, if you will, but there is a finish and a style about it that shows it is a jewel-box. . . . The style, for those who are particular about a style, may be called Italian renaissance." Within were such wonders as gold-encrusted doorways, red velvet walls "profusely embroidered, and studded with cut crystals of every shade," and in the vestibule, reproductions of the Ghiberti doors in Florence—the bronze overlaid with gold. A Japanese parlor was done in a lacework of bamboo with "enormous jewelled dragonflies, motionless among the innumerable reeds as if the tropical summer were too warm to let them . . . stir." A mural in the drawing room, by the French painter Pierre V. Galland, depicted "knights at the tournament, with the fair ladies who watch them." Even the pantry had its splendors—fireproof safes, two stories high, in which to lock up the family plate. In all, "the effect is gorgeous in the extreme: everything sparkles and flashes with gold and color. . . . "

Herter was also responsible for the additions to and interior of the John Pierpont Morgan house at Madison Avenue and Thirty-sixth Street. A number of years after Herter's death, his daughter-in-law lunched aboard Morgan's yacht, the *Corsair.* In a family letter she wrote that Mr. Morgan had spoken of Christian Herter "almost reverently" and had said: "He painted for me in my library six panels for the ceiling—painted them *himself,* with his *own hands!*" And the story has also been told of the admiring J. P. Morgan exclaiming to his decorators when the house was renovated in 1893, "Renew, by all means, but retain the original designs of Herter. You cannot improve upon them."

46. *Sketch by Jelliff for a Renaissance Revival table*

47. *Above: an armchair by Brooks & Co.*

48. *Opposite: cabinet in the Renaissance Revival style by Giuseppe Ferrari*

The Fashions of the Renaissance Revival

For more than a quarter of a century, from before 1850 to after 1875, what contemporaries referred to as the "Renaissance style" maintained a broad popularity. Apparently no one found it necessary, or possible, to define "Renaissance" with any precision. It was rather, noted one critic, a word that "would seem to cover almost anything." The three illustrations on these pages suggest how disparately the style was interpreted. Thomas Brooks & Company of Brooklyn made the heavily upholstered armchair (47), with its incised frame topped by a pair of carved dolphins supporting a crest. A design for a table (46) was sketched about 1860 by John Jelliff, a Connecticut Yankee who worked for scores of years as a prominent cabinetmaker in Newark, New Jersey. A rich vocabulary of Renaissance ornament was carved, applied, and gilded on the cabinet (48) wrought in exotic and native woods by Giuseppe Ferrari of New York. Ferrari came to America from Italy in 1872 and spent more than two years preparing the piece for exhibition at the Philadelphia Centennial, where it was honored "for good design, superior carving, and fine workmanship."

In the years before the Civil War the observant New York diarist George Templeton Strong complained of the "tyranny of custom" which led those who had enough money to spend it on furnishings in the latest French taste. However, for the interior decoration of the boudoir of his own expensive new *palazzo*, he—like other fashionable New Yorkers—turned to the *émigré* Léon Marcotte. A columnist writing for *The American Architect and Building News* in 1876 reported that the Renaissance furnishings produced by the firm of Léon Marcotte exhibited "the highest degree of refinement and luxury," and that the displays of that company splendidly illustrated "the latest phases of decorative art, as employed by the French in the adornment of house interiors." Family tradition maintains that the parents of Theodore Roosevelt also turned to Marcotte for furniture. The bed (49) and dresser (51) from the Roosevelt house (built about the same time and near Strong's home), handsomely made of satinwood and rosewood, both have a broken-scroll pediment surmounted by an ornamental crest. That architectural theme is echoed on a smaller scale in the crest rail of a chair (50) from the set.

49, 50, 51. A bed, a chair, and a dresser of satinwood and rosewood, said to have been made by L. Marcotte & Co. for the New York home of the parents of Theodore Roosevelt. Some variations of design among separate elements of a suite were common in this period.

52, 53. *Two tables with carved, inlaid, and gilt ornamentation, in the Renaissance Revival style*

54. *Rosewood cabinet with inlays of lighter wood. The vase-shaped ornament has a pineapple finial.*

One editor tried to explain to his readers that, in addition to France, Germany and Spain (not to mention Italy) also provided historical sources of design for the revival of Renaissance styles. However, in the decades that followed the Civil War the most sophisticated American cabinetmakers continued to look closely to France for models and in their best work matched the achievements of Parisian craftsmen in the quality of their performance (see pages 20–21). The rosewood cabinet shown here (54), made about 1870 in New York, with its delicate inlays of lighter wood and gilded, incised lines, fairly reflects French fashions of the period as they were interpreted here. The two small tables (52, 53), with designs of inlaid woods on their tops and, again, with incised motifs, are separate variations on the same theme. Both were probably made in Grand Rapids.

Like the ornamental element in the niche of the cabinet just discussed, the legs of a carved and inlaid table (55) also resemble tall, handled vases of classical style (55a) in their outlines. Rodlike elements bound together by knotted ribbons and with acorn finials provide further carved decoration. In the course of his visit to America, Anthony Trollope was dismayed to notice the continuing prevalence of French influence in American furnishing, as in the American cuisine and conversation and the comforts and discomforts of life in general. On the other hand, about fifteen years later one reporter observed that however faithfully Americans modeled their *décor* on French precedent, the American home provided delights unknown abroad. "Who ever tried to get a bath in Paris," she asked, "that did not regret the hot and cold water of New York houses?" Seated in the rather cluttered library of her New York home, Mrs. Charles A. Lamb (56) is surrounded by a table, chair, and stand, all apparently versions of the French Renaissance style. A small, inlaid table (57) from the Roosevelt house presents another variant of the style. Serious interest in furniture from the years just before and after the Civil War has been revived only in relatively recent years. Although the talents of such men as Marcotte were widely publicized during their lifetimes, very few remaining examples of their work have been positively identified at the present time.

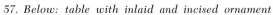
55a. Opposite: detail of a leg from the table at left

55. Left: carved and inlaid table with decorative elements typical of the Renaissance Revival style

56. Below: Mrs. Lamb with her Renaissance Revival furniture; a detail from a painting by C. A. Fassett

57. Below: table with inlaid and incised ornament

58, 59. *Dresser and bed of walnut and walnut burl. Linear motifs, incised and gilded, often ornament such Renaissance furniture.*

Very few American-made pieces in the Renaissance Revival style so closely resembled an actual model of the sixteenth or seventeenth century as the ornate cabinet, illustrated on page 55, wrought by the recent Italian immigrant Giuseppe Ferrari for display at the Philadelphia Centennial. Nonetheless, many of the forms so labeled did owe some debt—however remote—to the elaborate, architectural designs of European furniture from those earlier centuries. At no time since the Renaissance, in any case, did furniture achieve such massive solidity as it occasionally did in the post-Civil War years. "We have been making our furniture so heavy of late," wrote Clarence Cook in the 1870's, "that the amount of solid wood in it added to the carving, inlaying, and veneering with different woods, has made it very expensive." The walnut dresser (58) and bed (59) from a suite made about 1875 by Berkey & Gay Furniture Company of Grand Rapids, with their monumental, crested pediments and huge proportions, are impressive reminders of what Cook had in mind.

60. *Above: oak canterbury; provincial version of the Renaissance style, with flat-sawn, incised elements*

61. *Right: walnut* méridienne, *or day bed, also with flat-sawn, incised members, upholstered in horsehair*

"Grand Rapids" Renaissance

As the nation continued to surge westward in the decades following the war, manufacturers developed nomadic habits of their own, moving along with the general flow of the population and tailoring their products to the requirements of the rapidly growing market of the hinterland. Even before the war the Studebaker brothers in South Bend, Indiana, and Cyrus McCormick in Chicago were already enjoying a flourishing trade in wagons and reapers suited to the needs of life in the West. When Berkey & Gay's great bedroom suite (see pages 62–63) was shown in Philadelphia in 1876, Grand Rapids was quickly acknowledged as an important furniture-manufacturing center. There and in other western towns the prevailing styles were interpreted in homely, machine-made versions (60, 61) as well as in forms in the grand manner.

A sharply critical report in *The American Architect and Building News* for January 13, 1877, complained that "vulgar renditions of the French Renaissance" made up the stock in trade of nineteen out of twenty contemporary furniture manufacturers. In another acid note, about the displays at the Philadelphia Centennial, the same journal sincerely hoped that "such an array of vulgarity in design as emanated from the thriving city of Grand Rapids will never again bring disgrace upon the American name at an international exhibition." The provincial machine-made versions of the Renaissance Revival style were hardly to be compared to the elegant concoctions of Marcotte and his peers, but they satisfied the taste of a general public whose domestic economy seriously considered price tags along with matters of style and comfort. In the mid-1860's Grand Rapids firms were turning out large quantities of goods for sale throughout the Midwest, and by the next decade Grand Rapids furniture was finding its way as well to South America, the Philippines, Canada, and Hawaii.

62. Opposite: a marble-topped walnut plant stand with red and black painted decoration

63. Above: upholstered sofa; part of a set

64. Right: chair from the same set, made 1860–70. All three pieces are machine-carved variants of the Renaissance Revival style.

67

65. *Left: walnut secretary with burl walnut
panels and carved Corinthian applied columns*

66. *Above: an inexpensive bedroom suite in the
Renaissance Revival style; advertisement, 1875*

As early as 1861 the architect Samuel Sloan noted the "immense trade" in relatively inexpensive furniture that had recently sprung up in the southern and western states and the great number of large steam-powered factories that were engaged in meeting the demands of that trade. At the time, New York State, followed by Massachusetts and Pennsylvania, produced by far the greatest quantity of furniture of all types. However, as one example of western expansion, the value of the output at Grand Rapids increased more than tenfold between 1860 and 1870, and again almost sixfold in the next decade. In 1872 it was reported locally that "every manufacturer in this city has to enlarge his shop as often as once in two years." An extension dining table (67) of walnut, made by Berkey & Gay in 1873, and a mirrored secretary (65), probably made in Grand Rapids about the same time, typify the substantial forms made not for special exhibition but as stock-in-trade furniture for the public at large.

67. A solid walnut extension dining table, made in Grand Rapids   69

68–75. An assortment of side- and armchairs illustrating variations of the Renaissance style

Some furniture companies were established with the single purpose of manufacturing chairs. As early as 1851 one Grand Rapids furniture manufacturer contracted to deliver ten thousand of them to a Chicago firm. His equipment for producing some types of chairs was so efficient, he claimed, that he could almost throw "whole trees into the hopper and grind out chairs ready for use." However, machinery did not altogether eliminate the need for handwork; the early carving machines achieved only crude results, which had to be hand finished, a job often entrusted to craftsmen brought from Europe. The need for individual workmanship led at least one company to deliver its chairs to homes where women—or children—could cover seats for "remunerative" wages.

70

71

72

73

74

75

76. *Above: a combined desk and sewing table with angular supports and stretcher and incised panels*

77. *Below: a walnut bed with a maple burl panel*

As we are often reminded, from its very beginnings America has felt the need of short cuts to production—of quicker and easier, if not always better, ways of getting a job done. Steam-powered machines for hurrying and simplifying the manufacture of furniture were in operation at least as early as the 1840's; in 1848 Cincinnati alone boasted of seven factories so equipped for turning out forms of every description "from the common bedstead to the most costly articles." In spite of the continuing need for some handwork for finishing details, the machine inexorably took over more and more of the functions required for run-of-the-mill, mass-produced furniture. In 1866 a visitor to one Grand Rapids factory reported "the sight and sound of lathes and saws," the "purring and snarling" of planing machines, "scroll saws eating out ornamental designs," and a gauge lathe "turning out spindles and ornamental turning as fast as three men could on ordinary lathes." In their simple shapes, with almost geometric profiles and relatively flat surfaces, the forms thus produced constituted a distinctive style in their own right.

78. A walnut dresser with incised, stylized floral ornament and adjustable mirror. This example typifies the way in which the machine modified the Renaissance style.

Iron for Public Places

Shortly before the Civil War one American author announced that the use of iron was the "social barometer" that gauged the "relative height of Civilization among nations." At the moment (1857), he observed, the iron industry in the United States was second in production only to that of England. In spite of certain disadvantages as a building material, the metal had a tensile strength that encouraged designs impossible to realize in materials such as stone and wood. When it was used imaginatively in its own right, without regard for traditional formulas, iron could be given forms of unusual grace and novel character—as the designers' studies for telegraph poles (81) in Union Square, New York, for a "suspended lamp" (79) in the same city, and for the Ladies Pavilion (80) in New York's Central Park make amply clear. Central Park, completed in 1876 according to the inspired designs of Frederick Law Olmsted and Calvert Vaux, was in itself a work of art—environmental art in its purest and best sense.

79. *Opposite: a design for a streetlamp*

80. *Above: detail of a design by Jacob W. Mould for a cast-iron pavilion, 1871*

81. *Above, left and right: preliminary study for telegraph poles in New York, 1872*

82. *Right: an architect's drawing for a flower garden in Central Park, New York City*

83. Left: a painted, iron doorstop cast in the form of a ribboned basket of flowers and leaves

84. Above: a cast-iron matchsafe, patented 1872

85. *Above: cast-iron garden bench made by Eugene T. Barnum in Detroit*

86. *Below: a detail from a catalogue illustrating cast-iron furniture*

Ferromania: Iron to Meet All Needs

The recent rapid growth of the iron industry, it was explained, was largely due to the tireless ingenuity with which Americans produced "the utmost variety of articles fitted for use in our houses, our fields, our gardens, stores, counting-rooms and summer resorts." Iron could be cast in virtually any conceivable design, and since a foundry mold from which the casting took its shape could be used almost endlessly, a form could be reproduced over and over again at relatively small cost. And it could be easily and effectively painted in gay colors. In short, it had what one nineteenth-century architect referred to as a "happy adaptability" to decoration. During the Civil War a new, high, cast-iron dome was raised over the Capitol. Proponents claimed that architectural elements in the classical style, when cast in iron, were cheaper by far than brownstone cut in the same manner, and cast-iron buildings by the hundreds were raised in the principal cities of the land, often with simulated classical details; buildings that could be erected "with extraordinary facility" and "taken to pieces with . . . despatch."

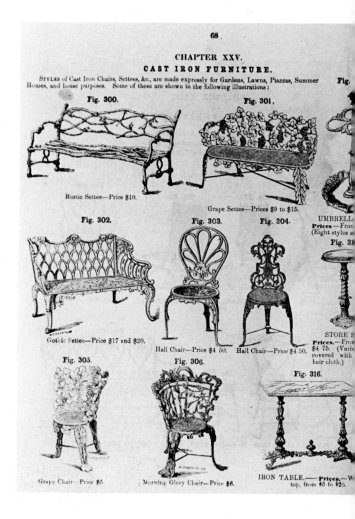

68

CHAPTER XXV.
CAST IRON FURNITURE.

STYLES of Cast Iron Chairs, Settees, &c., are made expressly for Gardens, Lawns, Piazzas, Summer Houses, and house purposes. Some of these are shown in the following illustrations:

Fig. 300.

Rustic Settee—Price $10.

Fig. 301.

Grape Settee—Prices $9 to $15.

Fig. 302.

Gothic Settee—Price $17 and $20.

Fig. 303.

Hall Chair—Price $4 50.

Fig. 304.

Hall Chair—Price $4 50.

UMBRELL
Prices—Fro
(Eight styles

Fig. 3

STORE
Prices.—Fro
$4 75. (Varie
covered with
hair cloth.)

Fig. 305.

Grape Chair—Price $5

Fig. 306.

Morning Glory Chair—Price $6.

Fig. 316.

IRON TABLE.—Prices
top, from $5 to $25.

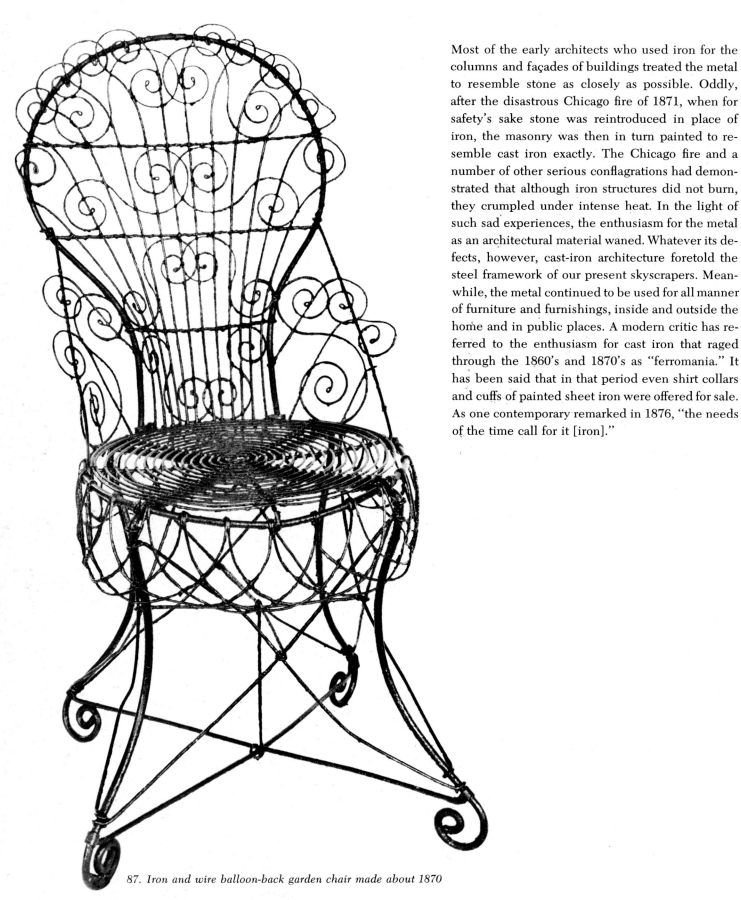

Most of the early architects who used iron for the columns and façades of buildings treated the metal to resemble stone as closely as possible. Oddly, after the disastrous Chicago fire of 1871, when for safety's sake stone was reintroduced in place of iron, the masonry was then in turn painted to resemble cast iron exactly. The Chicago fire and a number of other serious conflagrations had demonstrated that although iron structures did not burn, they crumpled under intense heat. In the light of such sad experiences, the enthusiasm for the metal as an architectural material waned. Whatever its defects, however, cast-iron architecture foretold the steel framework of our present skyscrapers. Meanwhile, the metal continued to be used for all manner of furniture and furnishings, inside and outside the home and in public places. A modern critic has referred to the enthusiasm for cast iron that raged through the 1860's and 1870's as "ferromania." It has been said that in that period even shirt collars and cuffs of painted sheet iron were offered for sale. As one contemporary remarked in 1876, "the needs of the time call for it [iron]."

87. Iron and wire balloon-back garden chair made about 1870

88. *Above: cast-iron stool designed by Joseph Peabody*

89. *Below: advertisement of an iron-manufacturing firm, showing a design for a column with Corinthian capital*

90. *Right: combination carved-wood buffet and marble-topped, cast-iron radiator cover, with accouterments*

93. *Above: bowl in the Horn of Plenty pattern*

94. *Opposite: pitcher in the Honeycomb pattern*

91. *Above: pressed-glass whale-oil lamp in the Comet, or so-called Horn of Plenty, pattern, made by various firms*

92. *Right: compote in a pattern known as Lincoln Drape*

Pressed & Patterned

Throughout most of the last two thirds of the nineteenth century mechanically-pressed glass tableware was probably produced in greater quantities and was used more widely for domestic services in America than in any other country of the world. Starting about 1840 such tableware, pressed in relatively simple forms and patterned with bold designs broadly similar to those familiar on more expensive cut glass, was issued in the form of complete table settings. Over the decades that followed the variety of patterns multiplied in bewildering profusion, in colored as well as clear glass. The names under which the patterns were originally advertised have often been arbitrarily changed by modern dealers and collectors. For instance, the pattern known as Comet (91, 93) a century or so ago is now known as Horn of Plenty. Glass manufacturing was a highly competitive enterprise and almost every pattern that won popularity when it was produced by one company was quickly copied more or less exactly by other firms in different sections of the country.

Unlike a large number of other American industries the manufacturers of pattern glass did not need tariff protection to enjoy a virtual monopoly of the domestic market. American sands produced glass of lustrous clarity and, offsetting the high wages paid to workmen in this country, American pressing devices were on the whole more efficient than those used abroad. In the 1860's, at Wheeling, West Virginia, soda ash and lime were first successfully used to replace lead and other fluxes, a development that drastically reduced the cost of production and forced most other factories throughout the land to follow suit. A decade or so later, in the aftermath of the panic of 1873, one Pennsylvania firm that specialized in goblets and tumblers developed a large market for its wares overseas, especially in Great Britain. Some Englishmen were puzzled by the fact that in spite of high freight rates and high labor costs in America, English soda was shipped to western Pennsylvania and glass was returned that sold at lower prices than local makers could manage for their own neighborhood markets.

95. *Above: pressed cordial glass, in the Argus, or Thumbprint, pattern, produced in New England and the Midwest*

96. *Right: Magnet and Grape patterned goblet; one of several variant designs featuring grapes and grape leaves*

97. *Elements of various pressed-glass services; from a catalogue of McKee & Brothers, Pittsburgh, about 1867*

98. *Dish in the Ribbon pattern supported by a frosted-glass dolphin; made by Bakewell, Pears & Company, Pittsburgh*

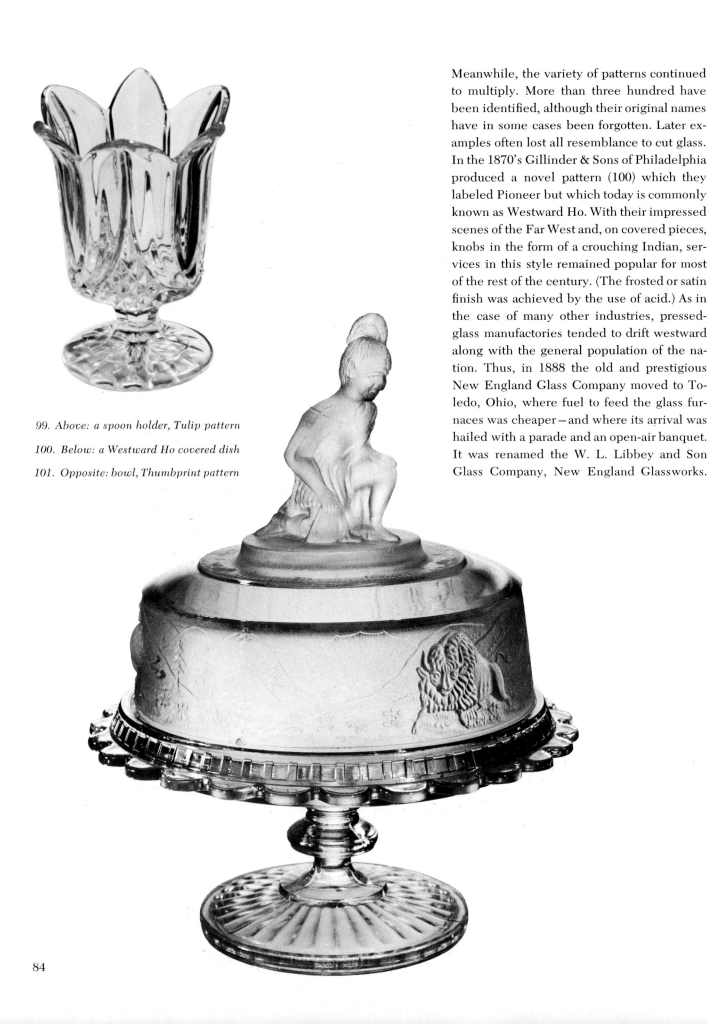

Meanwhile, the variety of patterns continued to multiply. More than three hundred have been identified, although their original names have in some cases been forgotten. Later examples often lost all resemblance to cut glass. In the 1870's Gillinder & Sons of Philadelphia produced a novel pattern (100) which they labeled Pioneer but which today is commonly known as Westward Ho. With their impressed scenes of the Far West and, on covered pieces, knobs in the form of a crouching Indian, services in this style remained popular for most of the rest of the century. (The frosted or satin finish was achieved by the use of acid.) As in the case of many other industries, pressed-glass manufactories tended to drift westward along with the general population of the nation. Thus, in 1888 the old and prestigious New England Glass Company moved to Toledo, Ohio, where fuel to feed the glass furnaces was cheaper—and where its arrival was hailed with a parade and an open-air banquet. It was renamed the W. L. Libbey and Son Glass Company, New England Glassworks.

99. *Above: a spoon holder, Tulip pattern*

100. *Below: a Westward Ho covered dish*

101. *Opposite: bowl, Thumbprint pattern*

Some Glass with Built-in Magic

Because he could take inert, opaque substances—sand, flint, alkalies, and the like—and transmute them into transparencies of crystal clarity and delicate design, the glassmaker in centuries past was considered by many to be a magician. The magic of his art, or mystery as it was long called, is nowhere more clearly demonstrated than in those paperweights that, with their exquisitely patterned fantasies in brilliant colors, enjoyed such a great vogue in the last century. Following precedents in France, Bohemia, Belgium, Italy, England, and elsewhere, American craftsmen—some of them were emigrants from those countries—fashioned quantities of these popular, functional ornaments at Sandwich, Philadelphia, and other centers in the East and Midwest. The techniques involved in floating these often wondrously intricate and ornamental colored designs in their surrounding bed of crystal glass were rooted in ancient practices, but now—that is, toward the middle of the last century—they were developed to a new and complicated state of refinement. Paperweights were built, rather than blown, by a variety of intricate processes. As one example, glass rods of different colors might be assembled in a desired pattern, fused together, and the resulting semi-molten mass drawn out into a very thin "cane" whose section showed the original pattern reduced to a delicate miniature. Any number of such multi-colored canes could then be placed on a pad of molten glass in a mold, arranged to resemble sprays of tiny flowers, and coated by pouring clear glass into the mold. The resulting mass was dipped in molten glass to build it up to the required size.

102. *Red overlay over white, faceted, with enclosed canes. The New England Glass Co.*

103. *Fruit and leaves on a lacy (latticinio) background. Probably New England Glass Co.*

104. Strawberry, leaf, and floral forms. The Mt. Washington Glass Co., New Bedford, Mass.

105. Blue cherries on a leafy stem. Made at the Boston and Sandwich Glass Co., Mass.

106. Sulfide cameo of Zachary Taylor on blue underlay. Made at the New England Glass Co.

107. Weight in form of an apple on a plate, or "cooky," base. The New England Glass Co.

108. Red and white casing over a clear body, enclosed ornament. New England Glass Co.

109. *Above: Rip Van Winkle meets the gnome, one of three statuettes drawn from Irving's tale*

110. *Top right: advertisement from* The Century

111. *Opposite: Lincoln, Grant, and Stanton in Rogers' highly popular group,* Council of War

The Images of John Rogers

"His art is for the people," wrote a contemporary of John Rogers', the sculptor, in 1869. "All can understand it; all can appreciate its meaning; all can perceive its truth, and respond to its feeling." Originally trained as a draftsman and mechanic, John Rogers (1829–1904) was unable to pursue his artistic bent until the age of twenty-nine, when he went to Europe to study. Most American sculpture at that time remained "but a vapid foreign echo of an echo," bound by neoclassic conventions that depicted Presidents and senators, for example, in togas and crowns of laurel. In Rome Rogers quickly realized his aversion to the classic style. "I do not take to it," he declared, and returned to America to make a name for himself with his homespun plaster statuettes, the first success entitled *The Slave Auction*. As Rogers defined his philosophy in 1863, he had "cut adrift entirely from the old school of allegory and mythology."

89

Sculpture, to Rogers, was a narrative art. Here (112) a southern gentlewoman is portrayed taking the oath of allegiance from a Union officer in order to draw rations. In *Coming to the Parson* (115), Rogers' delight in humorous touches is typified by the cat and dog on the brink of a spat and the parson's newspaper aptly named *The Union*. Rogers' gift for portraiture is exemplified by the figure of Lincoln (111), regarded by Robert Todd Lincoln as the finest sculptured likeness of his father. Coupled with Rogers' extraordinary talent for warmhearted realism and appealing native themes was the modest price of his work. "Large sales & small profits" was his avowed motto. The putty-colored plaster groups, cast in glue molds made from bronze master models, were sold at an average price of fourteen dollars. Between 1860 and 1893 an enthusiastic public bought close to eighty thousand copies, and in a wry anecdote of the day, a tramp described his family as so pitifully impoverished, they could not, alas, even afford to buy a Rogers group for the parlor.

112. Above: Rogers' commentary on the pathos of the Civil War, Taking the Oath and Drawing Rations, *continued to sell for thirty years.*

113. Right: Mail Day, *also a popular war piece*

114. Above: Coming to the Parson *shown in a contemporary photo of a New York parlor*

115. Right: sales of Coming to the Parson *amounted to 8,000 copies in about 20 years.*

Celebrating the Centennial

"The opening of the Centennial Exposition was a scene of confusion," wrote one visitor. "The heat was terrible, food difficult to get and the visiting diplomatists were extremely glad when it was over. . . . The diplomatists were asked to come in uniform and that meant coats padded and buttoned up to the chin. The Baron de Santa Ana, the Portuguese Minister, looked like a vivid flamingo, and Madame de Hegermann Lindencrone wrote that the Chamberlain, her husband, resembled an enormous poppy in his red uniform; the sun blazing through the glass roof almost set him on fire." But in spite of the unseasonable heat, a crowd of close to two hundred thousand people massed in Philadelphia's Fairmount Park on May 10, 1876, to cheer and huzza for Generals William T. Sherman and Philip H. Sheridan and President Ulysses S. Grant. Dom Pedro, the emperor of Brazil, and his Empress were roundly greeted by the mob. (The handsome Dom Pedro was reportedly an indefatigable sightseer, rushing "from one exhibit to another with his perspiring escort at his heels.") Four thousand digni-

taries gathered on the speaker's platform, the diplomatic corps glittering with decorations, the "numerous ladies elegantly costumed," and the band struck up a world-wide medley of national airs, to be followed by the "American Centennial March," composed for the occasion by Richard Wagner. ("Perhaps one of the most original things Wagner has written since Tristan," wrote the *New-York Tribune*.) Program highlights included a hymn with words by John Greenleaf Whittier, a cantata by Sidney Lanier, and President Grant's address, concluded amid further wild cheering, "the Emperor of Brazil rising in his seat and joining in the demonstration by waving his hat." The choir sang Handel's "Hallelujah Chorus," a salute of one hundred guns was fired, bells chimed, and the band led the way to Machinery Hall. Here was the mechanical wonder of the exposition, the Corliss engine, prime mover of all the machines in the building. With Grant at the left throttle and the Emperor at the right, the giant engine was set in motion. The crowd roared. The fair had officially begun.

116. Above: needle-point slipper holder shown at the Centennial

117. Opposite: a souvenir kerchief of the Centennial Exhibition

118. ÓVERLEAF: One Hundred Years of Progress, oleograph, 1876

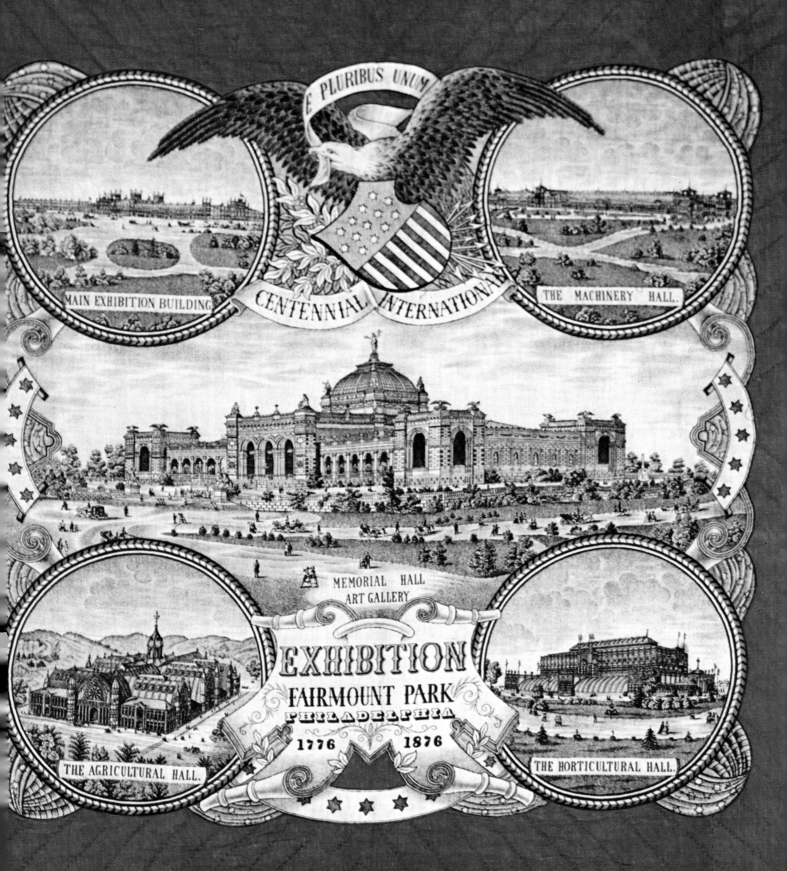

TO PHILADELPHIA

119. *Left: kerosene lamp with an 1876 Philadelphia Centennial Liberty Bell base*

120. *Top: detail from a cotton fabric bearing a Centennial print. "To Philadelphia," reads the legend, as a smiling citizen flies to the fair on his eagle.*

121. *Above: Centennial washstand set, white china banded with gold and pink, the Liberty Bell in tones of brown and gold; the original cost, forty dollars*

96

In honor of the Centennial, a rich assortment of gim-crackery and souvenirs were manufactured, as well as a variety of commemorative household objects. Furniture, for example, made from so-called "historic woods" was enthusiastically exhibited: a hat rack and chairs from the wood of Andrew Jackson's old home, the Hermitage; a set of chamber furniture made "in the style of 1776" from a maple that had grown on Independence Square. This armchair (122), with a needlework figure of Washington, was made from a limb of the tree in Cambridge, Massachusetts, under which Washington took command of the Continental Army in 1775. But for the average American, a visit to the Centennial was an eye opener. Not only were there wondrous exhibits in every branch of the arts, science, agriculture, and industry (although William Dean Howells suggested that a "half-mile of sewing-machines" seemed a good deal), but what had been proclaimed as a "national celebration" was, in fact, an international exposition. Fifty foreign countries were represented—their art and artifacts, culture and traditions. "The provincial belief," wrote one contemporary, "that nothing really worth while existed east of the Atlantic seaboard began to dissipate itself."

122. *A carved armchair made from the Washington elm*

"As compared with the exhibits of other nations," declared a judges' report on the Centennial, "one is struck with the ambitious pretension of our designs, overloaded as they too often are with meretricious ornament." The sterling silver Century Vase (124), fraught as it is with symbolism, allegorical figures, and historical emblems, exemplifies this generalized comment on American artistic endeavors on display at the fair. However, Gorham Manufacturing Company's "functionless vase," over four feet in height, was one of the hits of the exhibition. It represented time and money and industrial persistence. Not only was the vase valued at twenty-five thousand dollars in 1876, but it had taken five years, thirty-eight weeks, and twenty-two hours to complete the sterling extravaganza. "No one is so direct and efficient as the American workman," *Godey's Lady's Book and Magazine* editorialized, and then regretfully concluded: "no one goes so far astray in elaborate ornamentation."

FIELD 1877

123. *Above: Buffalo Hunt, shown by Meriden Britannia Co.*
124. *Opposite: the Century Vase created by Gorham Co.*

Matters of Taste & Sincerity

Styles between Fairs (1876-1893)

The Civil War sharply accelerated changes in American life that had begun to develop twenty or thirty years earlier. Barely a decade after the war was over, the great international fair held at Philadelphia made dramatically clear how large and portentous those changes had by then become. It was manifest that the Machine Age had arrived and that the United States had assumed a high rank among the industrial nations of the world. A foreign visitor to the fair, a German journalist and historian, pointed out that since the United States had been so poorly represented at earlier, European fairs, the outside world had thus far no proper conception of the "young giant" that had so quickly grown so large and strong in the western hemisphere. Most important, the exhibitions at the Centennial demonstrated how insistently mechanization was modifying the daily habits of the American people. At every turn the visitor was confronted by some new or improved machine or appliance, from threshing and reaping machines that were transforming the traditional pattern of agricultural life beyond recognition to the inexpensive pocket watches that kept the city man on the regular, hourly schedule imposed by an industrial society. For the young there were delights promised by soda fountains, often beguilingly composed of polished stones and glittering metals; for older folk there were the comforts promised by artificial teeth, among all the other "amiable apparatus of dentistry" in which America excelled. For royalty, along with the rest, there were still other excitements to savor. One high point for Dom Pedro II, the emperor of Brazil, was his introduction to the telephone. "My God! It talks!" His Majesty exclaimed when he heard Alexander Graham Bell's voice through the transmitter, and his surprise was immediately and exultantly reported throughout the nation. The London *Times* referred to the new contraption as the "latest American humbug." Some years later, however, Arnold Bennett was startled and frightened by the "efficiency and fearful universality" of the instrument. It was, he thought, America's most practical achievement.

The symbol of America's expanding industrial prowess was the great Corliss steam engine, the most powerful and probably the most handsome machine that had ever been constructed by man and the prime mover of the mechanical part of the exhibition. Made of highly refined metals, shaped to a mammoth size yet to precise detail, with its cylinders bored to a diameter of more than a yard, gear wheels thirty feet in diameter (the largest cut gears ever made), and great piston rods of tireless speed and efficiency, the seven-hundred-ton engine performed

Opposite and above: details of an interior from the William H. Vanderbilt house, 1882

The giant Corliss engine at the Centennial

Armchair, made by Morris and Company

with the quiet perfection of a good watch as it produced up to twenty-five hundred horsepower. As one exuberant spectator remarked, it was enough "to run anybody's ideas up into majestic heights and run 'em round and round into lofty circles and spears of thought, they hadn't never thought of runnin' into before."

For a large majority of the Americans who visited the fair, as the editors of *Godey's Lady's Book* reported, the experience was "simply stupendous." In Machinery Hall, where the Corliss engine rhythmically pulsed out power, the native population felt more or less at home, familiar as it had become with the ever-novel mechanical gadgets that were offered for sale. But in other areas they were introduced to "a new and wonderful world," a world that took them far beyond their common experience, a world of alien and exotic delights. Among other things, they were exposed to the largest display of the arts that had ever been held anywhere. "Seldom has there been, even if ever," concluded one reporter, "so complete an opportunity for the cultivation of good taste and sound ideas concerning industrial art as the Centennial Exhibition afforded."

To most qualified observers it was all too clear that America had much to learn along these lines from the rest of the world. For all their mechanical ingenuity, the Americans had not yet successfully married the machine to the arts. The best exhibits of American silverware, furniture, and other household accessories could challenge anything shown by European exhibitors. However, as one disenchanted reporter complained, the American department at the fair "was largely crowded with badly-designed, tawdry, and vulgar work, only fit, at the best, for the drawing-room of a *parvenu,* or the glittering saloon of a North River steamboat." It would be charity, wrote another critic, somewhat extravagantly, to consign most of the exhibits to "an unfathomable limbo."

England had been initiated into the complex problems of the Industrial Revolution earlier than the United States, and had already faced the dilemmas posed by machine production. In that country a variety of earnest reformers and critics had for several decades past sought solutions to those problems. Among the most earnest and most influential was the art critic John Ruskin, whose pronouncements won a phenomenally wide audience in America (although he heartily disliked most Americans) as well as in England. In 1855, as he wrote the editors of the newly founded American journal *Crayon,* Ruskin thought his audience in the United States was more significant than that in England. By 1887 it was "numbered by tens of thousands." Like another English critic, Augustus Welby N. Pugin, Ruskin sought to demonstrate that good design was basically a matter of sound and honest principles, not a matter of style. Pugin had believed that design was a moral act, and this note of moral purpose in the practical arts was repeatedly struck by other reformers throughout the rest of the century. Along with his somewhat younger contemporary William Morris, Ruskin condemned the machine on principle as a dehumanizing agent and urged a return to the handicrafts to assure those faithfully and honestly made products that were essential to human satisfaction and welfare. Morris apparently designed very little furniture commercially, but he is lovingly remembered in America for the adjustable armchair that bears his name — a type that was first manufactured and popularized in 1866 by the company Morris had founded five years before. Early in its history, the most admired furniture produced by that company were the cupboards and cabinets of simple, basically Gothic form, decorated with paintings by Morris himself and by Ford Madox Brown, Dante Gabriel Rossetti, Sir Edward Burne-Jones, and other members of the Pre-Raphaelite Brotherhood. (As the name implies, these artists looked back to the work of Italian painters before Raphael for the principles of probity they chose to emulate.) Although this sort of product was too expensive for the general public, it incorporated principles that were becoming increasingly popular. "One good painted panel," it was pointed out by a critic of the times, "is worth ten thousand times more than all the meretricious carving with which so much of our modern furniture is filled."

There were others, just as deeply interested in sound construction and good design, who felt that the machine should and could be mastered to realize those ends. One of the first of those pioneering industrial designers, Sir Henry Cole, was an organizer of the Crystal Palace Great Exhibition at London in 1851 and editor, from 1849 to 1852, of *The Journal of Design*, through which he promoted his views. Whether he liked it or not, man's welfare was increasingly and inextricably bound to the machine and Cole's approach to the problems of the day inevitably succeeded in the market place. "The growth of mechanism has been so rapid, so overwhelming," *The Art Journal* announced in 1877, "that the region of pure handicraft grows less and less. . . . It may be frankly admitted that we can never return to the primitive conditions of production by simple hand-labour." That was not altogether true, but the crafts continued to be practiced only along the margins of the economy.

Cabinet designed by William Morris and painted by Burne-Jones, 1861

Through the influence of such men, theorizers and practical men alike, changes were effected in English design that were widely admired in the exhibits at the Centennial. "We have before our eyes," one critic reported shortly after the fair had closed, "the spectacle of a great people, who in our own time, finding themselves outstripped by their neighbors in the arts of decoration, and learning that to the highest success in these arts there is needed a certain basis of principle, have proceeded from this discovery with an energy born of a high sense of duty, have gradually unfolded one by one the secrets of art." Judging from the evidence, our own generation would hardly accept such an extravagant estimate of English accomplishment. But for many and at least for a time English influence replaced French as the strongest influence on the development of the American decorative arts. As one periodical devoted to furniture and interior decoration complained in 1885, America was experiencing "a remarkably unreasonable Anglo-mania."

Following the lead of the pioneering English reformers, "authorities" in this country formulated rules for good taste in the household arts. One of them, echoing the judgment just quoted, urged his compatriots, when they selected furniture, to consider more than just comfort, taste, and cost; they must consider "certain higher duties," the most prominent of which was "the principle of *truth of construction*." This meant, according to another pronouncement citing English models, that the designer must "make manifest to the eye all the details of his joinery. . . . Every joint must be plainly confessed, and every part must have its function distinctly declared, not only by its form and by its position, but by its ornamentation. . . . [The designer] acknowledges, in short, no *order* but that of truth and construction." "Thus," it was elsewhere explained, "a tenon passing through a mortise-hole and pinned on the other side with a practicable peg is one of the accepted traits of moral cabinet-work." Hypocrites nailed or glued pegs onto tenons separately as a show, and this sort of deceit simply had to be avoided. Veneered surfaces (which might disguise shoddy workmanship), applied moldings (instead of moldings carved in the solid wood), mitered joints, and unnecessary curves were all to be eschewed as nonconstructive in practice and principle.

Illustration of "truthful construction," 1868

An engraving of a drawing room from B. J. Talbert's Gothic Forms Applied to Furniture

To find models for such exemplary practices, men like Ruskin and Morris had turned to the work of medieval craftsmen, not because they believed that Gothic styles need necessarily be followed or revived, but because in that work could be found the fundamental principles of honest construction. "The revival of mediaeval principles in furniture," reported one American journal, "must ever be regarded as the most significant incident in the history of this branch of art; and this not because the principles are mediaeval, but because they are principles." The course of styles and fashions was indeed capricious and beyond the rules of reason, but that mattered little if the workman and his patrons cleaved to those enduring, basic, and commendable principles that alone produced furniture fit to live with, and houses fit to live in. That furniture could serve a moral purpose as well as a useful function—that its functionalism (a word unknown in the nineteenth century) was indeed inseparable from its moral qualities—was a concept that in retrospect we find hard to accept. However, in the 1870's and, particularly, in the 1880's the notion carried widespread conviction.

The apostles of these ideas whose message reached the largest American audience with the greatest persuasion were Bruce J. Talbert and, specially, Charles Locke Eastlake. Talbert's published designs, which were largely responsible for the general public acceptance of the new styles in England, were quickly reproduced in this country. But it was Eastlake's book, *Hints on House-*

104

hold Taste, which ran through eight American editions from 1872 to 1890, that spread the gospel throughout the land. "Suddenly the voice of the prophet East-lake was heard crying in the wilderness," editorialized *Harper's Bazar.* "Repent ye, for the Kingdom of the Tasteful is at hand!" The voice was indeed heard far and wide, although as the *Bazar* confessed some years later, not everyone clearly understood what it was saying. Writing in 1878 Mrs. Harriet Prescott Spofford observed that every marrying couple who could read English consulted Eastlake's book and accepted its dicta as gospel truths. The book occasioned, she wrote, "a great awakening, questioning, and study in the matter of household furnishing." There was an immediate demand for furniture in the "Eastlake style" and, as a contemporary journal reported, "as if by united accord" the manufacturers produced furniture they so labeled.

Eastlake did design some furniture but, as his book emphatically reminded his readers, he was less concerned with external forms, or style, than with "constructive principles" and "sincerity" of purpose. He did recommend simplicity of form (and as a partial consequence a relatively inexpensive product that was still in "good taste"), and this made it easy for manufacturers to travesty his ideas—which they apparently did in good measure. In 1877 one critic who had become wearied by so much talk of "principles of art" pointed out to his readers that "Mr. Eastlake has the misfortune to have his name associated with more ugly furniture, we suppose, than the world ever saw before in equal time"—a misfortune of which Eastlake himself was sadly aware. However, in the hands of such master craftsmen as Christian Herter and Léon Marcotte, Eastlake's doctrines were interpreted in good faith—but expensively—in America.

The search for evidence of the true spirit of medieval craftsmanship led to unexpected and exotic sources. In 1862 the first important exhibit of Japanese art and artifacts was shown at the International Exhibition held in London. It made news for the Occidental designer. "If the visitor wishes to see the real Middle Ages," wrote the English architect William Burges, "he must visit the Japanese Court, for at the present day the arts of the Middle Ages have deserted Europe and are only to be found in the East. Here in England we can get mediaeval objects manufactured for us with pain and difficulty, but in Egypt, Syria and Japan you can buy them in the bazaars." In the years immediately following that observation the vogue for Japanese prints, lacquers, pottery, and the like developed rapidly, and importing such treasures became a large business. (Liberty's in London was an outgrowth of this trade.) There also developed an Anglo-Japanese style of furniture combining both Gothic and Japanese elements in lightly framed forms, which won public favor and which were adapted in some of the furniture sold as "Eastlake."

Commodore Matthew Calbraith Perry in 1854 had opened the way for large-scale trade with Japan. As early as 1863 the American artist John La Farge had imported Japanese prints into this country. And about that same time the American expatriate James McNeill Whistler became the first important artist in Europe to incorporate Japanese motifs into his paintings. But the American public at large had its first real introduction to Japanese culture at the Centennial Exhibition. An initial shock at the outlandish costumes worn by the Japanese attendants and the curious methods of the Japanese workmen quickly gave way to admiration of what they offered for sale and what they made. "The Japanese are quite as peculiar in their tools and implements as they are in every other incidental of their life," one journal reported. They rarely used nails and those they

Japanese builders at work at the Centennial

did use, strange of shape to western eyes, they carried in "small wicker baskets, hung to a sash worn around the waist." Another observer judged the Japanese dwelling to be the best-built structure at the fair, and its exotic charms were soon reflected in the decoration of elaborate city mansions and of plain vacation houses in the eastern regions of the country. By then English design books featuring the Anglo-Japanese style in furniture were current in America. The vogue had taken hold at every level.

In America as in England the enthusiastic quest for "good taste" and "artistic" expression in domestic trappings became something of a craze in the 1880's. It was, in fact, known at the time as the "Artistic Craze." Never before had people of professed refinement been so acutely self-conscious of those "aesthetic attitudes" by which they judged the world about them—attitudes which were so delightfully lampooned in the popular operetta *Patience* by Gilbert and Sullivan. The "too utterly utter" personification of aesthetic attitudes was Oscar Wilde, who had studied under Ruskin at Oxford and whom the producer of *Patience*, Richard D'Oyly Carte, sent to America in the winter of 1881–82 (as a sort of advance agent) to lecture on the very subject that was so happily burlesqued in the play. Wilde was the model for that

> . . . most intense young man,
> A soulful-eyed young man,
> An ultra poetical, super-aesthetical,
> Out-of-the-way young man!

about whose adventures all America was singing that season to the tunes of *Patience*. After a year of often farcical episodes Wilde returned to England, discouraged enough by his reception across the land to consider giving up his knee breeches and cutting his hair. ("If Mr. Wilde will leave the lilies and daffodils and come west to Cincinnati," one reporter had promised, "we will undertake to show him how to deprive thirty hogs of their intestines in one minute.") Wilde's departure was, concluded one member of the press, "the end of the aesthetic movement" in America. Whether that was true or not, the movement as it had grown under William Morris, Rossetti, and others, and as it was represented in its more colorful phases by Wilde and Whistler, had a lasting influence on the decorative arts. The very word "art" had taken on certain new and precious connotations that persist in today's usage.

One further addition to the cultural scene was the evolution of what, for reasons not clear, was called the Queen Anne style in architecture. The name was applied to some of the English buildings seen at the Centennial, buildings that with their open halls and great fireplaces recalled Elizabethan and Jacobean structures, if not those of Queen Anne's own time. During the decade following the fair, the style was transformed into the American vernacular, characterized by light frame construction, irregular picturesque outlines, sharply peaked roofs, spindled verandas, upper-story balconies, and large, open interior spaces. Such designs, it was felt, were "sincere," "artistic," and "practical," and at the same time, a fitting complement to Eastlake furnishings; they were comparable in some ways to Japanese constructions. Here, in short, was a style for the times, and since it could be adapted to almost any level of architectural pretension it became popular almost at once, "not only among the educated, but even among the rustic populations."

Those "rustic populations" were a rapidly diminishing tribe. In the last

Flower stand, Anglo-Japanese style

quarter of the century people continued to swarm into American cities from all directions, from country and village and from foreign lands as well. To cope with the problems of congestion in New York City, apartment houses, or "French flats" as this novel expedient was early called, were brought into being. These were, in effect, high-class tenements for the well-to-do urbanite, who earlier had had to buy a single house or resort to the dreariness of a boardinghouse. As early as 1870 the architect Richard Morris Hunt had constructed the Stuyvesant, on East 18th Street, with dumb-waiters—another novel convenience. For from one thousand to fifteen hundred dollars a year the Stuyvesant offered suites of six rooms and a bath—and a substantial savings in servant hire. Within a relatively few years such accommodations were commonplace. New York's first "luxury" apartment house, called the Dakota and still standing, was put up on West 72nd Street in 1884, when this part of the city was considered as remote from the center as the Dakota Territory. Elsewhere in the city Hunt and others were designing châteaux of almost unprecedented magnificence for the Vanderbilts, the Astors, and other patrons of great wealth—châteaux whose splendid furnishings had little of the "sincerity" of Eastlake but much of the opulence of Louis XIV. One aggressive little journal devoted to Ruskin's ideas, *The New Path*, declared that it would wage relentless warfare against those gaudy embellishments favored by the merchant princes, but the princes did not heed. The day of the professional designer had dawned. Speaking of such elaborate homes, a representative of the prominent firm Pottier & Stymus reported to the press in 1882: "We generally get a house from the mason, that is, when the mason work has been finished, and have charge of the entire woodwork decoration. . . . Sometimes we get *carte blanche* for everything—style, design, quality and price." Their rich customers, he pointed out, preferred furnishings in the Louis XIV, Louis XVI, and Renaissance styles.

That year, 1882, Christian Herter finished his work on the William H. Vanderbilt house (see page 100), of which a detail from one room is shown in the opening illustration of this chapter. Herter was architect, designer, *and* decorator of this elaborate establishment, which one contemporary, somewhat blinded by its magnificence, claimed "better than any other possible selection, may stand as a representative of the new impulse now felt in the national life." This was, he added reverently (Vanderbilt had paid for the publication from which these quotations are excerpted), "a typical American residence, seized at the moment when the nation began to have a taste of its own, an architecture, a connaisseurship [sic!], and a choice in the appliances of luxury, society, culture." It was but one of the series of Vanderbilt family homes that, with increasing size and splendor, continued to rise farther up Fifth Avenue, in Newport, Rhode Island, and—the largest of all—in Asheville, North Carolina. Viewing that Fifth Avenue scene some years later a French visitor to New York commented on those "vast constructions which reproduce the palaces and châteaux of Europe. . . . The absence of unity in this architecture," he remarked, "is a sufficient reminder that this is the country of the individual will, as the absence of gardens and trees around these sumptuous residences proves the newness of all this wealth and of the city. This avenue has visibly been willed and created by sheer force of millions. . . ."

Not far from the city's most palatial monuments were other "typical" American residences, the drab tenements and billets that were unfit for human habitation but that did actually house a sizable part of the population. Other

THE SIX-MARK TEA-POT.

Æsthetic Bridegroom. "It is quite consummate, is it not!"
Intense Bride. "It is, indeed! Oh, Algernon, let us live up to it!"

Humorous commentary on the "Artistic Craze"

The interior of a Queen Anne house, 1878

cities showed the same pattern in reduced scale. The slum-mansion combination had become a characteristic aspect of urban "development."

However many came into the city from the farms, there were not enough Americans to service the growing industrial machinery of the nation, so much of it concentrated in urban areas, and a cry went up for more immigrants to man the flaming forges of the mills, to ply needles and work sewing machines in the garment houses, and to dig coal in the outlying mines. And they came by millions— Italians, Croats, Czechs, Magyars, Poles, Greeks, Russians, and still others along with the English, Irish, and Germans. During the 1880's alone, wrote one observer, America had "suffered a peaceful invasion by an army four times as vast as the estimated numbers of Goths and Vandals that swept over Southern Europe and overwhelmed Rome." There were those who feared that the invasion of those "gross little foreigners," as the expatriate American Henry James on a return visit to Boston snobbishly referred to them, would end by seriously changing and corrupting the character of American society. Nevertheless, those people came to the New World with the same mixed motives that had brought the early settlers and, however different their physical appearance and background, they had no less biological efficiency than the firstcomers. In addition, the typical newcomer displayed an almost pathetic eagerness to adapt himself to American patterns of thought and outlook, and to find some kinship, however remote, with the Founding Fathers.

In both native born and immigrant the Centennial aroused a poignant nostalgia for the early American past, specially for the colonial period that was so eloquently summarized in the centennial edition of George Bancroft's *History of the United States*. The nation had grown big and complicated since 1776 and the colonial scene recalled the wholesome simplicities of life in America's ancestral past. "Going back to Boston [and seeing its colonial relics]," wrote one author, ". . . begets a feeling that our ordinary world is too large." This looking backward involved more than nostalgia, however. It was also a search among all the possibilities that were opened to the architect and designer for a new and indigenous style. "If ever America is to become possessed of an historical style," observed one sympathetic Englishman, "it must spring from the work of the old colonists." The acceptance of that point of view led in two directions: toward colonial "revivalism," including a growing passion for native antiques and reproductions that never has abated, and toward new experiments using for inspiration colonial art and architecture.

If any one person was responsible for the change toward an indigenous American architecture, major credit would probably go to Henry Hobson Richardson. He was, as Lewis Mumford has written, a man who "in stature, ideas, and habits of mind . . . was a curiously close counterpart of William Morris"; a man with "the build and driving force of a bison." More firmly than any other contemporary American architect, Richardson came to terms with his times. He designed buildings of every purpose, from frame dwellings to tall commercial structures of masonry, all of them (at least those of his mature years) freshly conceived in terms of their functions and all graced with a sense of fitness. He died in 1886 at the age of forty-seven, at the very dawn of the age of steel construction, whose qualities he was approaching in masonry during his last years. Ironically, it was the influence of two of his own pupils, Charles Follen McKim and Stanford White, in the buildings at the World's Columbian Exposition held at Chicago in 1893, that set off a new trend back toward the historical revivalism from which

Richardson had so successfully escaped in his quest of a living architecture.

McKim, White, and other architects and artists who created the White City on the Chicago fairgrounds were men, some with a Beaux Arts background, who shared a devotion to the "pure ideal of the ancients." Henry Adams thought that their imposition of classical standards on the raw, lusty Midwest was a "rupture in historical sequence." Whether it represented a thin, impermanent veneer on that regional culture or a solid shift of American ideals, as he rather hoped, he could not determine. Some others were more decided and hoped otherwise. "Arcadian architecture is one thing and American architecture is another," wrote one critic. "Men bring not back the mastodon. Nor we those times."

If the dominant architecture of the Columbian Exposition looked to the classical past for its inspiration, there were other important manifestations of times to come. The fair was a herald of the Age of Electricity. Here for the first time the man in the street got an impressive notion of what electricity would do for him. Several cities had already installed electric street lights, and electric trolley cars were already running along more than two thousand miles of track in America. But even sophisticated folk were somewhat bewildered by the queer brightness that could be enclosed in a glass bulb and turned on and off by pressing a button, and by cars whirring through the streets without any apparent means of propulsion. Mysteries were involved beyond ordinary understanding. To Henry Adams the dynamo that made it all happen became a symbol of infinity, a moral force as strong for its time as the Cross had been in earlier centuries.

The World's Columbian Exposition at night

125. *Left: hall and furnishings, New York City*

126. *Below: an armchair of inlaid ebonized wood*

126a. *Opposite: crest detail from the chair below*

Inlaid Elegance

Despite the reformers' cry for simplicity and sincerity in furniture design, the Gilded Age rolled on with its princely tastes and dazzling *décors*. *The Art Journal*, 1877, in describing the library of one Fifth Avenue mansion—"ebony inlaid with ivory"—pointed out that the art of inlay had become a "favourite reproduction of a past fashion; it demands infinite nicety, skilled and patient labour." Parquet, or inlaid floors, had already "taken a strong hold on public taste, as represented among the wealthier classes," and was particularly touted for having been "in use for centuries among the upper classes in France and Germany." Inlaid furniture, as well, continued its marked revival. This opulent armchair (126) was made for James Lenox, the New York philanthropist and bibliophile, and carries an inlay of the Lenox coat of arms on the back. A similar chair, which may be by the same unknown cabinetmaker, was pictured in an interior view (125) of Dr. I. Wyman Drummond's house.

127. *Left: rosewood table, mother-of-pearl inlay and gilt*

128. *Top right: a chair from the John D. Rockefeller house*

129. *Center right: inlaid mahogany chair, Pottier & Stymus*

130. *Bottom right: carved mahogany chair with inlaid panels*

The Decorator and Furnisher, in 1886, offered a definitive list of colored woods suited to inlay and marquetry: "lime, holly, box, maple, beech, poplar, for white; lignum-vitae, walnut, teak, partridge wood, for brown; fustic and satinwood for yellow; tulip, purplewood, amboyna, mahogany, logwood, camwood for red; ebony, or stained wood for black." The article further suggested that it would be well for furniture makers to seek out and study ancient examples of marquetry, "the beauty of the old work lying in the charming feeling for color and tenderness of treatment." Mrs. Spofford had earlier given fair warning to her readers: "Today the Dutch counterfeit those early marquetries, and sell them at high prices to those unable to detect the forgery." And Clarence Cook gave special notice to Italian chairs of contemporary manufacture, "inlaid all over with mother-of-pearl," as well as to similarly inlaid stools from Morocco and Egypt.

131. Brass-footed table with a marble top and a rosewood border inlaid with mother-of-pearl

132. Adjustable mirror and dressing table with a velvet footrest

In 1884 when Mrs. Arabella Worsham (formerly of Alabama) married railroad magnate Collis P. Huntington (formerly a grocery clerk in Oneonta, New York), she sold her New York town house to oil tycoon John D. Rockefeller (formerly a bookkeeper in Cleveland, Ohio). The Rockefellers took possession of the brownstone house, lock, stock, and barrel—rugs, furniture, and draperies. Inlay, on woodwork and furniture, was a principal aspect of the *décor*, with delicate patterns on a door or mantel, for example, matched by inlay on a bedstead or chest of drawers. On this panel (134), a detail of the exquisite woodwork in a dressing room, the inner decoration (carved in relief) has a vine border that was repeated on a side chair (133). The mirror and dressing table (132) were also among the furnishings, as was the chair (128) on page 112, part of a set designed for a Moorish parlor.

133. Above: inlaid chair with tufted upholstery

134. Opposite: paneling with a border of inlay

Eastlake & Honesty

"In adopting the Eastlake method of furnishing," wrote one critic during the 1890's, "we step out of our luxurious carriage to take a bracing walk upon the firm earth." The "sincere" principles of construction popularized by Charles Eastlake were chiefly based on medieval and Early Jacobean forms, and represented a complete reversal from the curvaceous styles that had been in vogue, particularly in furniture of French inspiration. Eastlake's philosophy of design, that beauty was inherent in simplicity and usefulness, set off a burst of interpretations — also variously known as neo-Gothic, modern English Gothic, domestic Gothic, and "the homelike style." Furniture makers emphasized straight lines, eschewed the "sham" of veneer, and made a great display of "carving of an ultra-Gothic type, and an appearance of the most ingenuous truth-telling in the construction." The examples shown here are solid, freely translated versions of Eastlake's ideas. Attributed to Allen & Brother, Philadelphia, these pieces of ebonized cherry wood, some with insets of Minton tiles, were reportedly bought at the Centennial. The complete set included no fewer pieces than two spring-seat side chairs, a bureau, night table, towel rack, washstand, window cornices, curtains, and draperies.

135. Wardrobe with a full-length mirror

136. *Left: bed with blue damask panel overhead*

137. *Above: platform rocker, or "patent rocker"*

138. *Inlaid side chair, one of a pair*

139. *Left: an inlaid wardrobe branded "Herter Bro's"*

140. *Above: a mirror, part of the Herter bedroom set*

141. *Above: matching bureau finished with marble top*

142. *Opposite: mirror with a frame of beveled glass*

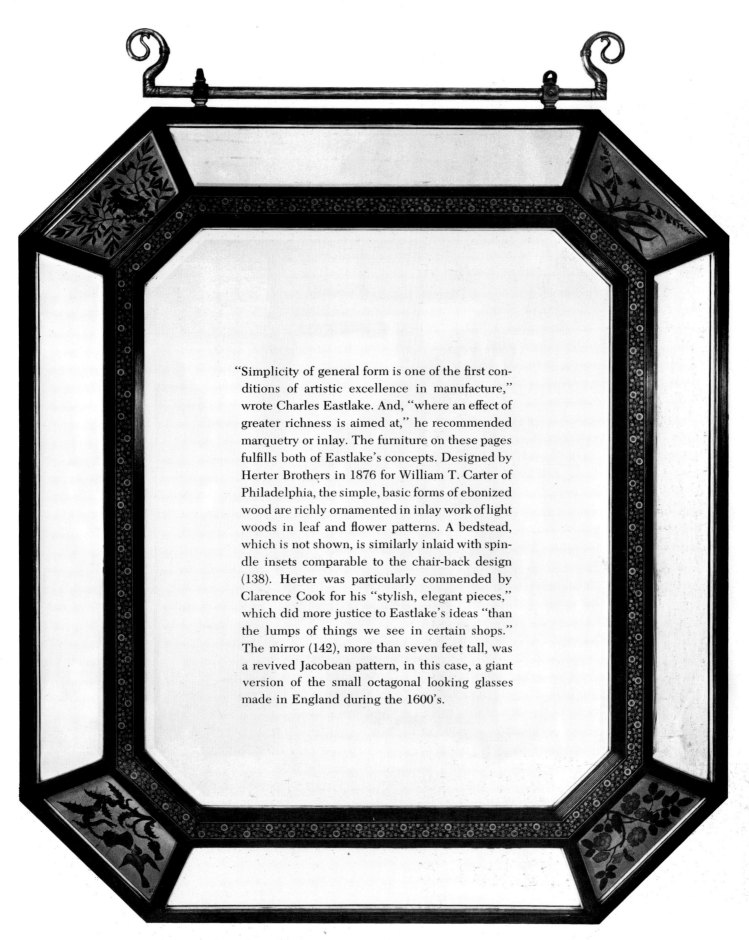

"Simplicity of general form is one of the first conditions of artistic excellence in manufacture," wrote Charles Eastlake. And, "where an effect of greater richness is aimed at," he recommended marquetry or inlay. The furniture on these pages fulfills both of Eastlake's concepts. Designed by Herter Brothers in 1876 for William T. Carter of Philadelphia, the simple, basic forms of ebonized wood are richly ornamented in inlay work of light woods in leaf and flower patterns. A bedstead, which is not shown, is similarly inlaid with spindle insets comparable to the chair-back design (138). Herter was particularly commended by Clarence Cook for his "stylish, elegant pieces," which did more justice to Eastlake's ideas "than the lumps of things we see in certain shops." The mirror (142), more than seven feet tall, was a revived Jacobean pattern, in this case, a giant version of the small octagonal looking glasses made in England during the 1600's.

A. Kimbel & J. Cabus, 7 & 9 East 20th Str. New-York.

120

"Sideboards and bookcases of mediæval design," rhapsodized *Appletons' Journal* in 1876, "with lovely keys which Lucretia Borgia might have worn at her girdle, and which Benvenuto Cellini may have originally designed, lock up the tea and sugar from pilfering domestics. Doors swing not on modern hinges, but on long brass ornamental bars." A roomful of just such furniture was shown by Kimbel & Cabus, a New York City firm, whose designs and stock of pottery certainly appear to have met Eastlake's standards. In *Hints on Household Taste*, he wrote that if a sideboard "were constructed in a plain and straightforward manner, and were additionally provided with a few narrow shelves at the rear for displaying the old china vases and rare porcelain, of which almost every house contains a few examples, what a picturesque appearance it might present at the end of a room!" Narrow shelves, in fact, tucked away hither and yon on so-called Eastlake furniture, became one of the earmarks of the style, as did spindling, so extensively used for decorative balustrading. Both chairs in the Kimbel & Cabus illustration combine spindles with upholstery, a motif found in designs drawn by Eastlake himself.

143. *Above: the Kimbel & Cabus showroom, 1877, with up-to-the-minute stock of Eastlake styles*

144. *Right: a cupboard, shown in a photograph pictured in a Kimbel & Cabus furniture catalogue*

Photographs from a catalogue of Kimbel & Cabus:

145. Right: cupboard made with Japanesque tiles

146. Below: a conversation chair, or tête-à-tête

147. Opposite: bookrack topped with carved owl. As one lady of the press wrote: "The soothing influence of an Eastlake bookcase on an irritated husband has never been sufficiently calculated."

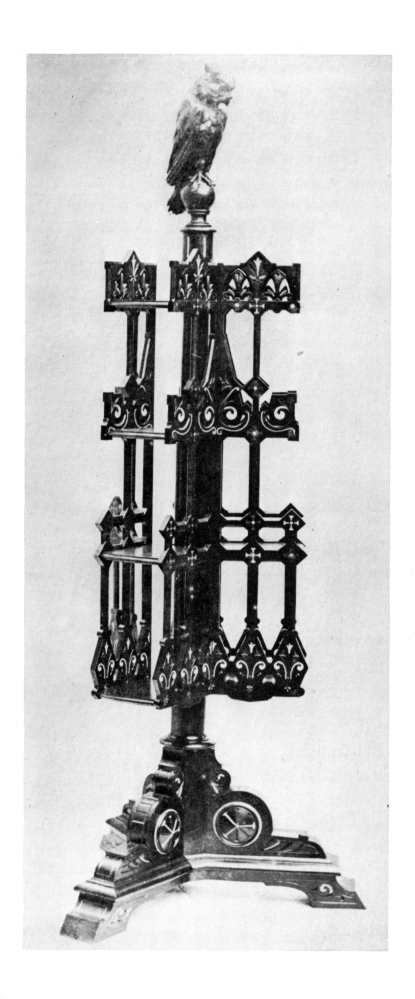

Eastlake recommended tiles for flooring and even for hall wainscoting, especially the encaustic tiles by Minton, Hollins, & Co., the English ceramic firm. And with the tile exhibits at the Centennial, a new decorating fad began. Tiles were used everywhere, in woodwork and on furniture, in parlor, bedroom, and bath. One New York town house was acclaimed as "a paradise of tiles" by *The Art Journal*, and *Appletons' Journal* raved about furniture in a Boston shop with tiles of "pale green ground-tint, with the common wild-rose and cat-o'-nine-tails" and "Japanese tiles of storks and sprays of peach-blossoms." Here, a conversation chair (146) has insets, apparently of tile, with such beguiling devices as mice and a butterfly on the wing. Fireplaces and mantelpieces particularly lent themselves to tiled ornamentations. One columnist, who extolled the "morality in a tile," urged her readers to build "Æsop's fables, with their immortal teachings, into your fireplace." By 1881 the fad reached such proportions that an English architect suggested that impecunious ladies, devoted to artistic pursuits, take up tile painting as an "honourable means to gain a livelihood."

"The natural grain of such woods as oak, rosewood, walnut, &c., is in itself an ornamental feature," wrote Eastlake, "if it be not obscured and clogged by artificial varnish." *Harper's Magazine,* in 1876, in an article on "Modern Dwellings," added a firm moral footnote by declaring that "want of honesty" in the treatment of wood was "a great evil." This bureau (149) and bedstead (150) again demonstrate Christian Herter's success in interpreting the Eastlake style. Here, the natural grain of bird's-eye maple provides an ornamental feature—an "honest" treatment of the wood—highlighted with insets of Japanese hand-painted tiles and the popular spindle motif.

Eastlake also approved of carving in low relief as one of the "legitimate modes of decoration." Incised designs, comparable to those of the Renaissance Revival, were frequently used on neo-Gothic "art furniture," the pattern picked out in gold. This technique was used on the easel (148), also ornamented with blue and black. Easels had become a fashionable fixture, a touch of the artist's studio transplanted to the parlor, and were used to display prints, paintings, and portraits. Often, in unrestrained bursts of decorative fervor, the easel and its picture were hung about with draped swags of plush, or even overgrown with strategically planted twining vines and mosses.

148. Walnut easel with incised carving

149. *Above: a bureau, part of a bedroom suite*

150. *Below: a bed, also a part of the same set*

125

152. *Japanese bazaar and teahouse at the Centennial exhibit*

Japanese Embellishments

In preparation for the Centennial Exhibition, Japan shipped fifty carloads of building materials, objects for display, and a native work crew to Philadelphia. Bystanders gawked at the "peculiar construction" methods and building tools "of eccentric uses" employed by Japanese carpenters. Street crowds, it was said, so harassed Japanese in native dress that many abandoned their "own outlandish gear" for western clothing. But with the opening of the fair, American amusement at Nipponese ways was transformed into admiration and wonder. The Japanese dwelling was deemed "the best-built structure" on the fairgrounds, "as nicely put together as a piece of cabinet-work." The Japanese bazaar (152) was thronged with customers who pored over such exotic ware as "antique bronzes, curious specimens of porcelain, and pottery, wood and ivory carvings, and lacquer work." The craze "for all one sees that's Japanese" had struck. In England James McNeill Whistler, the expatriate American painter, had already fallen under the rising spell of Japanese art. In this canvas (151), one of several painted during the 1860's with predominant Japanese motifs, a young woman in a kimono, seated before a *yamatoe* screen, gazes at a collection of Japanese prints.

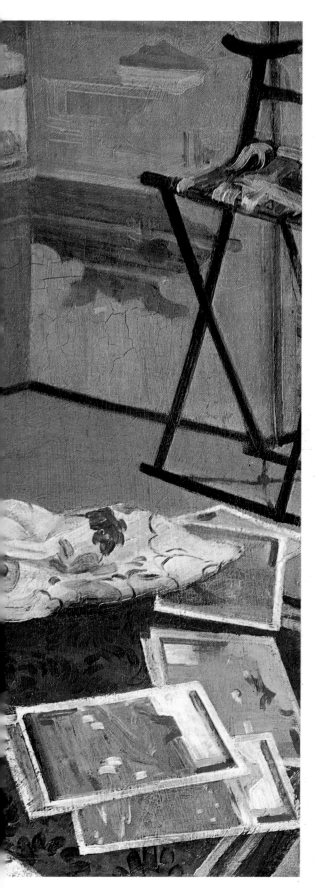

151. *Painted by Whistler,* Caprice in Purple and Gold, No. 2: The Golden Screen, *dated 1864*

127

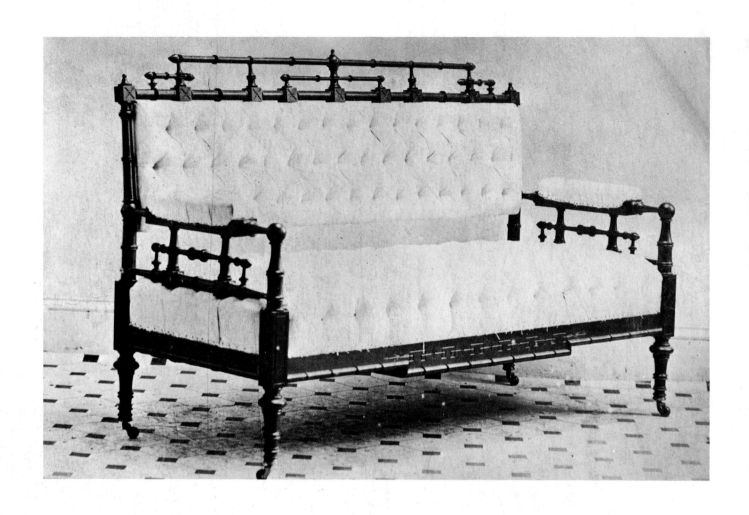

153. *Above: settee designed in the Japanese mode*

154. *Right: a Japanese style hanging wall cabinet*

155. *Opposite, above: English furniture patterns*

156. *Opposite: an étagère in the Japanese style*

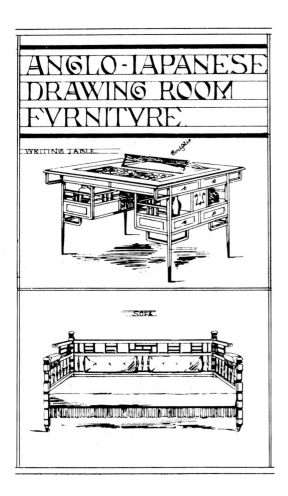

Following the Centennial exhibit Japanesque details soon appeared in American architecture—upturned eaves, overhanging eaves, lattices and trelliswork. By the end of the century, out-and-out imitations of Japanese houses and gardens were abundant. One such effort in Salem, Massachusetts, was a nostalgic rendering by a Japanese art dealer, Bunkio Matsuki, married to a Salem girl and settled in America. And from the outset of Frank Lloyd Wright's career in the 1890's, his work evinced his interest in and admiration of Japanese art and architecture. Among furniture designs inspired by the Centennial, Japanese trends were evident on every hand. These illustrations (153, 154, 156) are reproduced from photographs in a Kimbel & Cabus catalogue. The settee, with latticed arms and cresting, reflects a similar pattern (155) from *Art Furniture Designed by Edward W. Godwin*, London, 1878. Godwin, in fact, was so enamored of Japanese traditions that the ladies of his household reportedly dressed in kimonos.

During the 1880's and 1890's such magazines as *The Decorator and Furnisher* deluged readers with articles on every aspect of Japanese design. ("What," they exclaimed, "may our little neighbors across the wide ocean have still in store for us?") Those who could not afford embroidered or painted screens, porcelains, or rare bronzes, (159) were given inexpensive decorating tips. Japanese fans, for example, could be arranged on a dado, pinned to picture frames, affixed to drapery brackets. No parlor, in truth, from Maine to California was considered complete without a Japanese fan. *The Art Journal* extolled Japanese pottery as "finished and learned." Clarence Cook praised the delicacies of Japanese embroidery, as opposed to "eye-scratching" German colors. Mrs. Spofford acclaimed the "freshness" of Japanese art, not yet "injured by European demands." And in England, Gilbert and Sullivan merrily composed *The Mikado*.

157. Top: kerosene lamp with bronze base and painted globe decorated in Japanese patterns, about 1900

158. Above: a side table with Japanesque latticework

159. Opposite: Japanese "treasures" at the Centennial

For Softer Sitting

Improved textile manufacturing and printing machinery, as well as the rapidly spreading use of sewing machines, drastically reduced the cost of many forms of fabric products in the third quarter of the nineteenth century. Never before had the upholsterer had such ample opportunities to practice and expand his trade. How completely he could monopolize the decoration of an interior was indicated by the exhibit of Carrington, De Zouché & Co., Philadelphia, at the Centennial (160). For the first time the upholstery on furniture was more important than the structural frame; indeed, the frame tended to disappear altogether in the abundance of fabric covering. The perfecting of spiral metal springs led to their increased use for chairs and sofas (and beds), and to accommodate them a deeper frame was required for the seat than in earlier upholstered forms. Tufting the fabric helped to keep thick layers of stuffing material in position. The soft comfort of allover upholstered chairs encouraged some men to lounge in a manner that was deemed offensive to ladies of proper sensibilities.

162. Upholstered armchair, about 1885

160. Opposite: exhibit of Carrington, De Zouché & Co. at the Centennial

161. Above: a "conversational" seat

133

Hints & Notions from The Decorator & Furnisher (1882-1889)

"People do not shun expense so long as they get what they want. This change in taste dates from the Centennial Exhibition, and has been developed by travel principally. The desire for decoration amounts to a perfect craze, and no one can tell when it is going to end."

❖

Bullion embroidery is the name of a new upholstering material introduced by Mr. Cornelius V. Smith, of London. It is the application of the gold bullion, such as is employed on military uniforms, against a black or other dark colored satin ground. The effect is said to be very rich, as may be readily believed. It is thought this will in a great measure replace the now popular Persian saddle bags.

❖

Dogs, in shades to match the furniture, are said to be favored in fashionable houses.

❖

Waste-baskets in split bamboo are now decorated with large bunches of artificial flowers tied on with gay ribbons. Occasionally variety is obtained by the use of vegetables instead of flowers, bunches of Spring carrots, asparagus, etc., being used.

❖

The tambourine is turned to many uses; a frame for a friend's picture, the background of a musical programme, or a dinner menu, a hold-all for letters and a wall decoration. A pretty notion is to encase a friends effigy in the center of one's guitar.

❖

Coats of mail, helmets, spears and other remembrances of feudal times, are being employed more than ever in decoration, and those unable to buy these ornaments in steel may find excellent imitations in papier maché.

❖

Why not make electricity a study in our technical schools? There is every indication that this force will be the great motor for the world, and the sooner its capacities are understood, the better for the people generally.

❖

Swinging Couches are now very luxurious. These are made sometimes of brass, sometimes of heavy wire, handsome curtains of satin or velvet being hung on silver rings, to be drawn aside when the occupant wishes to recline in them.

❖

Genuine Tapestries, such as Gobelins, or Aubusson, or Beauvais, used in connection with deep-toned woods of choice varieties, such as Circassian walnut, San Domingo mahogany, or German walnut, are suitable for Renaissance furniture.

❖

A gypsy table is decorated by covering the top (circular) and legs with plush. At the intersection of the legs, and knotted, is added a scarf of plush embroidered with gold and fringe. The edge of the top is trimmed with heavy silk.

❖

Paper hangings are made to resemble leather so closely that the imitation can only be detected by the touch. They appear in plain dark colors, neutrals, and in the more elaborate semblance to the metals, and are of sufficient stability to admit of sponging with water, when soiled, without injury. . . .

❖

"The lady who wears her initials in diamonds on a brooch is vulgar."

Moon parasols are being revived in Paris.

❖

The display of fancy furniture has never been greater and more satisfactory than it is at this time. . . . The report seems to be in every direction that rosewood will gain in favor for parlor suites, and a table in this wood is shown by one manufacturer, supported by three recum-

bent lions. The chair to accompany this table has lions heads at the arms, with the mane drooping over the breast, and the conception and workmanship is most creditable. A small centre table is upheld by three storks, and a corner cabinet has its lower shelf resting upon the outstretched wings of a bat.

❀

Stamped Japanese Quilts are in active demand. They are sold for use in the gardens in summertime. "Lawn spreads" is the term sometimes given them.

❀

Peacock feathers stitched or glued to satin and set in the panels of a door, make a very pretty decoration.

❀

A Set of Smoking-Room Curtains is made in cigar brown satin sheeting, embroidered with the pale green leaves and flowers of the tobacco plant. . . . The curtains are bound with amber-colored galoon, mounted with rings on a wooden

bar, suggesting a "long-nine" cigar, and looped back with strings of large imitation amber beads.

❀

Window shades have field flowers or vines painted upon them.

❀

A "Mauve dinner" was recently given at a fashionable uptown residence. The cloth was of lace, through which a delicate lining of mauve silk was visible. The light shone through dainty shades of the same color, ornamented with wreaths of lilacs and silver lace. The napkins were bordered with lace, the flowers consisted of orchids and deep-tinted lilacs.

❀

Ribbon is not invited to fashionable tables so often as formerly. Time was when every lady-finger and every piece of rolled bread had its waistband and bow of narrow ribbon, but these articles now appear unbelted in good society.

❀

In the centre of a lady's work table is a gilt brass lamp stand bearing a tulip shade to which a savage bronze dog, in the act of endeavoring to break bounds, is attached by a chain.

❀

Ladies in buying chairs, pose in them before a looking-glass to see whether the style agrees with their mode of posture.

❀

A new mantel cover of golden brown silk serge has a scarf covering the shelf and hanging over each end half way to the floor. These ends are embroidered with Japanese roses in shaded yellows. Across the fronts of the mantel is a straight lambrequin gathered up very short at each corner of the shelf and

fastened to the scarf with a large bow of wide gold-colored ribbon. Across the centre of this lambrequin is a spray of the yellow roses.

❀

"Chicken down" is the name of the newest color, a delicate yellow.

❀

Geranium red has replaced cardinal.

❀

A miniature railway train of burnished silver, copper and steel, the cars loaded with fruit, has made its appearance as a dessert service on a millionaire's table. The locomotive is apparently complete in its appointments.

❀

Since the Montreal carnival, snow shoes have become popular articles of wall decoration. . . . A trophy composed of a pair of snow shoes, a couple of lacrosse sticks, and one of the red and blue woolen caps which have such a jaunty effect in a Canadian snow scene, would make a very striking and pictorial ornament indeed for a smoking-room wall.

❀

A very pretty and inexpensive protection for gilt picture or mirror frames is the pink mosquito net . . ., looped back each side of the picture and fastened with a bow of pink ribbon.

❀

A hat rack of spears is a novelty.

❀

Storks made of wool, and with wings widespread, are suspended by invisible wires in a recess or bay window.

❀

The numerous articles of Swiss carved work in white wood afford ladies good opportunities for hand-painting.

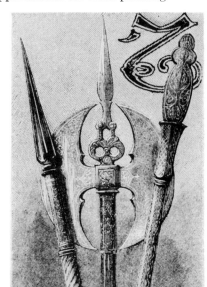

Art & Fancy Glass

During the years between the two fairs at Philadelphia and Chicago, and for some years after to be sure, the glass blowers of America made remarkable efforts to quench the thirst for beauty that was so typical of the times. This was, as one highly susceptible lady of those times observed with barely controlled rapture, the "fine summer of perfected art." Blown glass blossomed out in a wide variety of new colors and shapes that caught the popular fancy under such alluring, descriptive names as Peachblow, Amberina, Pomona, Agata, Burmese, and many others besides. The search for novelty, so distressing to sterner critics, led to extravagant experiments that tried the technical skills of the glassmaker to the utmost. Some craftsmen were brought over from Europe to supplement, with their special talents, the efforts of native craftsmen.

Peachblow attempted to simulate in glass the color and character of the Chinese porcelain that was finished with what is today known as a peach bloom glaze. In 1886 an eight-inch vase of this porcelain was sold at auction for eighteen thousand dollars, a price that "exceeded all anticipations" and that created a sensation of sorts. Ladies were soon appearing with Peachblow complexions, Peachblow jokes abounded, and Peachblow glass, produced at various factories in different shades and shapes, became a popular fashion. The auctioned vase and other Oriental porcelain forms were reproduced more or less faithfully at several glasshouses, which also turned out such prosaic, Occidental conveniences as whiskey tumblers, butter dishes, and finger bowls in the same ware.

Fruit bowls made of "richly decorated glass" and in "assorted colors," often with ruffled rims and mounted on silver-plated supporting stands (163), were apparently first marketed by the silver-plate manufacturers around 1886. They remained popular throughout the rest of the century.

163. *Above: bowl with gold decoration on silver-plated stand*

164. *Opposite: vase patented 1886 by the New England Glass Co.*

165. Above: Crown Milano cracker jar, 1886–95; the silver-plated cover by Pairpoint Manufacturing Co.

166. Right: Royal Flemish vase, made 1890–1900

167. Opposite: Amberina footed bowl, about 1885

In the summer of 1885 it was reported that American glassmakers were aware of a great demand for "artistic glass" and that a large amount of money had been invested in costly experiments with it. "The point of it is," the reporter concluded, "that our people love artistic things. . . ." He singled out the New England Glass Company for the surprising results it had achieved, including the widely popular Amberina (167), a ware of yellowish-amber tone shading to ruby. The unusual color was first accidentally achieved when a glass blower's gold ring slipped off his finger into a gathering of molten glass. A few years later the Mount Washington Glass Company was advertising its Royal Flemish line, a variously colored ware distinguished by fanciful designs in raised lines of heavy enamel (166). The same New Bedford firm also produced what they called Crown Milano (165), a painted and enameled white opal glass with ancient precedents.

Still another novelty of the Mount Washington works was named Burmese, a ware which, like Peachblow, was opaque and resembled porcelain rather than glass. A gift of Burmese glass so pleased Queen Victoria that she ordered a tea service and some vases from America, and when a patent licensee produced similar glass in England she permitted it to be called Queen's Burmese Ware. In 1885 Joseph Locke of the New England Glass Company patented what he called Pomona glass. A contemporary description refers to its surface as "treated in such a manner as to produce feathery forms, ice crystals, and all the effect of the fantastical 'Jack Frost' ice tracery." Agata, with its mottled surface resembling small oil slicks (170), was also patented by Locke in 1887. In an account of the New England factory's output *The Decorator and Furnisher* concluded that "the designs are all new, showing our native resources of invention, and that we are not entirely dependent on the foreigner for ideas."

168. *Left: a pattern-molded Burmese candlestick*
169. *Above: a Pomona vase with etched floral designs*

170. *Top: Agata bowl, a ware made for less than a year at the New England Glass Co.*

171. *Below: an Amberina bowl lined, or plated, inside with opaque white glass*

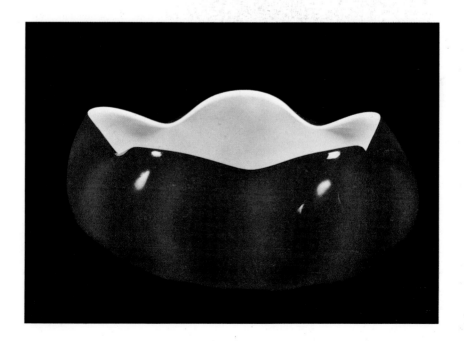

Throughout the last two decades of the nineteenth century art glass was produced, from East to West, in an almost bewildering abundance of rich colors and different shapes. Burmese appeared as bowls (173), candlesticks (168), pitchers, vases, salts, and still other forms. And so did Peachblow and the many other ornamental types. Toward the end of the 1880's Hobbs, Brockunier & Company, of Wheeling, West Virginia, capitalizing on the sensation caused by the price paid for the Chinese porcelain vase at the New York sale, reproduced the piece in Peachblow—or Coral, as it was also called (172)—and soon other companies followed suit. One New York house was selling the reproduction for ninety-eight cents each. "Peachblow is the prevailing craze," it was reported a month or so after the auction, ". . . and between the 'celebrated peachblow cat,' shown in a Broadway window, to the modest peachblow lamp shown in another, there is a wide field, both in the matter of distance and scope . . . for the introduction of the color into other decorations."

172. Opposite: Peachblow version of a porcelain vase

173. Above: Burmese bowl; applied, tooled decoration

Art & Ceramics

The Decorator and Furnisher was gratified to note, in 1884, the rising "taste in domestic crockery, glass, and china." Critics had lamented American prejudice against American ceramics, and it was not uncommon for domestic potters to forge an English trademark—or leave their work unsigned—to assure sales. But American pottery and porcelain, like American art glass, came into its own after the Centennial and fulfilled the Victorian craving for "civilizing, refining, and elevating" *objets d'art*. The ewer (175) was made at the Greenwood Pottery Company, Trenton, New Jersey, and the plate (174) at the Faïence Manufacturing Company, Greenpoint, New York, both with the type of rich blue praised by experts as comparable to the color achieved in European factories. The plate was painted by Francis Lycett, son of Edward Lycett, director of the Faïence Manufacturing Company.

174. Above: porcelain plate, painted about 1890

175. Opposite: porcelain ewer, made about 1885

176. A shell and seaweed plate of majolica

177. Left: a faïence vase, gold
and bronze gildings and veinings

178. Above: lotus ware rose bowl

Majolica, a brilliantly glazed earthenware, lent it-self to rustic patterns—basketry, twining vines, tree trunks, cornstalks, cabbage-leaf plates, and cauli-flower teapots, to list but a few. "Low, vulgar, even barbarous," stormed one critic of the majolica ex-hibit at the Centennial. But rustic fancies appealed to Victorians. Griffen, Smith & Hill, Phoenixville, Penn-sylvania, manufactured Etruscan majolica (176)—now a collector's favorite and once given away with baking powder. Cherubs, also beloved in Victorian arts, waft across this bowl (178) by Knowles, Taylor, & Knowles Company, East Liverpool, Ohio. The bowl, a potpourri, is lotus ware, a fine bone china the firm exhibited at the Columbian Exposition—"exquisite pieces . . . decorated in dainty colors, . . . with jeweled decora-tion and open-work effects." This little vase (179) with the frog and the pitcher plant (found in American marshlands) was designed for the Union Porcelain Works, Greenpoint, New York, by the staff artist Karl Müller, who was born in Germany and educated in Paris. The dolphin-handled vase (177)—"a fine example of artistic treatment," wrote a contemporary expert—is from the New York Faïence Company, and was made by Joseph Lycett, yet another son of the director of the firm.

179. Vase by the Union Porcelain Works, Greenpoint, N.Y.

Possibly the most influential ceramic firm of its day
was the Rookwood Pottery, Cincinnati, Ohio. Founded
in 1880 by Mrs. Maria Longworth Nichols (later Mrs.
Bellamy Storer), Rookwood was the outgrowth of what
had begun as a ladies' class in china painting—then
a nationwide Victorian fad. Operating on a principle
of art for art's sake, Rookwood specialized in a connoisseur's pottery—hand-thrown, one-of-a-kind ceramics—that by 1893 was "found in almost every home of
culture and refinement and in every prominent art museum." The coffeepot (183) by Mrs. Nichols, the vase
(181) by Albert R. Valentien, a Cincinnati artist, and the
jardiniere (182) all exemplify the rich underglaze color
achieved at Rookwood and the highly Japanese flavor
created by the informal placement of plants and animals. There were many Rookwood imitators. This
example (180), trademarked Louwelsa ware, was made

at the Weller Pottery, Zanesville, Ohio.

180. *Opposite: vase, Louwelsa pottery*

181. *Above: vase, with birds on snowy branches, from the Rookwood Pottery*

182. *Above: jardiniere, also Rookwood*

183. *Below: Rookwood coffeepot with Japanese motifs so popular in ceramics*

Diverse Forms in Silver

184. *Above: racing trophy by Tiffany & Company*

185. *Below: a pencil and ink design for a repoussé silver teapot, drawn by Frank Shaw, 1885*

A report of the judges at the Centennial pointed out that the enormous production of silver ore and an unprecedented public demand were stimulating the manufacturers of silverware as never before. What was more, "a growing æsthetical taste" in the country was insisting upon "the highest possibilities" in this useful art. To meet this challenge some silvermaking firms, like some glasshouses, brought in European-trained craftsmen and designers. As in the case of glass, silver assumed an almost bewildering variety of forms and patterns. And no orderly progression of styles can be traced in the resulting profusion. "Changes of fashion constitute the life of the . . . silversmith's trade," one trade journal conceded in 1887. At least one aspect of the "æsthetical taste" of the times called for allover *repoussé* decoration, as in the case of the teapot (186) and coffeepot (187) shown opposite.

150

186. Top: silver repoussé *teapot, about 1890*

187. Left: coffeepot with repoussé *decoration by Tiffany & Company, New York, about 1885*

151

188. *Above: sterling salt shaker by Tiffany & Company, made about 1880*

189. *Right: plated self-pouring teapot*

190. *Left: plated nut bowl, about 1880*

191. *Above: sterling silver wine ewer*

By the 1880's virtually all types of tableware made in sterling silver were also produced in plated ware. "Even families where there is an abundance of ancestral silver," observed *The Decorator and Furnisher* in 1888, "have their pieces duplicated in fine plate and lock up the solid ware in strong boxes and safe deposit vaults for greater security." (By the end of the century a large number of the smaller silver-plating firms in Connecticut had been brought together by the Meriden Britannia Company and finally consolidated as the International Silver Company.) One novelty produced in 1886 by the Meriden company was a "pump pot" or "self-pouring teapot" (189); a plunger attached to the knob on the lid pumped the tea through a strainer and then out through the spout. In their search for ever more novel forms, designers were advised to turn to "the open book of nature," which they did at times with capricious and whimsical spirit (188, 190).

192. Cup with a scene from Die Meistersinger *given to Anton Seidle, conductor of The Metropolitan Opera*

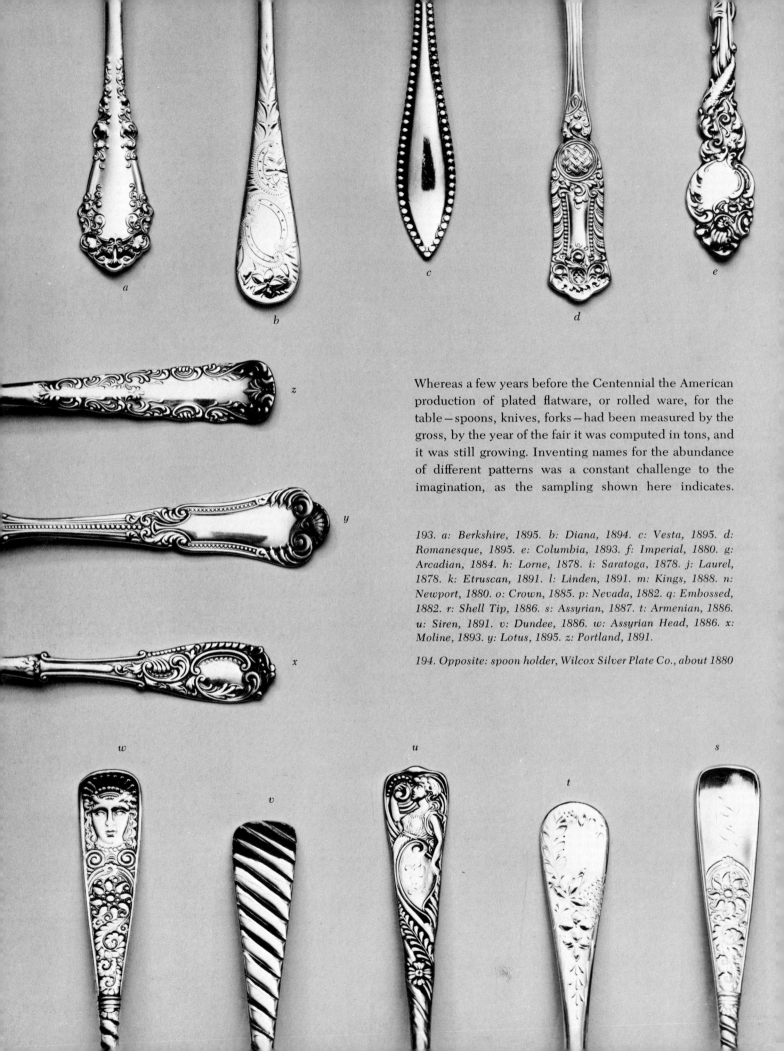

a

b

c

d

e

z

y

x

Whereas a few years before the Centennial the American production of plated flatware, or rolled ware, for the table—spoons, knives, forks—had been measured by the gross, by the year of the fair it was computed in tons, and it was still growing. Inventing names for the abundance of different patterns was a constant challenge to the imagination, as the sampling shown here indicates.

193. *a: Berkshire, 1895. b: Diana, 1894. c: Vesta, 1895. d: Romanesque, 1895. e: Columbia, 1893. f: Imperial, 1880. g: Arcadian, 1884. h: Lorne, 1878. i: Saratoga, 1878. j: Laurel, 1878. k: Etruscan, 1891. l: Linden, 1891. m: Kings, 1888. n: Newport, 1880. o: Crown, 1885. p: Nevada, 1882. q: Embossed, 1882. r: Shell Tip, 1886. s: Assyrian, 1887. t: Armenian, 1886. u: Siren, 1891. v: Dundee, 1886. w: Assyrian Head, 1886. x: Moline, 1893. y: Lotus, 1895. z: Portland, 1891.*

194. *Opposite: spoon holder, Wilcox Silver Plate Co., about 1880*

w

v

u

t

s

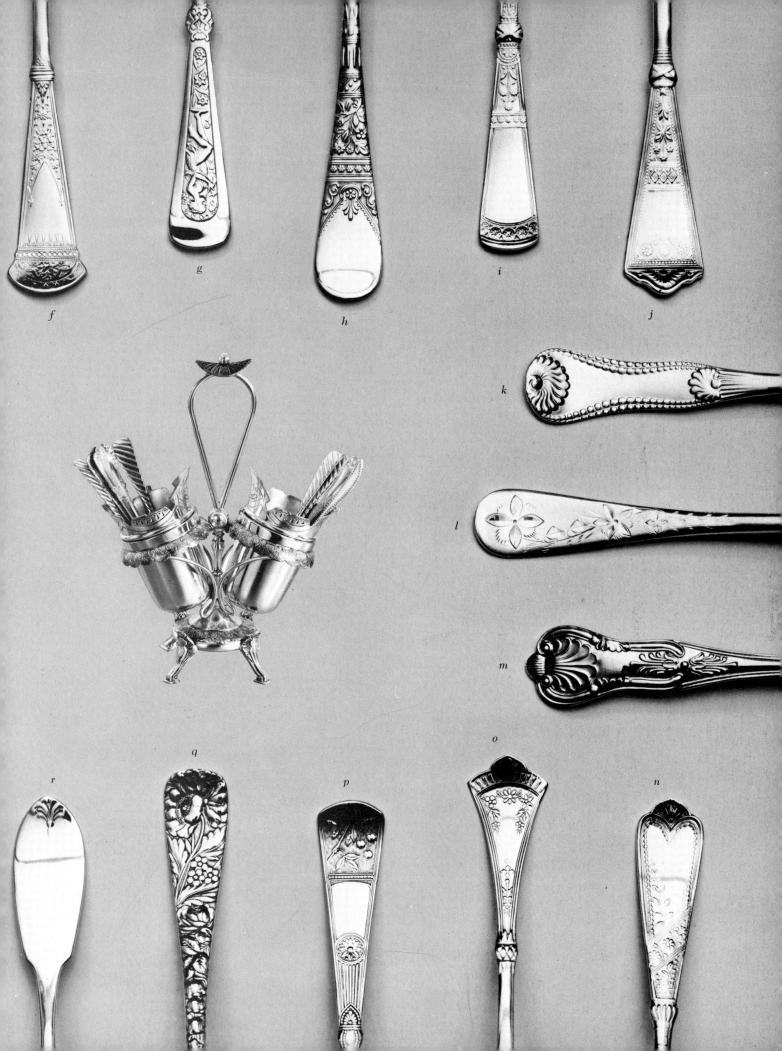

f

g

h

i

j

k

l

m

o

q

r

p

n

195. *Above: silver-plate spoon holder with Tree of Life pressed-glass bowl*

196. *Below: plated caster stand with Daisy and Button pressed-glass bottles*

Still other novelties of design were achieved by combining the pressed and "fancy" glass of the period with silver-plated mounts. "Card receivers are quaint and interesting as to pattern, and are shown in great variety," it was reported in 1888. (Two years earlier the Meriden Britannia Company catalogue had listed fifty-eight different designs.) The complicated practice of leaving calling cards with different corners turned down to indicate a personal visit, an adieu, condolence, or whatever was introduced from Europe shortly after the Civil War. Caster sets with colored and decorated bottles were also designed in "scores of styles, shapes, sizes and prices," prices that in the winter of 1888 ranged from $2.75 (for a luncheon caster) to $25 (for a salad set). A spoon holder (195) was an indispensable element of the tea service. Occasionally one was equipped with a bell for calling a servant.

197. Plated and ornamental glass calling card receiver

"Types of design [in silverwork] follow each other in public favor," wrote a reporter in 1887, "Egyptian, Greek, Etruscan, Byzantine, Assyrian, the severely classic, then capricious mediæval fancies, successively disappear and reappear, perhaps giving way for a time to styles essentially eclectic." That list could have been extended almost indefinitely. The long-necked after-dinner coffeepot (199) made about 1880 by Gorham probably corresponds to those that the company advertised a few years later as being of "odd and unique designs, Turkish, Moorish, and Old English decoration. . . ." In 1894 Tiffany & Company designed and made a pair of vases, one of which is illustrated here (198), of almost Pompeian elegance. These were a wedding present to Annie Louise Lamont who married Harry Harkness Flagler that year. The exuberant, naturalistic, *repoussé* ornament of a salt shaker (200) covers and all but conceals what is essentially an eighteenth-century form. All three pieces are sterling; obviously the popularity of plated ware did not discourage adventures in the solid metal. Indeed, explained a writer in *The Art Journal*, "the production of the artistic designs of the Meriden Company, and other electroplating corporations, appears to have stimulated a taste for the beautiful" in solid silver.

198. One of a pair of sterling vases, 1894

199. *Top, left: coffeepot by Gorham, 1880*

200. *Top, right: salt shaker made about 1890*

201. *Right: an electroplated card receiver, by the Meriden Silver Plate Co., about 1885*

202. *Opposite: a detail from* Spring on the Susquehanna   203. *Above:* Going to Church, *after a painting by Durrie*

Prang's Pretty Pictures

In 1871 Mr. Philip Gilbert Hamerton, "the most practical if not the most fertile writer in England about matters of art," complained that the machine carving on American furniture was utterly without charm. "You might as well try to paint by a machine," he cautioned. An American writer retorted that had Hamerton visited Mr. Louis Prang's flourishing chromolithograph factory in Boston he would realize that, there, paintings were in fact produced by machinery or, as he might better have said, reproduced by machinery. Over several decades Prang's was only the most prominent and prolific of the American establishments that were issuing large editions of inexpensive color reproductions of popular subjects by printing a number of separate colored impressions from as many different plates, or stones, on paper. (Earlier color prints, as in the case of Audubon's

Birds of America and most Currier & Ives, were hand-colored over black-and-white prints.) In their very popular book, *The American Woman's Home,* Catharine E. Beecher and her sister, Harriet Beecher Stowe, recommended that chromos by Prang after the work of the best American artists be bought with the twenty or thirty dollars budgeted for pictures in the furnishing of a parlor. At a time when the huge and colorful mountainscapes of Albert Bierstadt were selling for very high prices, the authors pointed out that one could purchase a copy of his *Sunset in the Yosemite Valley* by Prang, as one example, for twelve dollars. "These chromos [by Prang and others] being all varnished," they added, "can wait for frames until you can afford them." They also pointed out that resourceful homemakers could make their own frames.

204. OVERLEAF: *a chromolithograph after Albert Bierstadt*

PRANG'S CHRISTMAS CARDS

At its best, chromolithography resulted in highly creditable approximations of the original paintings that were copied. The biographer James Parton claimed that when Prang hung his chromos side by side with the original art "not even the artist who painted the picture could always tell them apart," and he was not alone in such forgivably extravagant appreciation. "It is not too much to say," wrote another contemporary, "that he [Prang] has done more to create a popular knowledge and appreciation of what may be called every day art than any other man in America." The distinguished author and clergyman Edward Everett Hale took his "grand friends," like the high priest of the Zuñi nation, to see Prang's place. In the face of heavy competition from cheap, and poor, color prints, Prang ultimately turned to producing greeting cards. In 1890 Hale reported that millions of these every year were finding their way to all parts of the globe.

207. *The portrait of a champion, by an unknown publisher, after a painting by Thomas B. Welch*

205. *Opposite: a romantic announcement of Prang's cards*

206. *Above:* The Old Kentucky Home, *after E. Johnson*

A Viennese Bent

One of the most popular and enduring styles of the past several centuries is the bentwood furniture first manufactured by Michael Thonet in Austria around 1840 and still being made in various places, including America, for general use. Thonet's innovation consisted of bending a piece of steamed wood by means of metal straps into the extravagantly curved elements of his forms. These components could be inexpensively made in large quantities by semiskilled labor and shipped to more or less distant markets, there to be assembled with screws. Thonet's furniture was displayed before a large public at the Crystal Palace exhibition at London in 1851, and it was soon being duplicated by American manufacturers. In 1890, remarking on its continuing popularity, *The Decorator and Furnisher* pointed out that bentwood furniture had obtained "a certain status . . . owing to its neatness, finish, lightness and great strength," although its lines did seem excessively curvaceous—beyond "those limits which the eye follows with pleasure."

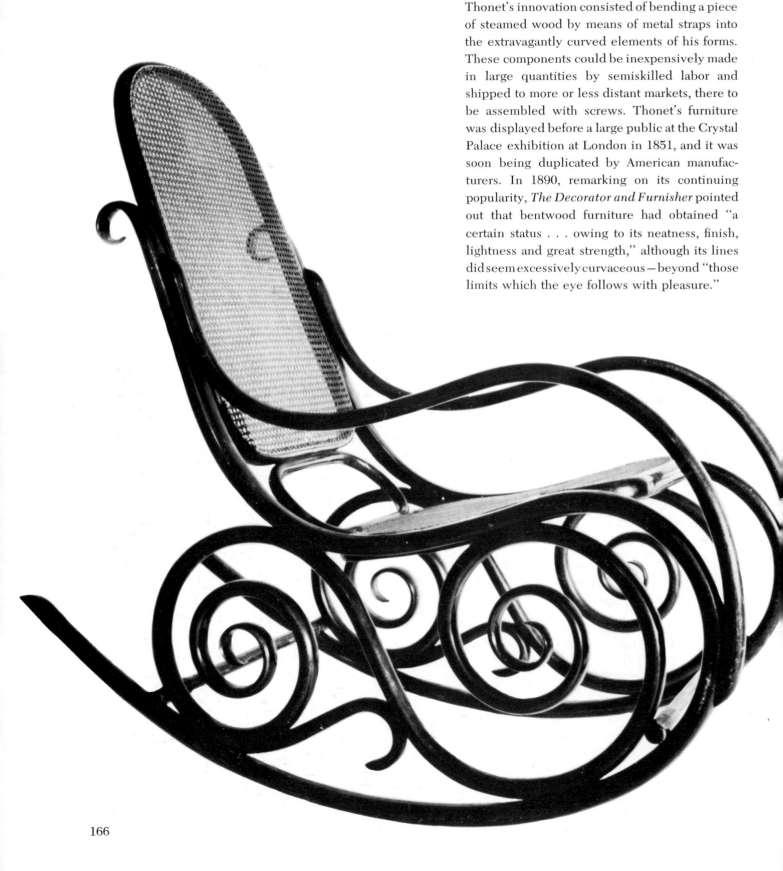

166

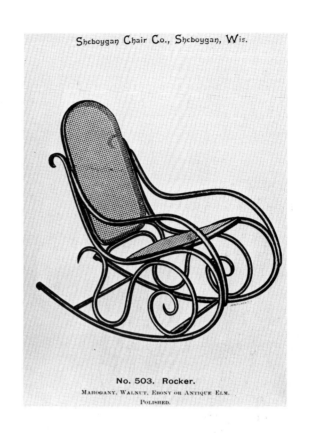

No. 503. Rocker.
MAHOGANY, WALNUT, EBONY OR ANTIQUE ELM.
POLISHED.

208. *Opposite: Thonet rocking chair, about 1860*

209. *Above: bentwood chair in an "Eastlake" room*

210. *Right: bentwood chair advertisement, 1891*

211. *Below: a room at Olana with bentwood chairs*

A Fresh Bent in Rattan & Wicker

Intricately structured pieces of rattan and bamboo, similar to the settee illustrated (212), were exported from various Far Eastern ports to America from the earliest days of the China trade. In the years following the Civil War the manufacture of rattan furniture was undertaken in earnest in this country. The domestic products grew in popularity until, in 1886, it was reported that one or two pieces were considered "indispensable in modern apartments." At first, apparently, the sheath, or cane, of rattan was woven about mechanically bent frames. (When he visited one Massachusetts factory, a son of Thonet's remarked that the firm had the best machinery for bending wood he had ever seen.) When it was discovered that the pith, or reed, of rattan that had earlier been discarded could be bent into stable shapes, designs became progressively more elaborate (215). Ultimately, wicker replaced rattan as the common material for this light and open type of furniture (213), which still retains its popularity.

212. A rattan settee made in the East or in the Oriental style, 19th century

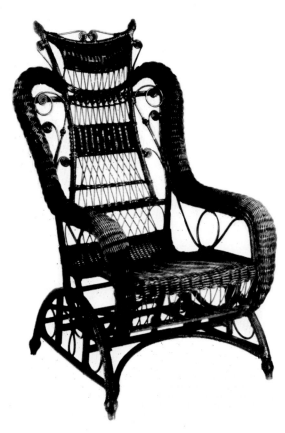

213. *Top: painted wicker platform rocking chair*

214. *Above: a merchant's trade card, about 1875*

215. *Right: a music stand made of reed in 1895*

A Bamboo Style

Running through the sources of supply for the fashionable house furnisher, Clarence Cook observed around 1880 that there was always a supply of bamboo furniture imported from China or Japan at Vantine's New York emporium, among other places. Such furniture, he pointed out, had the merit of being "strongly made and easily kept clean." Elsewhere in the city and in other urban centers, bamboo cane from the Far East was made to order after any practical designs that were submitted. As *The Decorator and Furnisher* counseled its readers in 1886, bamboo furniture was always in demand "among people of artistic tastes," and five years later the magazine reported that its use was becoming daily more widespread. Between times, in spite of those comments, the editors pointed out that furniture made of wood to simulate bamboo was actually *the* most desirable on the market.

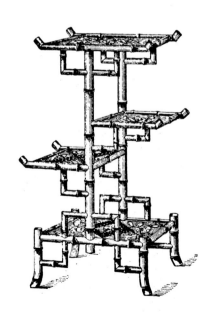

216. *Left: a bamboo-framed chest of drawers made by Nimura & Sato Company, Brooklyn*

217. *Above: a design for a Japanese stand*

218. Above: gilded stool of simulated bamboo

219. Right: a maple table, turned in imitation of bamboo, one element of a suite

For centuries past the Chinese had produced wooden furniture turned and carved in imitation of bamboo. In America the vogue became firmly established in the 1880's, and before that decade was out it was growing "more and more fashionable with every passing season." "The so-called 'bamboo' furniture," according to one report in 1887, "is made almost entirely from birds-eye maple, so turned in the lathe as to look like bamboo. It is sold to some extent, especially in the Southern states, at prices rather above those for plain furniture. As the natural color of the wood is retained, the bedroom sets are unique and cheerful." Actually, such pieces were sometimes gilded (218) or stained in different shades of color to resemble other woods. Also, bamboolike elements were commonly used in the construction of western forms that had little or no relation to Oriental design, as in the case of this bedroom suite.

220, 221, 222. Chair, bed, and bureau; the frames are made of turned, imitation bamboo maple; parts of a suite that includes the table shown on page 171

223. Opposite: design of an imitation bamboo chair priced at $8.67; by Kilian Bros., New York, 1876

Among the more exotic attractions of the Centennial were those offered by the Turkish Bazaar and Café, where one could savor rich Mocha coffee, as "fragrant as the perfume of 'Araby the Blest.'" There, too, the men, at least, could loll in deep-cushioned ease and smoke the long-stemmed Turkish pipes called chibouks and narghiles. In the years that followed, to the end of the century and beyond, other colorful and sybaritic forms and fancies associated with the Turkish, Moorish, Syrian, and East Indian ways of life were widely adopted and adapted by American furnishers and homemakers. Well-appointed homes (and more than a few clubs and hotels) gave way to the extravagant clutter of a "Turkish cozy-corner," a "Moorish den," an "Oriental divan," or some such apartment devoted to an assortment of "eccentricities" that may or may not have come from those strange and distant lands—inlaid Damascus tables, hookahs, incense burners, brass trays, Turkish carpets, and related impedimenta.

Turkish Corners
& Moorish Modes

224. *Opposite: Moorish hall in Mr. E. Lauterbach's home, New York*

225. *Left: an inlaid Damascus table similar to the one shown opposite*

226. *Above: a clock in the Oriental style from the Rockefeller house*

227. *Above: an armchair from the Rockefeller house*

228. *Below: "Turkish" armchair with rug upholstery*

229. *Right: a tufted ottoman that rests on casters*

230. *Opposite: an upholstered and tasseled couch*

"The great sense of rest that impregnates Moorish belongings in particular," reported one journal, "is very grateful to our Western people, who . . . must have a chamber specially furnished for wakeful rest." In such chambers the prevalence of soft, inviting furniture encouraged relaxed postures that were frowned upon by the formal etiquette of the day. When one young Occidental visitor to Istanbul sat primly on the edge of a large, colorful divan, drawing her skirts about her and "with two neat little toes" touching the floor for balance, her native escort broke into laughter. "Sit on your foot," he suggested, "curl it comfortably under you, so. Now be seated, far back, build a wall of cushions about your shoulders, and know true happiness." The tired American businessman who sat bolt upright all day in his office chair, it was pointed out, had a right to return home to at least one room where he could relax in the luxuriant restfulness of Oriental furnishings, where he could find peace, and where his heated nerves could be "soothed and cooled to the proper temperature." It was just one indication of the trend of the times that most of the important furnishing houses of the period were referred to as "upholsterers."

231. *Black lacquer and gilt wall cabinet with "Moorish" designs*

Interest in various Oriental styles had been evident long before the Centennial, but the fashion reached a near-epidemic stage in the 1880's and 1890's. In 1894 one Broadway warehouse displayed seven interiors illustrating Persian, Japanese, Indian, Chinese, and Moorish decoration, which were considered "complete object lessons in the study of the home furnishings of the Oriental people." *Objets d'art* imported from the various countries of the Orient and European and domestic manufactures in those styles were available in shops and warehouses scattered from Grand Rapids to Boston. The New York home of John D. Rockefeller, Sr., had a "Moorish" sitting room, whose decorations and furnishings were designed more or less obviously after diverse eastern sources. The New York banker and art connoisseur Lewis G. Tewksbury had in his Fifth Avenue apartment an "Oriental divan" that, with its tapestries "representing Eastern dancing girls in the most luxurious attitudes," its Damascus tables, pipes and pots of incense, and a sonorous Japanese bell, recalled to one visitor the fabled splendor of *The Arabian Nights*.

232. *Opposite, below: Dr. Henry Abbott, with hookah*

233. *Top: papier-mâché and mother-of-pearl book cover*

234. *Above: painted table with Oriental style motifs*

Who might have furnished and decorated the Tewksbury apartment and the house taken over by the senior Rockefellers, with their mélange of real and pseudo-Oriental elements, has not yet been determined. However, there were firms such as A. A. Vantine & Co. in New York that specialized in creating such "highly artistic effects." At Vantine's Oriental bazaar one could purchase "everything that belongs to a genuine Moorish interior," from imported hookahs and Moorish fretwork screens to Persian carpets and art metalwork, all "in bewildering variety." Oriental lamps in the "newest and controlled patterns" could be had from $3.75 up, Turkish coffee tables inlaid with mother-of-pearl from $7.25, and Indian seats, "easy and artistic," at $3.50 each; everything needed to "transform a modern house into an earthly paradise." Vantine's was also prepared to suggest the best placement and proper background for everything they offered for sale. A contemporary of Rockefeller's, the artist Lockwood De Forest, went so far as to establish a shop in Ahmadabad, India, where he had ninety craftsmen in wood, stone, and brass working under one Muggunbhai Huttushing to supply De Forest's New York studio-salesroom with "artistic creations" for the American market.

235. Above: a European brass clock in the Oriental style
236. Opposite: detail of a door from the Rockefeller house

A Monumental Man H. H. Richardson

"There has been very much vain groping and vaporing after a 'national' style, to supply which Classic and Gothic have alike failed," wrote an art critic in 1887. However, the article continued gratefully, "after Mr. Richardson, American architecture has become distinctly Romanesque. Our ablest architects are treading in his footsteps." As one of his contemporaries later recalled, Henry Hobson Richardson had "burst upon an astonished world as a sort of savior," and rescued American architectural design from its postwar low of "vulgar, self-satisfied and pretentious . . . frontier ideology." Richardson Romanesque, as his interpretation came to be known, did indeed serve for a time as the national style. "Richardsonians" throughout the country designed countless buildings in imitation of the master's technique—rounded arches, grouped pillars, vaulted ceilings, profuse carvings, and the buildings themselves constructed massively of stone blocks. Romanesque was eminently suited to high Victorian ideals. "Its dignity, its splendid adaptability, its marvellous richness and sober beauty," read one paean of praise, "recommend it for the monumental expressions of a mighty people."

Richardson himself was monumental in every way—his girth (boldly highlighted by his yellow waistcoats), his gusto and jovial good humor, his hearty pleasure in the delights of the table, his unbounded hospitality, and unflagging energy. Even his writing paper and handwriting were outsized. And he roared with laughter at a remark made by a German admirer: "Mein Gott, how he looks like his own buildings." Despite a chronic nephritic ailment that plagued him most of his life and was responsible for his early death at the age of forty-seven, Richardson was impatient with doctors' orders and prescribed diets. "One dreaded to see the long 'schooners' of iced beer set before him, and order upon order for ices," wrote a traveling companion, concerned by Richardson's indomitable indifference to his health.

Above all, Richardson, his buildings, and his business methods suited the politicians, tycoons, and industrialists who swamped him with commissions. He was thoroughly in tune with his era,

aware of the rising needs in a busy nation, and he turned his attention to such hitherto ignored projects as railroad stations. He designed the Pittsburgh jail and a warehouse for Marshall Field in Chicago. He sketched plans for an icehouse and a lighthouse, and declared: "The things I want most to design are a grain-elevator and the interior of a great river-steamboat." While his fame rested principally on his church architecture, library designs, and other such public buildings, Richardson also excelled in private homes, using wooden construction and creating the same indefinable medieval aura that was always evident in his masonwork. As the master architect, Richardson employed such first-rate artists and sculptors as John La Farge and Augustus Saint-Gaudens, to whom he entrusted major elements of decoration. Among his young architectural assistants were Stanford White and Charles McKim. "Briefly told," wrote an admirer in the 1880's, "the lesson of Mr. Richardson's work is structural truth, artistic handling of masses, obedience to use." And as a later critic summed up his relationship to his times: "To live in a house built by Richardson was a cachet of wealth and taste; to have your nest-egg in one of his banks gave you a feeling of perfect security; to worship in one of his churches made one think one had a pass key to the Golden Gates."

Henry Hobson Richardson was born in 1838 in the parish of Saint James, Louisiana. His father, whose forebears had been early Bermuda settlers, was in the cotton business. His mother was the granddaughter of the English chemist and philosopher Joseph Priestley, who had discovered oxygen and had been drummed out of England for his radical political theories. Richardson's boyhood was passed with winters in New Orleans and summers at the family plantation and such gentlemanly pursuits as fencing, riding, and playing the flute. Had it not been for a speech impediment—a stutter—Richardson would have been accepted at West Point, presumably to follow a career in the Army. But he entered Harvard instead, "full of creole life and animation," slim, handsome, popular, and famed for his skill at chess. It was said, in fact, that Richardson

could play several games at once—blindfolded. Although he had planned to study civil engineering, his interests changed in Boston and he chose architecture as his lifework. Following his graduation in 1859, and a summer tour of the British Isles with two classmates, Richardson enrolled in the Ecole des Beaux Arts in Paris. Again, as at Harvard, he was an instant social success, "an excellent companion, . . . always ready for a dinner-party or a dancing-party." He also joined his friends in a student rebellion and was arrested though, as he explained later, thanks to the fine tailoring of his English clothes, he enjoyed a semiprivate cell and a night of merry conversation with the French poet Théophile Gautier.

Despite these diversions and seemingly unlimited funds from New Orleans, Richardson was a serious student. He worked with "the earnestness of a man for whom it was to be what the Germans call a 'bread-study,'" and after a party, no matter what the hour, Richardson returned to his rooms to finish up plans or drawings in progress. At the outbreak of the Civil War, the allowance from home was cut off. But with that formidable energy that characterized the man throughout his life, Richardson got a job in the office of a government architect and somehow continued his studies at night. "Economy is my hue and cry just now," he wrote his fiancée, Julia Gorham Hayden, daugh-

ter of Dr. John Cole Hayden of Boston. "I breakfast for twenty-five cents, dine for thirty-five, and pay fifty francs (ten dollars) a month for my room." In yet another letter to Miss Hayden, he wrote that in spite of hardships, he preferred to finish his European training, rather "than return to America a second-rate architect. Our poor country is overrun with them now. I never will practice till I feel I can at least do my art justice." At the close of the war Richardson at last returned home—after six and a half years in Paris—still impoverished. "Look at me," he once remarked cheerfully, "I wear a suit made by Poole, of London, which a nobleman might be pleased to wear, and—and—and I haven't a dollar to my name." In 1866 his fortunes changed. Through the in-

fluence of a college classmate and fellow member of Harvard's Porcellian Club, the young, unknown architect was invited to submit plans in a competition for the Church of the Unity in Springfield, Massachusetts—a competition Richardson won with a conventionally Victorian English Gothic design. When told the good news, he broke into tears: "That is all I wanted—*a chance.*" Richardson's career was launched. He and Miss Hayden were married, and he established an office in New York. His first use of the Romanesque idiom, which would make him nationally famous, was in the plan for Boston's Trinity Church, begun in 1872 and completed in 1877. Because his commissions largely centered in the Boston area, he moved to Brookline, Massachusetts. So great was Richardson's delight in his family, his friends, his students, and his work that he combined both home and office under one roof in 1878.

From then on—until his death in 1886—Richardson moved solidly forward, developing and dominating architectural trends. The age of steel-frame construction lay just ahead, and Richardson foretold its advent with his straightforward, functional designs. He also foretold the coming age of informality in his designs for country houses—the wide windows, inviting porches, and open, rambling rooms. "He began as a romantic architect," wrote Lewis Mumford, "but he was far more than that; . . . in the end, he was an able utilitarian and rational architect . . . the primitive source of modern architecture."

237. Top: oak armchair designed for the
Winn Memorial Library in Woburn, Mass.

238. Above: a bench, the Woburn library

184

Furniture &
Architecture

All too frequently, in the eclectic maze of high Victorian design, conformity between architecture and furniture was a catch-as-catch-can proposition. Henry Hobson Richardson, however, brought his driving concern for detail to every nook and cranny of his buildings. Exteriors, interiors, and furnishings were created as a harmonious totality—the grand tradition of architecture as practiced, for example, by such a past master as Robert Adam in eighteenth-century England. This Gothic church chair (240) was specifically patterned by Richardson to complement the essentially Gothic mode of the building. The library in Woburn, Massachusetts, the first of Richardson's notable series of libraries, was distinctively Romanesque, and Richardson's furniture—the trustee's chair (237) and the reading-room bench (238)—was suitably medieval in its basic design, fitting adjuncts to the library's vaulted ceiling and interior woodwork finished in carved and turned decorations. The dining table (239), with its massive base of clustered paw-foot legs, was designed by Richardson for use in his own home.

239. Left: dining table, mahoganized oak

240. Right: cathedra, or chair, for the Church of the Unity, Springfield, Mass.

185

241. An oak bench designed for a gatehouse porch

Light fixtures, umbrella stands, clocks, andirons, altar tables, a dressing table, the drinking fountain in a railroad station—no object was overlooked by Richardson. He created this large bench (241) for a gatehouse designed to serve as a guest lodge on the Frederick L. Ames estate in North Easton, Massachusetts. The lodge itself was a low, rambling structure made of rough boulders, suggesting "the work of some legendary Icelandic hero." For the library in Malden, Massachusetts—"a picturesque, individual, and excellent piece of work," as it was described in 1888—Richardson sketched a spindle chair (242). This vaguely Jacobean form was used in chairs (243) for the Crane Memorial Library, Quincy, Massachusetts—a building praised by a Richardson contemporary as having proved the "fitness of Romanesque art to meet the most refined demands of modern taste."

242. *Opposite: Richardson's sketch for a chair for Converse Memorial Library, Malden, Mass.*

243. *Above: library chair from Quincy, Mass.*

The Fair &
the Not So Fair

"Sell the cook stove if necessary and come," wrote Hamlin Garland to his parents on their Dakota farm. "You *must* see this fair." The World's Columbian Exposition, "as white and richly ornamented as a congregation of royal brides," was a marvel of technological progress. The wonders and countless uses of electricity were demonstrated on every hand; the fair itself, after nightfall, was ablaze with the dazzling magic of electric lights. The Hall of Manufactures and Liberal Arts, "a behemoth structure" covering some forty acres, was deemed one of the greatest engineering feats of the age, its semicircular roof upheld by arched steel trusses. Paradoxically, all such technological advances were displayed in a setting of Beaux Arts classicism, an architectural throwback adjudged by critics as "tawdry finery of the past," and likened to "schoolboy work." Only the Transportation Building (244), by Louis Sullivan and his assistant, Frank Lloyd Wright, represented the new and vital trend in American architecture, while dying but dogged holdouts of high Victorian design (see overleaf) were all too frequently on proud display.

244. Opposite: the Transportation Building with its "Golden Door"

245. Above: model of relief sculpture for the Electricity Building

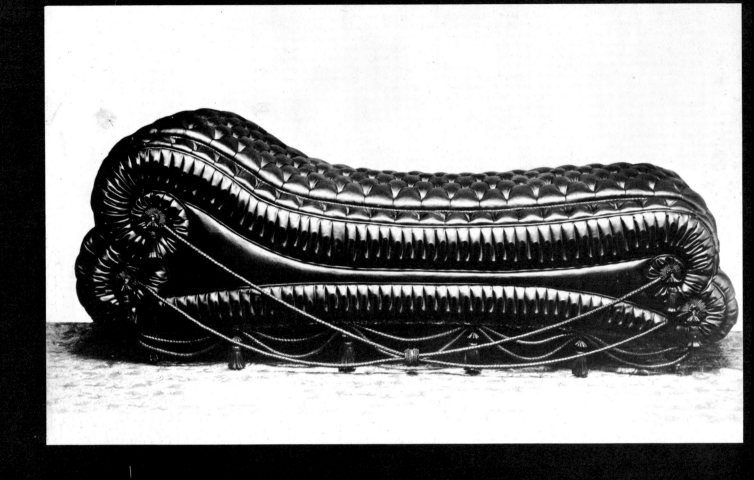

246. Tufted, fringed, and richly overstuffed furniture made by a
American manufacturer and displayed at the Chicago expositio

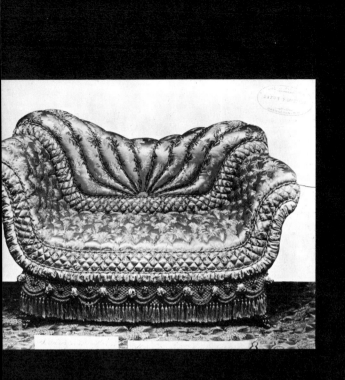

About the Turn of the Century

Styles of a New Order (1893-1917)

"What shall we do with our great cities? What will our great cities do with us?" Those questions, which were so urgently addressed to thoughtful Americans in the 1890's, remain largely unanswered to this day. We have become familiar enough with the distressing problems of our urban communities, if not altogether inured to the strains they put upon us. But in the 1890's the noise, confusion, and congestion of large and rapidly growing cities, the vice and crime and long list of other social blights, were relatively new developments—disturbing to a nation still inclined to revere the homespun virtues of its recent pioneering past.

But nothing moralists wrote or preached about the *Mysteries and Miseries of Americas Great Cities*, as one tract of the times was subtitled, slowed the torrential migration from the countryside toward those larger centers. Lurid stories of the sin and debauchery of city life, intended as warnings, no doubt excited the curiosity of country lads and lasses and led them on to unwonted adventures. In any case life on the farm was not what it had been, or was thought to be from the sweetly nostalgic depictions of Currier & Ives. In large areas of the West, at least, farming was becoming another of the nation's big businesses, with huge, mechanized, heavily capitalized operations and with migrant workers hired by absentee owners to handle the load at season's peak. The individual and independent tiller of the soil, the "oldest of nobles" and a vital figure in Jefferson's dream of an agrarian democracy, was losing his traditional status. And as he diminished in importance and influence, the words "rube" and "hayseed" crept into the vernacular of city folk. When the nation was founded, more than 90 per cent of its gainfully employed population was engaged in agriculture; by 1910 the proportion was less than one third and continued to decrease. Americans had literally gone to town, where the real excitement seemed to be.

The growing pains that accompanied the sudden rise of modern cities were not confined to America. London, Paris, Berlin, and other old European capitals had related problems caused by vastly increased populations, problems that called for new techniques of living and a new social philosophy. But in America the growth of cities was still more rapid and unsettling, and further complicated by the constant, large admixture of alien strains to the population; the newcomers tended increasingly to cluster and remain in cities when formerly they might more easily have drifted off to a farm in the country. Between 1890 and 1910 almost twelve and a half million immigrants reached America from countries

Opposite and above: details from a stained-glass window made by Louis Comfort Tiffany

about the globe. By 1890 New York City, with Brooklyn, already had half as many Italians as Naples, as many Germans as Hamburg, twice as many Irish as Dublin, and two and a half times as many Jews as Warsaw. One third of Boston's population and one fourth of Philadelphia's were foreign born. The number of foreign-born inhabitants in Chicago that year was almost equal to the total population of the city in 1880. At the same time, during a stay in Monterey, California, the Scottish visitor Robert Louis Stevenson had as daily companions a Frenchman, an Italian, a Mexican, and two Portuguese, and occasionally, as well, an Indian, a Chinese, a Swiss, a German, and a Midwesterner. America had indeed become not only a nation of cities, but "a teeming nation of nations." (As one reflection of those circumstances, by 1900 almost one thousand foreign-language periodicals and newspapers in twenty-five different tongues were being published in the United States.)

However bad those conditions were, and too often they were unspeakably sordid, the city also generated benevolent and progressive forces that were beyond the means of smaller communities. The very word *civilization* literally means the making of cities and urban life. With their great concentration of people and wealth and power, their vastly enhanced mechanical resources and intercommunications, not to mention a gradually developing social conscience, cities had become the creative centers of civilization, more importantly than they had ever been in the past. Cities were giving "the twist of progress to the age," as it was said, and nowhere in the world with more dramatic thoroughness and suddenness than in the United States.

For better and for worse, urban ways and habits, urban opinions and fashions prevailed across the land. The intrusion of city manners into the rural countryside was not always welcomed. As early as 1885 one observer warned the farmers that they must make a clear distinction between the false glitter of such manners and "true refinement," which could be as easily found in the country as in the city. However, there was great seduction in the offerings of the large mail-order houses, such as Montgomery Ward & Company and Sears, Roebuck and Company, whose illustrated catalogues reached the corners of the nation before the close of the century. In those "wishing books" the farmer's family could see not only the necessary equipment for the farm but as well the fripperies and accessories made popular by city fashions, from the "most stylish ladies' millinery" to "princely parlor furniture" that followed the latest designs, and including pressed glassware that looked just like cut glass and was as handsome as that displayed on the tables of the rich, it was claimed, but that cost on the average only seven cents apiece.

The huge Sears, Roebuck catalogues (or "Consumers Guides," as they were labeled), with the countless varieties of merchandise they proffered, were annual reminders of the enormous output that the American industrial machine had attained by the turn of the century. In fact, the nation had applied itself to the problem of producing more goods so earnestly and effectively that constantly increasing production was becoming an end in itself. There was, indeed, no simple way of keeping the machine from outracing the demands it had grown to satisfy. How to make the public want more material goods than it could decently be satisfied with, so that mines and factories might continue to increase their output, had become a serious problem. The rise of extensive and intensive commercial advertising in answer to that problem opened a new era in American culture. At the century's end that art, from its early, small, but promising beginnings, had

Advertisements from Sears' 1897 catalogue

burgeoned into a large and vital force in the American economy. Nevermore would the average citizen be spared the insistent claims of promotional material in myriad forms, claims that at times tested credulity and patience to the limit.

If an unprecedented and increasing abundance of material goods could be taken as the measure of progress, America was progressing at an accelerating rate. More and more of what had been considered the restricted luxuries of one generation were being converted by faster and more efficient machines into the commonplace necessities of the next. On a return visit to the United States early in the present century, Lord Bryce, the most respected British critic of the American scene, pointed out that in this land every class seemed rich compared to the corresponding class in the Old World, and life was more comfortable at all levels. At the one extreme of the social spectrum, he noted, pauperism was decreasing in relation to the total population; at the other, huge fortunes were "far more numerous than in any other country."

The gulf between those two extremes was abysmal, more profound than it had ever been in the American experience. But for persons who might be disturbed by such gross discrepancies in the human condition, comforting words came from the pulpit and other respected sources. God, it was pronounced, gave success and wealth to those best qualified to exercise the powers they implied. "Godliness," concluded Bishop Lawrence of Massachusetts in the 1890's, "is in league with riches"; according to a governor of that same state, unemployment was itself, to all intents, an act of God. The impoverished might best look to the nobles of industry for charity and direction.

With considerably less complacency and more understanding the French poet, novelist, and critic Charles Joseph Paul Bourget, during a visit to this country in 1893–94, took a sharp look at those richest of Americans and found them not altogether infallible in their tastes and pretensions. In the small resort section of Newport, Rhode Island, where he was told there were "more millions of dollars represented. . .than in all London and Paris altogether," he observed American "society" in its most concentrated and exaggerated state. In this exclusive enclave, built upon its cliff within the space of a few years by the caprice of mil-

lionaires, who vied with one another to see who should excel in splendor, he counted "twenty, thirty, forty different styles of construction," some of them more or less direct translations of English or Continental prototypes. Those structures, Bourget suggested, were so carefully and extravagantly designed that they might have been removed to Oxford, Versailles, or the banks of the Loire without disturbing the traditional, mellowed aspects of those parts of the world. "In this country, where everything is of yesterday," he wrote, "they hunger and thirst for the long ago. . . .The furnishings of the Newport houses betray a similar effort, — a constant, tireless endeavor to absorb European ideas." The desire of those Americans to surround themselves with furniture, silver, paintings, and tapestries that conveyed an idea of time and stability, concluded Bourget, was sincere to the point of being pathetic.

Godey's Lady's Book had made much the same point years before, in 1878, by citing the "latest mania among fashionable people" for collecting old furniture. "A curious feature of this fashion," the editors observed, "is the aid it affords people desiring to lay claim to a respectable ancestry." About that same time the critic Clarence Cook pointed out that in Boston "a polite internecine warfare" had for some time been raging between rival collectors of "old pieces." "The back country," he added, was being "scoured by young couples in chaises on the trail of old sideboards and brass andirons."

Architects had been among the first to call attention to the merits of colonial design. "In our early days all of us had a great interest in Colonial architecture," recalled William Rutherford Mead, later of the famous firm McKim, Mead, and White, which put a formal stamp on the times with its elegant and impressive structures in the classical revival style. In 1877, with McKim and White, he undertook a "celebrated" trip to New England in the course of which they all made sketches and measured drawings of colonial houses to keep in scrapbooks for future reference. Further interest in the colonial past was encouraged by the growing popularity of such venerable New England towns as Marblehead, Portsmouth, Gloucester, and, notably, Newport, where old buildings could still be seen, as summer vacation resorts. Bourget was pleasantly impressed by the trim,

Newport "cottage" of Cornelius Vanderbilt

A drawing of an 18th-century Newport house

simple houses in the old quarter of Newport, which contrasted so dramatically with the sumptuous "cottages" of the new quarter.

This interest in early American architecture and artifacts grew as the century advanced, and it has never abated. It led in various directions: to whimsical concoctions labeled "colonial," but often bearing only a tenuous resemblance to early forms (many of which were, in any case, from the postcolonial period); to carefully manufactured facsimiles, well-enough conceived and made to fool the unwary collector of today; and, ultimately, to the serious scholarship that resulted in such convincing and popular re-creations of the past as may be seen in the American Wing of the Metropolitan Museum of Art, Henry Ford Museum and Greenfield Village, Colonial Williamsburg, and elsewhere. Around the turn of the century *The House Beautiful* felt it advisable to warn its readers against an excess of enthusiasm for colonial styles. "Let it be admitted at the outset," the magazine reported, "that the furniture of our forefathers has certain undeniable qualities. . . .Those of us whose Connemara grandfathers kept the pig in the parlor, or whose German parents reached these shores in an emigrant-ship thirty years ago, set an even higher value on everything that speaks of deep-rooted Americanism. And this is most praiseworthy. But, O friends, it is a wearisome thing to visit living-room after living-room and find each aping the same period."

However, as already noted, in creating the White City that accommodated the great world's fair at Chicago in 1893, McKim and his associates had not been carried away by enthusiasm for the American colonial past. They reached farther back, to classical antiquity, to put together what Henry Adams termed an "inconceivable" architectural display. Thomas Jefferson, who had small regard for most colonial buildings and who was an avowed classicist in architectural matters, once stated that he preferred the dreams of the future to the history of the past. But even his enlightened imagination could not have previsioned this monumental extravaganza in the Midwest, with its glittering façades of plaster of Paris rising with fluttering flags on the shores of Lake Michigan. This, remarked Daniel Burnham, one of the architects, was "what the Romans would have wished to create in permanent form."

Others felt differently. To a number of critics the thin veneer of classical order imposed on most of the fair buildings, and which bore little or no relation to the demonstrations within, seemed like a sickly sweet frosting deposited by the chill, dead hand of the past. The Chicago architect Louis H. Sullivan, whose steel-framed skyscrapers had already won acclaim and whose nonclassical Transportation Building at the fair caught the special attention of foreign observers, thought that the influence of the fair on American architecture was all but disastrous. The epidemic of classicism that had germinated in the East, he wrote, had spread westward, contaminating all that it touched. "Thus did the virus of a culture, snobbish and alien" to the land of the free and the home of the brave, subvert the cause of progress. "Thus ever works the pallid academic mind, denying the real, exalting the fictitious and the false, incapable of adjusting itself to the flow of living things." Architecture would be a living art when form followed function.

Years before, both in England and in the United States, earnest efforts had been made to deliver art and design from thralldom to the past, to evolve styles that would speak importantly for the present. Ruskin and Morris, among other nineteenth-century reformers, were dedicated to this purpose, but their extraordinary reverence for the "honest" intentions and practices of medieval craftsmen and their distrust of the machine combined to limit their vision. Nevertheless, by

challenging the popular values and shoddy performances of their own day they helped prepare the ground for more realistic advances. And the influence of their ideas persisted into the twentieth century.

Morris' principles served as a guiding influence in the "Arts and Crafts" movement that flourished in England during the last quarter of the nineteenth century and that had counterparts in this country. The goal of such movements was, in part, to purify industrial design of its contamination by the machine. Beyond that was an intention to elevate all the crafts to the dignity of fine art, a term the Royal Academy preferred to reserve for oil paintings in gilt frames such as were hung in its exhibitions. A display of Arts and Crafts furniture, held at London in 1888, was, in the words of one critic, "full of things which seem to have been done because the designer and maker enjoyed doing them—not because they were calculated to sell well." Most of the work produced by members of the movement was, in fact, experimental in nature and varied in style. On the whole, however, it did emphasize simplicity as a virtue in design, even to what some critics thought was a fault. As one of them wrote, "the object now seems to be to make a thing as square, as plain, as devoid of any beauty of line as is possible and to call this art."

That observation might have served as an introduction to the so-called Mission furniture that enjoyed such an astonishing popularity in America during the first two decades of the present century and that, although associated with craftsman values in advertisements, was ultimately mass produced in very large quantities. Contemporary reporters seem to have disagreed as to whether the term "Mission" had a reference to the primitive furniture put together by Indian neophytes for the California Spanish missions, or whether it implied that the new style had a mission to perform in the decorative arts. In any case, it was hailed as America's first original furniture style.

Two men of highly disparate personalities were the most influential early propagandists of the Mission style, Gustav Stickley and Elbert Hubbard. Each

The Art Palace at the Chicago world's fair

Photograph of Elbert Hubbard taken in 1914

called the other a "fake" and each enjoyed some fame and some fortune until 1915, when Stickley's overexpanded operations led him to bankruptcy and when Hubbard lost his life on the ill-fated *Lusitania*. Apparently, it was Stickley's display of what he then called Craftsman furniture at the semiannual exhibition of 1900 in Grand Rapids that first called attention to the simple, rectilinear forms that later became celebrated as Mission furniture. In a summary explanation of his guiding principles he wrote: "I endeavored to go back to the beginning and seek the inspiration of the same law of direct answer to need that animated the craftsman of an earlier day, for the only way to find a new expression was to base whatever was made upon need alone, not the cultivated taste of the man learned in the great styles of the past, but the need suggested by the primitive human necessity of the common folk."

"Fra Elbertus," as Elbert Hubbard sometimes called himself, was a soap salesman and a Harvard dropout before he instituted a "cooperative brotherhood" that, among a miscellany of other activities, produced furniture in the Mission style. Hubbard's greater fame stemmed from his little magazine, *The Philistine*, which he filled with breezy, smart sayings, quotations, and homely apothegms and which became a widely read periodical throughout the country. His "A Message to Garcia," an inspirational piece published in 1899, attained a total printing of forty million copies, according to its author. Dedicated as he claimed to be to the principles of Morris, Hubbard was a very practical man. "Be kind," he advised "—but get the mazuma."

Stickley thought it unlikely that his furniture would go out of fashion as other styles had done, since his designs were not founded on fashion but on elemental structural principles. In their functionalism they rode a wave of the future. *The House Beautiful*, "The American Authority on Household Art," endorsed the style, pointing out that simplicity of design was winning favor "among the most cultured and educated of town and country." However, the successful reception of Stickley's stoutly made, heavy oak forms, and their stark simplicity, led to a host of imitations and approximations. Whole factories switched from whatever else they had been making to produce Mission furniture, much of it cheaply contrived and poorly finished. The basic simplicity of Stickley's designs also encouraged a "do-it-yourself" trend. Published drawings based on his models and ideas were used in the manual-training courses that were becoming a standard feature of public school education. (The incorporation of such courses in the regular curriculum of grade schools, instead of restricting them to the programs of vocational schools, recognized the influence of the Arts and Crafts movement; work with the hands, even "dirty" work, could contribute to the education and betterment of mankind, and at its best assume the dignity of an art, as Morris had claimed.) And in 1909 a book was published that illustrated ways to make chairs, tables, and other forms of square, Mission-like outlines out of orange crates and odd bits of lumber. Within a decade Mission had gone out of fashion, as other styles had done, after cutting a great swath through forests of oak.

The search for a distinctively modern idiom in design and decoration led in other directions. Before the Mission style enjoyed its vogue a totally different formula had developed in various countries, including America, that today is best known as Art Nouveau. In its own heyday, during the two decades just before and after the turn of the century, it was given more than a score of different names in various languages—Métro style, Inglese style, Yachting style, Modernismo, the Glasgow School, Jugendstil, and, of course, Art Nouveau among still

Ornament on the entrance to the Schlesinger and Meyer Department Store by L. Sullivan

others. This new style shared with Mission a respect for the teachings of William Morris and an intention to depart from the traditional commonplace, but little else. It was extravagantly ornamental and curvilinear rather than simply functional and rectilinear. It was highly sophisticated, capricious, and widely experimental instead of static and uniform. And it enjoyed international favor, as the various names listed above indicate. Each nation developed its own version, drawing from its separate experience and circumstance. Everywhere it represented a total decorative program in which all distinction between the fine and useful arts was ignored.

As early as the 1880's the progressive American architect Louis Sullivan had introduced decorative motifs in his constructions that in spirit, at least, predicted the flowing, organic forms of Art Nouveau ornamentation. In the next decade Boston-born Will H. Bradley was creating posters and other designs in the new style that won him international recognition. But it is with the work of the artist-craftsman-decorator Louis Comfort Tiffany that American developments of the style are most prominently identified. (His father, Charles Lewis Tiffany, was a goldsmith and jeweler who had founded a firm, still flourishing on Fifth Avenue, which the son chose not to enter.) Tiffany had started his radical experiments in glass in the 1870's, before he was out of his twenties, and his peculiar genius was early acknowledged abroad. He was commissioned to execute a series of colored glass windows after designs by such leading French artists as Toulouse-Lautrec, Vuillard, and Bonnard, a series that was shown at the Salon de l'Art Nouveau of 1895 in Paris. His work was soon widely imitated in Europe.

A dozen years earlier President Chester A. Arthur had called upon Tiffany to redecorate the White House. (To make room for the new installations, Arthur had more than twenty wagonloads of furniture removed from the mansion and sold at public auction.) Among other things Tiffany designed a great opalescent glass screen that reached from floor to ceiling in the hall. However, under Theodore Roosevelt's administration that handiwork was stripped away. Although it is not a matter of record, it seems unlikely that Roosevelt was an admirer of Art Nouveau. Actually, in America the style never enjoyed the popular vogue that it did in some European countries. Here the popular interpretation or extension of the style was undoubtedly "the Gibson girl," with her curvaceous outlines and her flowing mass of hair. This elegant creature, the brain child of the artist Charles Dana Gibson, led a charmed life through the pages of several periodicals from the 1890's through the early years of the present century. Then, with the approach of World War I, she, like Art Nouveau itself, passed out of fashion. As Louis Sullivan had observed, "our art if for the day, is suited to the day, and will also change as the day changes."

Miss Elsie de Wolfe, sometimes known as "The Chintz Lady" and elsewhere referred to as the first prominent lady interior decorator, looked back on the reign of Art Nouveau with horrid memories of "that avalanche of bad taste which burst upon us in 1900 and had its way until the beginning of the war." She remembered with dismay "those awful chairs and tables supported by flowers contrived to look as if they were growing from the ground" and "the mantelpiece of fleurs-de-lis and rushes." However, nowadays we look more charitably on the style, which is enjoying a revival of sorts. We tend to see in it one important phase of a rebellion against the staid conventions of the late Victorian period. Short-lived as the style was, by its radical departure from historical precedents and traditions, and by its invasion of virtually every phase of the fine and applied arts, it helped pave the way toward other, fresh, and more enduring modern concepts.

Miss de Wolfe was not in favor of change in any case. "We have not succeeded in creating a style adapted to our modern life," she wrote despairingly. "It is just as well! Our life, with its haste, its nervousness, and its preoccupations does not inspire the furniture makers." And she recommended to her wealthy clients an acceptance of the proven styles of the past, in antique form or in reproductions as circumstances favored. As in years past there were American agents of French firms to supply either, and there were other, American manufacturers who made all manner of reproductions and adaptations of eighteenth-century French, as well as early American, furniture. Such imitative work ranged from very close copies to gross caricatures of original, early forms.

Although she could neither appreciate nor approve of them, the roots of still newer styles had already been struck, and these would grow and come to flower in the decades following the war. In 1913, the year Miss de Wolfe published *The House in Good Taste* celebrating the genteel tradition, it seemed to some that the familiar world was at a point of explosion, which it was in several different senses. That year, just before the cataclysm triggered at Sarajevo, at the famous Armory Show held in New York, Americans at large experienced the shock of Fauvism, cubism, and expressionism as those movements had developed in advanced art circles in Europe. Even the spirit of isolation that settled over the nation when the war "over there" was won was not enough to spare Americans from the epidemic progress of "modern art" in all its phases and applications.

Nude Descending a Staircase, No. 2, *1912, by Marcel Duchamp; exhibited at the Armory*

201

247. Above: a Jacobean bench, or settle; around 1910

248. Below: Colonial Revival urn, Samuel Kirk & Son, 1885

A Return to the Colonial Past

"All this resuscitation of 'old furniture,'" wrote Clarence Cook in 1881, "is a fashion . . . that has been for twenty years working its way down from a circle of rich, cultivated people, to a wider circle of people . . . who have natural good taste." The Centennial, of course, had also fostered the colonial revival through such nostalgic views of the past as the New England kitchen (250) with its "quaint architecture" and "antiquated furniture." By 1884, *Cabinet Making and Upholstery* could report: "The manufacture of antiques has become a modern industry." The pieces illustrated here are thoughtful reproductions of "the beautiful work of the Colonial days." This silver urn (248), for example, revived a neoclassic form first used in the late 1700's in America; the fretwork, or gallery (here in 18-carat gold), is a motif associated with Philadelphia silversmiths of that period. The urn, one of a pair bearing the Bonaparte crest, was made for the American branch of the family, descendants of the ill-fated marriage between Elizabeth Patterson of Baltimore and Napoleon's youngest brother, Jerome.

249. Left: *Chippendale highboy of the late 19th century*

250. Above: *the New England kitchen at the Centennial*

With the growing enthusiasm for antiques and reproductions thereof, the word "colonial" assumed an all-purpose meaning, whether furniture styles under discussion actually fell within the colonial period or not. The medieval chair (256), for one, copies a simple form first made in England in the early 1500's, and the Sheraton chair (252), for another, was a post-Revolutionary pattern. But no matter. The revival was ablaze, encouraged no doubt by a certain snob appeal—the "good breeding" of colonial design, as *The American Architect* put it in 1876. Furthermore, "nice old-fashioned chairs . . . make a parlor look very cozy and old-timey," said *The Ladies' Home Journal* in 1888. And Clarence Cook, who praised the "staid and discreet appearance" of colonial furniture, welcomed it as a respite from the "whims and impositions of foreign fashions."

251. Left: country style chair

252. Above: a Sheraton chair

253. *A Chippendale armchair*

254. *Windsor, or stick, chair*

255. *Advertisement,* the Grand Rapids Furniture Record, *1902*

256. *Chair of medieval design*

257. *A banister-back rocker*

258. *Above: Saint-Gaudens'* The Puritan

259. *Right: sketch from* Harper's Weekly *of Paul Revere statuette by J. E. Kelly, 1882*

260. *Above, right: George H. Boughton's painting,* Pilgrims Going to Church, *1867*

As added impetus to the colonial revival, antiquarians and architects contributed their researches into early American design, and the restoration of eighteenth-century houses came into fashion—to remain in fashion ever since. One of the first such projects was undertaken by Charles McKim in 1875 in Newport, "the old kept wherever it was sound enough . . . and whatever new was added kept true to the spirit of the old times." History buffs contributed countless articles to countless periodicals on colonial days and ways, prominent colonial figures, Revolutionary battles, and accounts of visits to "unspoiled" colonial towns. The revival also offered inspiration in the arts. Augustus Saint-Gaudens' *The Puritan* was unveiled in Springfield, Massachusetts, Frederick MacMonnies' *Nathan Hale* in New York's City Hall Park, Quincy Ward's *Pilgrim* in New York's Central Park, and Daniel

Chester French's the *Minute Man* in Concord, Massachusetts. James E. Kelly, who did the *Monmouth Battle Monument* in New Jersey and *Count Rochambeau* in Southington, Connecticut, entered this statuette (259) in a Boston competition for a figure of Paul Revere. Revere, famed for his silver, was little remembered as a Revolutionary hero until Longfellow's poetic version of the "midnight ride." And the story has been told of an American lady, who—after many years abroad—was unaware of the impact of the colonial revival. She owned Revere silver and could understand a memorial to the distinguished craftsman. But why, she asked, was Revere so often represented with a horse? An English visitor, however, George H. Boughton, was historically *au courant* and painted a number of colonial scenes (260), as well as illustrating *Rip Van Winkle* and *The Scarlet Letter*.

207

261. *Below: rocker, Bishop Furniture Co., Grand Rapids, Michigan, the early 1900's*

262. *Above: an Empire sofa, the late 1800's*

263. *Opposite: advertisement for a chair, The Decorator and Furnisher, October, 1886*

264. *Opposite: dressing table of mahogany*

No. 970
Colonial Parlor Rocker.

QUARTERED OAK
AND MAHOGANIZED BIRCH.

WE can safely say that there has never been placed on the market a rocker of similar design and equal quality at so low a price as we ask for this. The back is handsomely carved and embossed, and the spindles hand turned. Seat is filled with highly tempered steel springs, guaranteed not to sag, and covered with figured imported tapestry or genuine leather, plain or embossed.

Retails for $10.00 to $12.00.

Price C. O. D. $7.65
Price cash with order 7.27

970

While many furniture makers conscientiously interpreted antique forms, there were those manufacturers—as there are today—who seized on "colonial" as a catchall category for indiscriminate variations, not to mention such sentimental novelties as this spinning-wheel chair (263). The rocking chair (261) also offered a bogus colonial design, complete for seven dollars and sixty-five cents, with an imported tapestry upholstery that depicted what appears to be the three musketeers in a medieval Parisian rathskeller. The dressing table (264), taken to the White House by Mrs. Woodrow Wilson, dips into at least four periods of design with its Chippendale legs, Sheraton and Hepplewhite brasses, Empire mirror brackets, and the whole crowned with a fringe of Gothic Revival cusps. The sofa (262), apart from techniques of construction that place it late in the nineteenth century, offers an overblown amalgamation of Empire motifs (winged-paw feet, curved arms) and the Rococo Revival (a curving back extravagantly crested with carving).

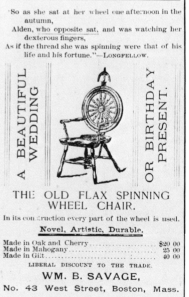
209

265. *Detail of a room in The Breakers, built in Newport, Rhode Island, by Richard Morris Hunt for Cornelius Vanderbilt II in 1892-95*

The Old World Styles

For those who wearied of colonial style furniture, *The House Beautiful* advised in 1902, "old French pieces" offered a refreshing change. Five years earlier the novelist Edith Wharton and the architect-decorator Ogden Codman, Jr., had published a book, *The Decoration of Houses*, in which they paid respect to the historic French styles in architecture and furniture. (Mrs. Wharton, who preferred the European purlieus of Paris, London, and Rome to her native New York, later referred to the book as fashion's "touchstone of taste.") In Paris, the authors pointed out, one saw "the most refined taste the world has known since the decline of the arts in Italy." And the American homemaker, they advised, could achieve satisfactory results "only by a close study of the best models."

Paul Bourget reported that the ladies of Newport kept up a constant refrain: "When I was in Paris"; "Then we go to Paris"; "We want to go to Paris to buy our gowns." And "among the freaks of decoration" borrowed from France was their taste for old things—things whose prices soared so high because of Americans' eagerness to buy, that few Europeans could compete for them. "Counterfeiting has followed," he added, "and second-rate articles are especially abundant." And in those Newport "cottages" he saw "too many tapestries . . . too many *bibelots*, too much rare furniture"—too much of everything that made itself "show off." "What a mosaic is the taste of this race which takes everything pell-mell from our civilization," the excellent along with deplorable caricatures.

266. *Above: Louis XVI bed, design drawn by Ogden Codman*

267. *Right: a 19th-century chair made in the Louis XVI style*

268. *Left: Louis XV bergère by A. Kimbel & Sons, N.Y.C.*

269. *Lower left: a gilded table in the Louis XV manner*

270. *Below: settee by The Brooks Household Art Co., Ohio*

271. *Opposite: American-made chair in the Louis XV style*

212

"No sooner is it known that beautiful furniture was made in the time of Marie-Antoinette," wrote Wharton and Codman, "than an epidemic of supposed 'Marie-Antoinette' rooms breaks out over the whole country." The "counterfeiting" that was practiced to meet such demand was carried on at many levels, with and without intent to deceive. French artisans never had ceased making furniture in eighteenth-century styles; some firms had agencies in America that imported their products or made them here with the help of craftsmen sent to this country for the purpose. The more faithful reproductions, like the genuine antiques, were beyond reach of all but the wealthy. Other, American houses manufactured approximate versions of the early French styles for customers with more modest budgets, and for clubs and hotels.

275. *A painted panel from a chest made by S. R. Burleigh, Providence*

272. *Above: carved, painted cabinet by Stetson and Burleigh, about 1894*

273. *Left: silver spoons by J. G. Aldrich*

274. *Right: a chair made by Burleigh*

Of Arts & Crafts

At about the same time that the gilded extravagance of Newport was coming to full flower, in nearby Providence, a group of artists and craftsmen, professionals and amateurs, was seeking a more direct and, as they earnestly believed, more sensible answer to the question of design and decoration. Paralleling the efforts of the English Arts and Crafts movement they sought to demonstrate the unity of all the arts and crafts; to show the vitality of the vernacular arts, in contrast to the pale authority of academic tradition; and to prove that art in the broadest sense could and should be part of everyday life. The three leading spirits of the group—the artists Sydney R. Burleigh and Charles W. Stetson and the industrialist (and artist and craftsman by avocation) John G.

Aldrich—came to call themselves the Art Workers' Guild. Like the equivalent societies in England, this group found in the teachings and practices of William Morris a corrective to the corroding influence of industrialism on all the arts. Like those others, too, they owned a romantic interest in the forms and principles of medieval craftsmanship. The carved and painted furniture, the silverwork, and other artifacts produced by these men and their associates had little direct effect on the development of American styles, but like the contemporary activity of the Rookwood Pottery in Cincinnati (see page 148) and the Tiffany Studios in New York (see pages 236–45) they expressed a point of view that filtered into the mainstream of art history with lasting results.

276. Top: a detail from a chest by Burleigh

277. Above: a chest with portraits of Shake-spearean characters, painted by Burleigh

Mission Style Furniture

"The day of cheap veneer, of jig-saw ornament, of poor imitations of French periods, is happily over," enthused *The House Beautiful* in 1900 in an article on Mission furniture — or Craftsman furniture, as it was called by its originator, Gustav Stickley (1857–1942). Stickley's plain, square-cut patterns were inspired by his idealistic concept of furniture made "solely for use and comfort and durability . . . the beauty that is peculiarly its own arises from the directness with which it meets these requirements." Stickley, a Wisconsin farmer's son, had worked in furniture factories and stores during his youth and rebelled against the "reign of marble tops and silk upholstery," recognizing the vitality of such simple forms as those made by the Shakers. He journeyed abroad to view Art Nouveau and the English Arts and Crafts movement at the source. Neither, however, met his high standards of functionalism. He considered Art Nouveau's "conventionalized plant-forms" to be merely worthless decoration.

He adjudged "Quaint" furniture, as the English described their current designs, to be far too quaint. Stickley created his own sturdy and primitive patterns, imbuing the project with a personal mystique — the cult of hand craftsmanship and a desire to build a "sane, reasonable, beautiful" civilization. Before going bankrupt in 1915, his enterprises had expanded to include the Craftsman Farms in New Jersey, the Craftsman Workshops near Syracuse, New York, *The Craftsman* magazine, and the Craftsman Building in New York City with its lecture hall, library, home-builders' exhibit, gardens, furniture, and textiles. Meanwhile, his popular designs were copied at random throughout the country, by amateurs and professionals alike. Both the chair (280), with the goatskin-covered cushions, and the lamp (278) were made in Michigan. And an imaginative piano firm, J. P. Seeburg, produced this coin-operated player piano (281), highlighted with a stained-glass landscape — in effect an early jukebox.

216

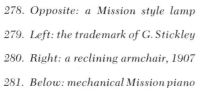

278. *Opposite: a Mission style lamp*

279. *Left: the trademark of G. Stickley*

280. *Right: a reclining armchair, 1907*

281. *Below: mechanical Mission piano*

282. *Above: Mission sofa, typically made of oak, 1900–1913*

283. *Below: leather-topped Mission desk, the legs secured by mortise and tenon, the paneling with butterfly wedges*

The Fra DeLuxe

284. Left: a Mission style standing clock

285. Above: caricature of Elbert Hubbard

Among the numerous imitators of Stickley's furniture designs—a list that included his brothers at their factories in Grand Rapids—was Elbert Hubbard (1856–1915), the colorful entrepreneur and self-styled medievalist. Hubbard produced "Craft-Style" furniture at his Roycroft Shops, East Aurora, New York, the base of his varied and highly successful ventures as an author, editor, printer, publisher, lecturer, and promoter of Roycroft handicrafts. "Fra Hubbard's" flamboyant appearance with flowing cravat and long locks, the nationwide popularity of his folksy writings, the scandal attending an extramarital romance, and his death on the *Lusitania*, made him memorable. Indeed, Hubbard's name is generally linked to the Mission style, rather than Stickley's.

No. 50
COPPER LAMP $18.50
21 IN. HIGH
DIAMETER AT BASE
7 IN.
THREE LIGHTS AND
PULL CHAIN

50

No. 513
ELECTRIC SCONCE
COMPLETE WITH MICA SHADE
COPPER OR BRASS . . $8 00
IRON $7 50
SCONCE 12 IN. HIGH, 6 IN.
WIDE

PROJECTION OF
BRACKET 6 IN.
BASE OF SHADE 4 IN.

513

No. 512
ELECTRIC SCONCE
(SAME DESIGN AND SIZE AS 513, BUT
FITTED WITH TWO LIGHTS)
COPPER OR BRASS $12.00
IRON $11.00

624

No. 624
LIBRARY TABLE, WOOD TOP . $41.50
HARD LEATHER TOP $58.50
29 IN. HIGH. HEXAGONAL 48 IN.

No. 682
DINING TABLE, 30 IN. HIGH
48 IN. TOP TO EXTEND 6 FT. . $34.00
48 IN. TOP TO EXTEND 8 FT. . $38.00
58 IN. TOP TO EXTEND 8 FT. . $42.00

633

No. 633
LIBRARY TABLE
WOOD TOP $30.00
HARD LEATHER TOP $48.00
29 IN. HIGH. DIAMETER 44 IN.

682

286. An advertisement of Stickley furnishings

287. *Above: Mission-furnished living room of the house lived in by Frank Lloyd Wright, about 1911*

288. *Below: a side chair by Wright, 1904, showing the influence of the Arts and Crafts movement*

Although Stickley's name has slipped into obscurity, his designs (286) and their wide influence on contemporary furniture were hailed in almost hallowed terms by any number of admirers. One ardent critic wrote: "This man rose, as it were, out of the forests, in answer to the cry: 'Who shall deliver us from the expensive living, the thralldom of extravagance, the hereditament of conventions?'" There were those, of course, who thoroughly disliked the Mission style. Frank Lloyd Wright, whose designs (288) — like Stickley's — were essentially functional, reportedly detested Mission furniture, although he was known to recommend it when nothing else was available. And Wright, himself, had lived amidst Mission (287) in Spring Green, Wisconsin, while his home and studio, Taliesin East, was being built.

Horns Aplenty

289. *A steer horn chair upholstered with leather*

With imaginations fired by western expansion, furniture makers, professional and amateur, turned to and created their own brand of American exotica—steer, buffalo, and elk horn furniture. A western trapper sent an elk horn chair to President Lincoln. A buffalo hat rack, in 1867, was commended at a New Jersey fair as the "handsomest hat rack ever made." The fad continued well into the 1900's. This parlor set (290), shown in a photograph taken around 1909, is merely a dressed-up version of an earlier steer horn chair (289). A similar chair, made about 1885, was given to Theodore Roosevelt, whose home, Sagamore Hill, at Oyster Bay, Long Island, abounded with such trophies of the hunt as a rhinoceros foot inkwell (291), elephant tusks, bearskin and tigerskin rugs—all in keeping with the zoological decorating fad. Alligator and prairie dog hides were recommended for upholstery in the 1880's. Stuffed foxes were mounted as "watchful guardians" on iron umbrella stands. And umbrella stands wrought from elephant legs were on sturdy display in any number of front halls.

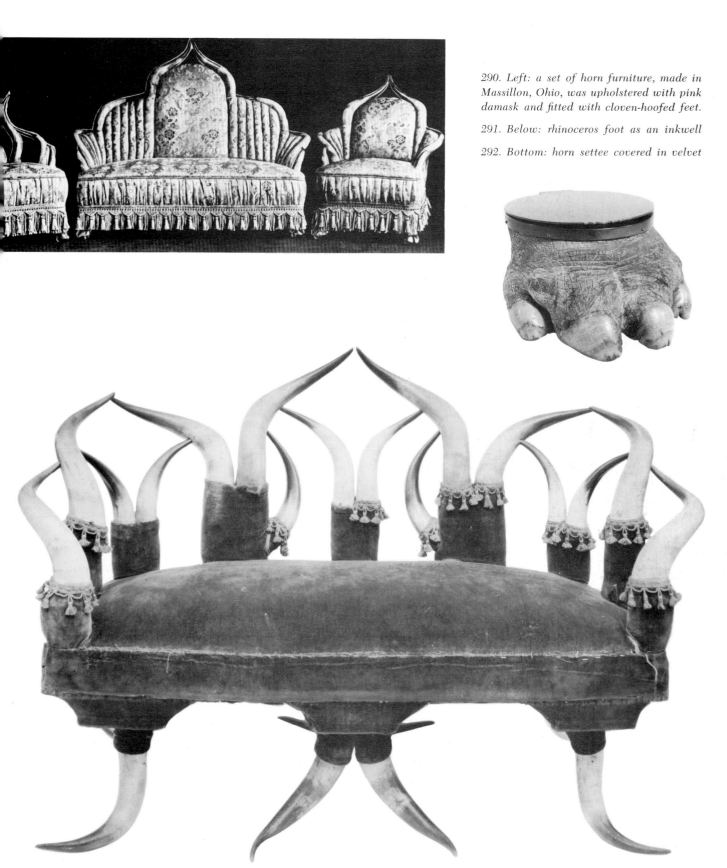

290. *Left: a set of horn furniture, made in Massillon, Ohio, was upholstered with pink damask and fitted with cloven-hoofed feet.*

291. *Below: rhinoceros foot as an inkwell*

292. *Bottom: horn settee covered in velvet*

293. *Above: a furnished room after a design by Will Bradley* 294. *Opposite: six designs for furniture, drawn by Bradley*

Further Missions

While Queen Victoria still reigned over her world-wide empire, in progressive circles the term "Victorian" had already taken on some of the derogatory overtones it holds for us today. Before the advent of the Mission style, magazines aimed at homemakers were calling for simplicity in interior decoration, for an end to what one editor called the "repellently ornate." That editor, Edward Bok, waged a vigorous campaign in *The Ladies' Home Journal* to "make the world a better or more beautiful place to live in." He launched a sharp attack against the dust-catching, plush-burdened, somber-toned extravagance of American Pullman cars. As part of his broader strategy, in 1900 he commissioned Will H. Bradley, one of the country's most prominent commercial artists, to prepare designs for a completely furnished house in a strictly contemporary style—a style to fit the tastes and needs of a new century. Bradley's designs may never have been put into production, but they expressed the questing spirit that, on both sides of the Atlantic, looked for a fresh, "modern" departure from the clichés of the past.

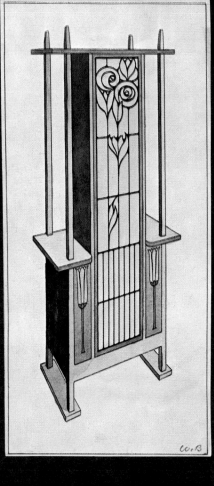

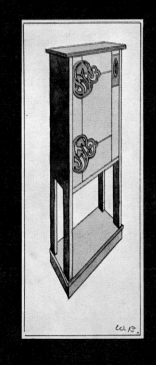

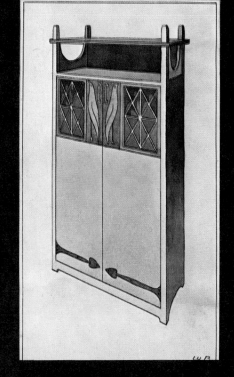

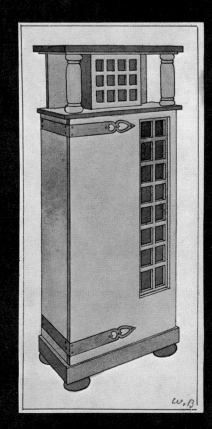

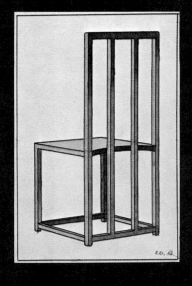

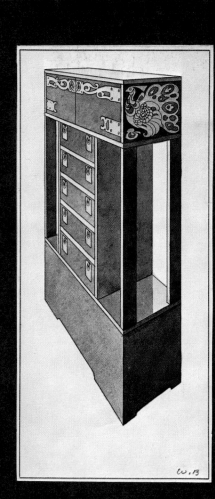

The New Art of Posters

The quest for new and vital design that marked the close of the Victorian period was exemplified in America by the Art Nouveau posters created by Will H. Bradley (1868–1962). Bradley achieved international acclaim as a designer with an exhibition of his posters at Bing's Salon de l'Art Nouveau in Paris, 1895. The poster—as an art form—had been earlier popularized in France by such masters as Pierre Bonnard and Henri de Toulouse-Lautrec, and by the 1890's had become a rage among the intelligentsia of the United States, who became avid collectors and gave—or attended—countless exhibits. "The modern poster is a thing of flamboyant beauty," *The Decorator and Furnisher* exclaimed in an article extolling artistic originality, excellence of technique, "the frisky line, and great patches of vivid color." Posters, of course, were not new in themselves. But the concept of an advertising medium as serious art was a radical innovation and presented a fresh field for artist-designers. In a successful poster, the message must be understood at a glance. Patterns, therefore, must be simple and the colors few and bold, words kept to a minimum. Art Nouveau, in particular, lent itself to these necessary ingredients. And Art Nouveau poster art lent itself to the *avant-garde* standards of the many little literary magazines that sprang up throughout the country during the nineties. Established and conservative publications were enlivened by such eye-catching covers and advertisements. While the rage for Art Nouveau affected even architecture in Europe, it found its most fruitful American expression in such forms as the poster, glassware, and silverware, metalwork, and pottery.

295. *Above: detail of a poster for* M'lle New York, *a magazine*

296. *Right: a magazine cover designed by Will Bradley, 1894*

The Chap-Book

WILL H.
BRADLEY '94

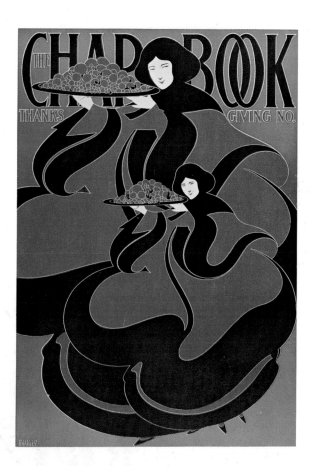

297. *Left: a cover for* Scribner's *magazine done by Max-field Parrish in 1897. The muted color scheme and seated figure profiled against the trees strongly resemble a poster with which he won a $75 prize in a cover contest sponsored by The Century Company a year earlier.*

298. *Above: this* Chap-Book *cover by Bradley, shown at a poster exhibition in New York in 1896, was praised for its "quaintly artistic whirl of lines in the draperies."*

299. *Right: ledger paper advertisement by Bradley, who also created advertisements for a stove company and a manufacturer of ink, as well as designs for wallpapers*

VICTOR

BICYCLES OVERMAN WHEEL COMPANY

BOSTON   NEW YORK   DETROIT   DENVER
SAN FRANCISCO   LOS ANGELES   PORTLAND ORE

300. *Left: a bicycle poster by Bradley. The floral border is of the sort he designed in varying patterns to be sold by the American Type Founders Co. With a number of these floral "cuts," a commercial printer could thereby devise his own artwork.*

301. *Above: John Sloan (1871–1951), later famed for his realism as a member of the Ashcan school of art, did this* Echo *cover in 1895 when he was working as a designer in the Art Nouveau style.*

302. *Above, right: Bradley cover,* Collier's Weekly

303. *Right: Bradley cover for* The Chap-Book, *1895, one of the many little magazines of the nineties*

231

304. *Above: another Bradley magazine cover that typifies his Art Nouveau technique of swirling lines and draperies. One critic, in 1896, was moved to declare that although Bradley was classed in the "Aubrey Beardsley" school, he far outdid "his English brother artist" with richer ideas and execution.*

305. *Right: a Scribner's cover by Robert J. Wildhack, born in Illinois, who came to New York to study art and became known in the 1890's for humorous line drawings and posters*

306. *Above: a further example of Bradley's covers for The Chap-Book, here a smiling nymphet with her reed pipes of Pan*

L.C. Tiffany In Quest of Beauty

The current revival of interest in Art Nouveau has, among other things, restored the reputation of Louis Comfort Tiffany close to the high level it had gained two generations ago. In the days of his greatest creative activity, as a result both of his skilled artistry and of his talents as a propagandist, Tiffany's name was a household word in America, standing for elegance, tastefulness, and beauty. No well-appointed home was without its Tiffany lamp, vase, or desk set, and for those who could not afford the genuine article the market abounded in less expensive imitations. For those of very substantial resources a house "done" by Tiffany was a declaration of superior taste. His fame overseas was hardly less. The work of no other American artist of the time was so well known, and so widely copied, in international circles. Around the turn of the century he was this country's most celebrated champion of the "modern" movement in design and decoration.

Tiffany was born in 1848, the eldest child of Charles Lewis and Harriet Young Tiffany of New York. His father could trace his ancestry to Squire Humphrey Tiffany, who had settled in the Massachusetts Bay colony about 1660. In 1837 Charles Tiffany had founded a small dry-goods and stationery store with a loan of one thousand dollars—a firm that by the time his son was grown had developed into the world-famous Tiffany & Company. As a child Louis was headstrong and volatile and his parents, unable to discipline their wiry, red-haired son, enrolled him at Flushing Academy on Long Island. At the age of eighteen the youth announced that he would rather study art than go to college. His formal education was over, and he did not enter the family business.

George Inness, the popular landscape painter, accepted the lad as his first and only student, and in the hours he spent in Inness' studio Tiffany was exposed to the company and the conversation of the leading American artists and writers of the time. The life of an artist, he decided, was the only one for him. He was a romantic with a love for nature, and he had a talent for painting landscapes. However, he could not abide criticism and preferred to work on his own. "The more I teach him," Inness declared, "the

less he knows." When he was turning twenty-one, Tiffany left for Paris to "study" in much the same manner at the studio of the French artist Léon Bailly, who was noted for his landscapes of North Africa and the Near East. There he remained only briefly before joining his friend, the American artist Samuel Colman, on a trip to North Africa. From Colman, Tiffany learned the value of water-color sketching and the interest in Islamic textiles. The decorative arts of the Orient and the Near East were much in vogue in Paris at the time, and Tiffany's sojourn there, as well as his travels with Colman, impressed him with the colorful designs of those exotic, distant lands.

Upon his return to America in 1870 he opened his own studio and immersed himself in the world of art and artists. His canvases, some based on European

and North African scenes, were favorably received and brought the young artist about five hundred dollars apiece. However, although painting remained a serious interest throughout his life, Tiffany soon turned to the crafts and industrial arts as offering a more promising career. After returning from a second trip to France in 1875, he decided to make "decorative work" his profession. "I believe there is more in it than in painting pictures," he remarked, and in 1879 he organized his own firm, Louis C. Tiffany & Company, Associated Artists, with Samuel Colman, Lockwood De Forest, and Candace Wheeler as the associates. De Forest was an artist and Orientalist who founded workshops for the revival of woodworking in India (see page 180); Mrs. Wheeler was primarily interested in embroidery and needlework. Their first order was for an embroidered drop curtain for the Madison Square Theatre, which Oscar Wilde praised as having been executed by "a master hand."

Tiffany had experimented with glass as early as the 1870's and his interest in this medium grew with the years. Although he continued his decorating business into the 1900's, his work with glass became a major preoccupation. He saw in glass windows and mosaics an opportunity to indulge his passionate love of color in producing a thing of beauty. He recalled the glorious medieval windows of France, but he wished to avoid the traditional methods of painting and leading in the creation of pictorial designs. To carry out his purpose, he remarked, "I took up chemistry and built furnaces . . . . By the aid of studies in chemistry and through years of experiments, I have found means to avoid the use of paints, etching, or burning, or otherwise treating the surface of the glass so that it is now possible to produce figures in glass of which even the fleshtones are not superficially treated—built up of what I call 'genuine glass.'"

With the considerable aid of expert craftsmen he brought to America from abroad, Tiffany perfected techniques that resulted in a variety of types of glass, all of which met his insistent demand that the designs, the colors, and even the textures of his subjects emanate from within the medium itself. By fusing molten glass of various colors, at times exposing it to fumes produced by vaporizing different metals, and by supremely skilled manipulation, he achieved an astonishingly wide range of effects. Thus he could suggest the effect of cloudy skies, of flowers and foliage, of folds of drapery, or of peacock feathers, without resorting to painted designs. Ultimately he called the new medium he had developed Favrile glass. ("Favrile" was derived from "fabrile," a Latin word meaning in effect handmade.)

For the World's Columbian Exposition at Chicago in 1893, Tiffany designed a "modern" Byzantine chapel which was furnished with mosaics of more than a million pieces of iridescent and opalescent glass together with pearls and semiprecious stones in a setting of white and black marble. Twelve stained-glass windows and a bejeweled sanctuary lamp provided light for this opulent creation which, along with Louis Sullivan's "Golden Door" for the Transportation Building, was widely considered the most sensational exhibition at the fair. Samuel Bing, a French dealer in Oriental art, who was a visitor to the display, thought so. Two years later, when Bing opened his Salon de l'Art Nouveau in Paris (his famous shop, L'Art Nouveau, provided the generally accepted name of the emerging new style in art), he gave a prominent place to work by Tiffany that he had commissioned and to other products of the American's studio. Bing became Tiffany's European agent, and for the next score of years and more Tiffany glass won awards at virtually every important international fair.

Both in his free adaptation of Oriental and Islamic forms and motifs and in his sensuously flowing designs derived from nature Tiffany was a true exponent of Art Nouveau, the dominant advanced style of the day. He was bent on providing well-designed and soundly made accessories for the American home and on educating the public in their merits. "It is all a matter of education," he remarked, "and we shall never have good art in our homes until the people learn to distinguish the beautiful from the ugly." And he prospered in his cause. Before the turn of the century the output of his atelier was enormous. In 1898 it was estimated that five thousand colors and varieties of Favrile glass were kept accessible in his stockrooms. In 1900 he established the Tiffany Studios and under that name, with the help of hundreds of female "craftsmen," he continued to produce a large assortment of glass, bronze, ceramic, and enamel objects which enjoyed a popular market. In each medium a seemingly endless variety of "properly beautiful" forms, from the smallest penwipers and pin trays to matched sets of stemware and elaborate lighting fixtures, were produced. A complete line of art jewelry, ranging from scarabs and charms of semiprecious stones to tiaras and necklaces of precious gems, was marketed through his father's firm.

Throughout his career Tiffany capitalized on dramatic gesture and on his flamboyant personality to impress the importance of his own ideas on others. His efforts in this direction were heightened by his colorful appearance, among other things by his flaming red beard worn pointed in Edwardian fashion. Of all his publicity schemes, his costume fetes attracted the most attention. In 1913 he staged an Egyptian costume party, transforming one area of his studio to represent the valley of the Nile. At this function "Egyptian beauties, bare-legged youths and Pinkerton men in Oriental guise" mingled with the hundreds of guests. *The New York Times* called it "the most lavish costume fete ever seen in New York." At the "Peacock Dinner," held on the eve of World War I, a course of peacocks was served to the male guests by young ladies clad in Greek garments who carried peacocks on their shoulders and formed a procession around the dining table. As a more durable form of self-presentation he commissioned *The Art Work of Louis C. Tiffany*, a privately printed book that was to serve as a memorial to his achievement and that Tiffany gave away to his "deserving" friends.

This endowed testimonial was pub-

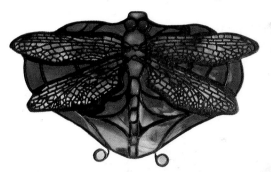

lished in 1914. The tides of taste were shifting and his own vision of what kind of art the world should have was wasted on the next generation. His firm continued in business for almost another quarter of a century, but its influence vastly diminished. In 1918 he established the Louis Comfort Tiffany Foundation, for which he converted his estate, Laurelton Hall, on Long Island into a retreat for artists. There was to be no formal instruction (such as he had so disliked in his own younger days), but he hoped the atmosphere of beauty in a beautiful setting would induce "art-by-absorption." "The most helpful thing I can think of," he observed, "is to show people that beauty is everywhere . . . up-lifting . . . health-giving."

Fresh Forms in Favrile Glass

Louis Comfort Tiffany's experiments were one phase of an international renascence in glassmaking that coincided with and was part of the development of Art Nouveau during the last two decades of the nineteenth century. The beginnings of the new movement were already apparent at exhibitions held in Paris in 1878 and 1889. At that time the unique and colorful creations of Emile Gallé of Nancy, France, (with whose work Tiffany was familiar) provided a tremendous stimulus to a new art in glassmaking. Even earlier, however, Tiffany had started his own experiments in this country, first in conjunction with his fellow artist John La Farge and then independently. He was initially concerned with stained-glass windows and mosaics, but soon broadened his operations in favor of bowls, vases, lamps, and other decorative objects,

and by the 1890's these were adding to his international reputation as a highly gifted, creative designer. In 1900 *The House Beautiful* exulted — with justification — that in Tiffany's Favrile glass "we possess a distinctively American product that is recognized wherever it is shown as an achievement in art." The mysteries of chemistry and manipulation by which such glass was produced were not known to the reporter, but this only added to the fascination of the results. "It is hardly possible to imagine the carnivalesque abandon of color exhibited in these gleaming trophies of art," the article continued. "A cabinet of Favrile vases has all the splendor of opals, emeralds, aquamarines, and chrysopras. There are colors stolen from hyacinths, tulips, and roses, from garnets, coral, and turquoise. Iridescence . . . [is] irradiated with purple and gold."

307. *Opposite: group of Tiffany Favrile vases of various shapes*

308. *Above: an iridescent vase in a jack-in-the-pulpit design*

In the closing years of the nineteenth century Tiffany undertook the production of lamps, combining cast-bronze bases with leaded-glass shades that were an obvious derivative from his stained-glass windows. The lead skeletons of the shades, with their flowing, unbroken lines, were skillfully contrived to accommodate irregular pieces of glass selected for their harmonious, shaded colors to suggest floral and other natural forms and patterns, as in the four examples shown here. These novel and varied accessories were largely designed to exploit the needs and possibilities introduced with the advent and the increasing popularity of lighting by electricity. Some were made to accommodate as many as twenty incandescent bulbs. The success of those highly ornamental and serviceable devices attracted a host of imitators on both sides of the Atlantic, until the term "Tiffany lamp shade" ultimately degenerated into a bland cliché for pseudo elegance.

309. *Opposite, left: a hydrangea floor lamp*
310. *Opposite, right: a dragonfly table lamp*
311. *Left: a table lamp with wisteria shade*
312. *Right: a table lamp, trumpet-flower shade*

313. *Five Favrile vases ornamented with lilies of the valley, vines, blossoms, and other naturalistic forms in various colors*

When Tiffany first launched his Favrile glass on the public market in 1896 he held what we would call today a press preview at his Fourth Avenue studios in New York. The reporters were mystified and enchanted by what they saw there. According to *The New York Herald* the effects he had achieved were "almost bewildering." "It is hard to understand," remarked *The House Beautiful* a few years later, "how these infinite gradations of tone and color can be applied to a single vase"—almost as if this vitreous substance were a growing and glowing organism caught and crystallized at some vital point of its development. Tiffany did not discuss the techniques of his operation, but Samuel Bing, his European agent and the impresario of the Art Nouveau movement in general, explained the matter obligingly but without disclosing any serious secrets. He described how the incandescent ball of molten glass, as it was withdrawn from the furnace, was slightly dilated, and flecked at the prearranged points with glass of different textures and colors—the seeds of the intended ornamentation. The ball was then reheated and similarly flecked as many as twenty times before it was blown large and manipulated to its final form and size, when each of the motifs introduced at the start had grown proportionately with the vase itself and each of the tiny, ornamented flecks filled "the place assigned to it in advance in the mind of the artist," forming perhaps a flower or a feather.

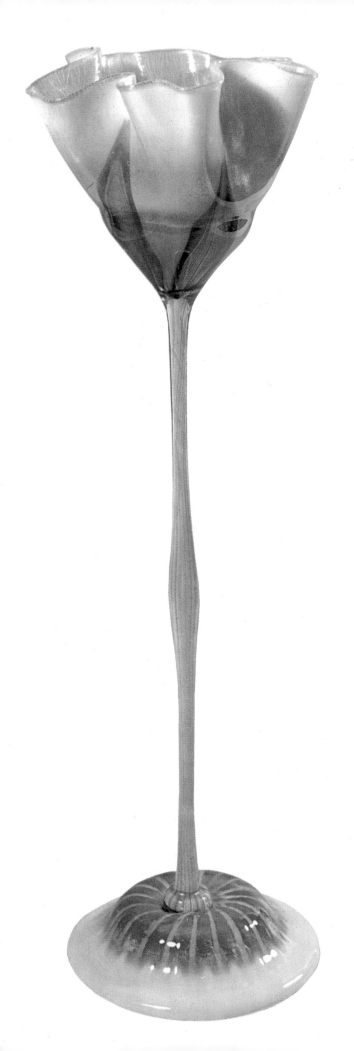

314. *Left: a tall vase in the form of a flower, 1898*

315. *Top: a bronze inkwell with glass ornaments*

316. *Above: a vase with naturalistic decoration*

After 1900 Tiffany's combinations of bronze and Favrile were developed in myriad forms. "Metal and glass are twin products of fire," wrote one contemporary reporter, "and their joint use is very appropriate"—and so it seemed to a large public that found not only Tiffany's lamps, but his desk sets, photograph frames, smoking sets (cigarettes were becoming increasingly popular), clocks, nut dishes, and scores of other accessories delightful complements to the art of living graciously and fashionably. More than ten different patterns of desk sets were produced; some consisting of bronze etched to simulate a greenish patina backed by amber or green marbleized glass, others incorporating enamel and mother-of-pearl. Meanwhile, Tiffany's decorating business continued to expand, and to meet its demands he enlarged his production to include furniture, pottery, and enamels.

317. *Surrounding: elements of a 19-piece desk set made of bronze and glass at the Tiffany Studios. Such sets were made in various patterns and colors.*

243

To produce so much and such varied ware Tiffany depended upon a large staff of craftsmen, designers, workmen, and workwomen, although his personal taste, judgment, and direction were reflected in virtually everything that issued from his studios. The most important of these helpers was the master glassworker, Arthur J. Nash, whom Tiffany had brought from England and whose contribution to the best results in glassware was substantial. In the relatively swift passage of glass from a plastic to a solid state the artificer has to control the material with extraordinary care to achieve the ornamental pattern conceived by the designer. Referring to the design here illustrated (320), Samuel Bing wrote: "this power . . . of assigning in advance to each morsel of glass, whatever its color or chemical composition, the exact place which it is to occupy when the article leaves the glassblower's hands— this truly unique art is combined in these peacocks' feathers with the charm of iridescence which bathes the subtle and velvety ornamentation with an almost supernatural light." This was, he observed, "Nature in her most seductive aspects."

318. *Left: an adjustable candleholder of bronze and glass*

319. *Above: a bronze candleholder with glass ornaments*

320. *Opposite: Favrile, peacock-feather vase, about 1896*

Silver in New Styles

Throughout much of the western world the arts and crafts were in a ferment during the last two decades of the nineteenth century. It almost seems, in retrospect, as if there were a widely felt, imperative need to discover a fresh vocabulary and syntax of design before the year 1900 ushered in the twentieth century. The rapidity with which the Art Nouveau style spread out over Europe and across the Atlantic to America was an expression of that spirit of expectancy and experiment. In the freely flowing, organic forms and ornament so typical of that style, it appeared to many that the modern world had finally cast off the bonds of the past; it had willfully and exuberantly turned away from historical precedent and confidently restated the principles of design in purely contemporary terms. And it raised the decorative arts to a parity with the fine arts, as Ruskin and Morris had urged must be done if art as such were to serve its vital social function and to flourish. Like glass, silver lent itself admirably to the sinuously curving, naturalistic configurations of Art Nouveau, as the French candleholder shown opposite (323), mounted with Tiffany glass shades, so handsomely demonstrates. The point is again emphatically made by a hand mirror (321) designed in Tiffany's studios. Its handle is in the form of a peacock's neck and head, brilliantly spotted with sapphires; on the back another peacock, in full plumage, is depicted in brightly colored enamels. A novelty that gained wide popularity in the 1890's and the following decade was created by depositing a pattern of thin silver coating on the outer surface of glass forms (322, 324). These swirling overlays, characteristically in the spirit of Art Nouveau, were further defined by engraved or etched details. Such ornaments appeared on every conceivable shape.

321. *Opposite: Tiffany silver hand mirror with enameled back*

322. *Above: a glass vase with engraved silver-deposit designs*

323. *Left: French silver candle-holder with Favrile glass shades*

324. *Above: glass decanter with silver overlay, made by Gorham*

Silver-deposit patterns were applied to wood, pottery, porcelain, book covers, purses, and other types of material as well as to glass. In the 1890's the famous Rookwood Pottery in Cincinnati sent quantities of the wares from its kilns to Providence to be overlaid with silver designs by the Gorham Manufacturing Company, and numerous other companies provided similar services.

In solid metal the female figure, nude or flimsily draped, sensuously modeled, who was often emerging from or afloat in some aqueous world where water plants abound, became virtually a symbolic motif of the Art Nouveau style. Female heads were inevitably crowned with luxuriant tresses that merged into all but abstract patterns of tendrils and flowers. In that fusion of natural forms and pure patterns Art Nouveau celebrated its complete freedom from classical conventions and restraints. A paperknife (327) by the Unger Brothers of Newark, New Jersey, with a mermaid, trident in hand, riding the waves on some scaly denizen of the water, summarizes that new freedom of design with obvious grace. A different sort of freedom is suggested by the head of a female on a cigar cutter (326); the lady's hair seems to drift off into smoke from her lips.

Opposite: 325. Tray by the Unger Brothers; 326. Cigar cutter; 327. Paperknife by the Unger Brothers; 328. Brooch made by Gorham

329. Above: bronze vase with silver overlay offered by R. H. Macy & Co., about 1911

Most of the silver and silver plate made in the United States around the turn of the century, like the bulk of furniture, was mass produced in approximations of conventional designs for a general public. However, as Louis Tiffany and others demonstrated, there was also a market for household furnishings expertly wrought in the advanced styles of the time. By 1901 the Gorham Manufacturing Company had developed a special line of silverware in which each item was a unique product of trained craftsmen. The metal used in this Martelé ware, as it was labeled, was softer and purer than the sterling standard and hammered into ornamented shapes that clearly reflect Art Nouveau influence. In earlier times the individual silversmith laboriously and meticulously planished away all evidence of the irregular marks left by his repeated hammerings in raising and shaping a form. In Martelé silver such marks were customarily left undisguised on the plain surfaces, possibly to eliminate all doubt in the mind of a public grown accustomed to machine-made products that these offerings were in fact fashioned by hand. (On cheap metalwork of later years such hammer marks were often deliberately imposed on pieces that had been turned out in volume by mechanical methods.) The guiding spirit in the development of Martelé was the English master silversmith William J. Codman, who had been brought to America by Gorham in 1891. Under his direction craftsmen were trained to produce a wide variety of individual forms from prepared designs. In those designs appear the undulating curves, the long-haired nymphs, the floral forms, and other elements that informed so much Art Nouveau decoration.

Martelé silverware by Gorham, from old catalogue photographs. 330. Cigar box; 331. Kerosene lamp; 332. Inkstand; 333. Coffeepot; 334. Centerpiece

250

330

331

332

334

Silver in the Art Nouveau style was more commonly produced in flatware than in hollow forms. The handles of brushes and mirrors for the dressing table and knives, forks, and spoons for the dining table nicely accommodated the sinuous patterns of tresses and floral growths that were essential elements of the style. A cake slicer (337), serving fork (338), and hairbrush (339), by different makers, incorporate such motifs in various forms and combinations.

The individualistic spirit that underlaid so much Art Nouveau design was also expressed in other terms during those years. In 1897 Tiffany & Company, which under the direction of Louis Comfort Tiffany's father enjoyed a growing reputation in the luxury trade, fashioned an unusual gold tea service (335, 336) for presentation to Samuel Sloan, president of the Delaware, Lackawanna & Western Railroad, by his employees.

335, 336. Gold tray and sugar bowl, parts of a tea service designed and made in 1897 by Tiffany & Co., N. Y.

337. *Top: cake slicer by R. Wallace & Sons Mfg. Co., Wallingford*

338. *Above: serving fork by Reed & Barton, Taunton, about 1900*

339. *Below: hairbrush by an unidentified silversmith, about 1905*

Jewelry Designs

340. *Attributed to E. Colonna, bejeweled, enameled earrings*

Largely due to the influence of the imaginative René Lalique, French Art Nouveau jeweler and glassmaker, many designers at the turn of the century were creating "non-traditional" jewelry. The value of the gems used was no longer of prime importance. A "ruthless mixture" of precious and semiprecious stones and metals had come into vogue, and enamelwork achieved new and brilliant color schemes. Original, if not bizarre, designs were the fashion — with serpents, dragonflies, lizards, bats, and scarabs offering inspiration. Wild flowers such as Queen Anne's lace, dandelions, clover, and thistle were copied in semiabstract forms. Louis Tiffany, as vice-president of Tiffany & Company, initiated a department of "artistic jewelry," whose patterns were those of his own firm, the Tiffany Studios. His scarabs of Favrile glass were one of the specialties, whether mounted in cuff links or watch guards, hatpins or bracelets, necklaces (345) or pendants (343).

Clockwise: 341. Colonna dragonfly pendant

342. Winged brooch made by Marcus & Co.

343. Tiffany pendant, glass scarab in gold

344. Gold and enamel floral brooch, Tiffany

345. Tiffany necklace, scarabs set in gold

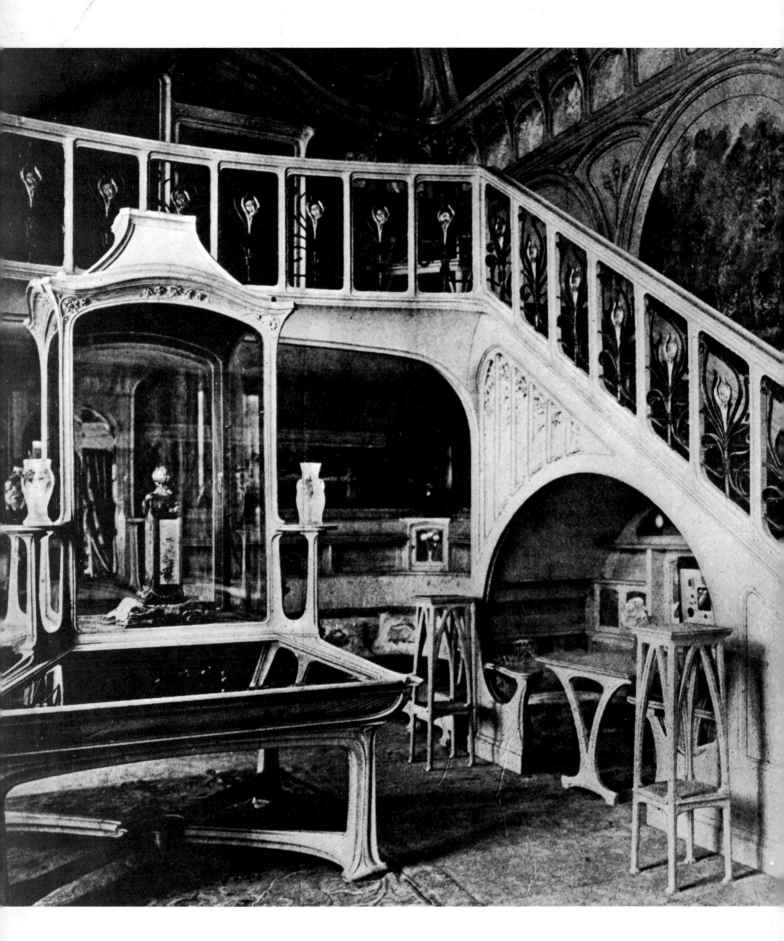

Other Forms of Art Nouveau

Divergent expressions of the "new style" in design were appearing more or less simultaneously in Europe and America. Although there was no apparent agreement in concept among various schools, there was—as one American architect pointed out in 1902—a mutual "protest against the traditional and the commonplace." In Glasgow and Vienna, for example, furniture patterns developed whose Gothic sources were comparable to the earlier Arts and Crafts movement in England. Victorian curves and furbelows were flatly discarded in favor of straight lines, squared corners, and an ascetic simplicity. On the other hand, the French and Belgian designs were dominated by serpentine plant and flower forms—those lush, undulating lines that evoked such caustic titles as "the style of the langorous noodle." This version of Art Nouveau, shown here in a contemporary photograph (346), was displayed at the St. Louis fair in one room of the French pavilion, which was otherwise largely devoted to a reconstruction of the Grand Trianon at Versailles. The sketch (347) for an Art Nouveau interior is by Edward Colonna, a leading designer for Bing's shop.

346. Above: French interior at St. Louis fair

347. Above right: interior design by E. Colonna

257

The career of designer Edward Colonna (frequently and mistakenly referred to as Eugene Colonna) offers an international itinerary of Art Nouveau influences. He was born in Germany, educated in Brussels, and held a United States passport, presumably having been naturalized during the 1880's. He worked at that time in Dayton, Ohio, designing railway car interiors, a job he later pursued in Montreal for the Canadian Pacific Railway. In 1887, while still in Dayton, he published a slim volume entitled *Essay on Broom-Corn*—broom-corn, a species of sorghum, serving as the motif of his twining Art Nouveau illustrations. Shortly before 1900, Colonna went to Paris and under the aegis of Bing became one of the outstanding adherents of French Art Nouveau fashions, as well as a designer of more geometric forms (350). The settee (349) and side chair (351), part of a set that included an armchair, are believed to be by Colonna. A photograph of his furniture, taken in Paris in 1900, shows strikingly similar pieces—if, indeed, not the same set illustrated here.

348. *Above: a table designed by E. Colonna about 1899*

349. *Right: a settee with Art Nouveau tendril carvings*

350. *Top: a sketch by E. Colonna for a marquetry table*

351. *Above: side chair matching the settee shown at left*

352. *Top: walnut table with metal inlay*

353. *Left: drop-front desk, also walnut*

353a. *Above: detail of inlay on the desk*

Concurrent with the hothouse curvatures of French Art Nouveau was the continuing appearance of straightforward, functional patterns—the "new style" that ultimately led to the angularities of the so-called modern decoration of the 1920's and 1930's. This desk (353) and table (352) were made about 1904 for Mrs. Curtis Freshel of Chestnut Hill, Massachusetts, and are possibly of her own design. (The first version of Tiffany's famed wisteria lamps, for example, was executed from an original design by Mrs. Freshel.) Both the desk and table, with their abstract copper and pewter inlays, are comparable in spirit to Will Bradley's work shown on pages 224 and 225. Similar pieces were also pictured in 1900 in *The Ladies' Home Journal*—the squared shapes decorated with twisting patterns, either painted or inlaid. The Tiffany table (354) offers basic simplicity, modified by abstract ornamentation.

354. A table made with patinated bronze legs and wooden top, a design created by Tiffany Studios

Illustrated here are the full-blown interpretations of Art Nouveau produced by the Gorham Manufacturing Company of Providence, Rhode Island. The Gorham furniture, extravaganzas of silverwork, reflects the French school of design in the use of cabriole legs, for example, and the unrestrained intertwinings of vines and leaves. Art Nouveau's symbolistic women with floating hair swirl in mermaidlike forms across the front of this dressing table (355). The dressing table and the chair (356), both chiefly made of ebony incrusted with silver and inlays of ivory, mother-of-pearl, and boxwood, won a grand prize at the St. Louis exposition in 1904. It is believed that William Codman, Gorham's head designer, worked on these pieces.

355, 356. *Above: a dressing table and chair in the Art Nouveau style, 1903*

355a. *Top right: detail, reverse side on mirror of dressing table (opposite)*

357. *Right: a dressing table made of silver with upholstered, silver bench*

The Cut of Elegance

In 1896 an article in *The Decorator and Furnisher* reported to the readers that "the articles of use and beauty produced in crystal have reached the acme of elegance." This was referring specifically to the brilliantly and deeply cut clear glass that was then available at one New York warehouse in "every conceivable form and variety of cutting" at prices ranging from six to over one hundred dollars, depending upon the size and design of the particular piece. Such glassware, housewives were reminded, constituted the "most showy, and, in many respects, choicest of table equipments."

Cut glass had been known to the ancients, as well as to earlier Americans, but in the decades just before and after 1900 it was developed in this country on an unprecedented scale to satisfy public demand. During this so-called "brilliant period," the glass was made of heavy, lustrous metal that was precisely cut from any one of innumerable available patterns with as many different names.

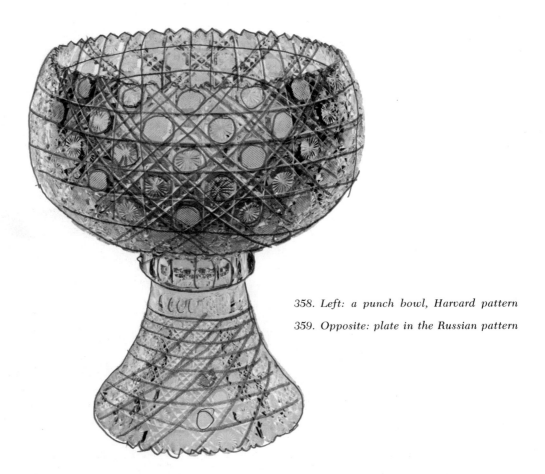

358. *Left: a punch bowl, Harvard pattern*

359. *Opposite: plate in the Russian pattern*

360. *Glass table produced at the Libbey Glass Company in 1902; cut by John Rufus Denman in the Neola pattern*

361. *Cut-glass standing lamp made at Libbey's in 1904. It is almost five feet tall and consists of five parts.*

362. Above: a punch bowl with its matching cups, made in 1904. 363. Below: a page from an 1896 Libbey cut-glass catalogue

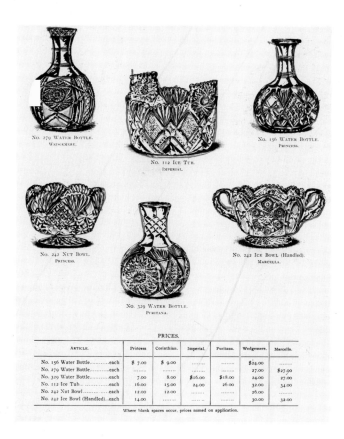

No. 279 WATER BOTTLE.
WEDGEMERE.

No. 112 ICE TUB.
IMPERIAL.

No. 156 WATER BOTTLE.
PRINCESS.

No. 242 NUT BOWL.
PRINCESS.

No. 329 WATER BOTTLE.
PURITANA.

No. 242 ICE BOWL (Handled).
MARCELLA.

PRICES.

ARTICLE.	Princess	Corinthian.	Imperial.	Puritana.	Wedgemere.	Marcella.
No. 156 Water Bottle............each	$ 7.00	$ 9.00	....	....	$24.00	....
No. 279 Water Bottle............each	....	....	....	....	27.00	$27.00
No. 329 Water Bottle............each	7.00	8.00	$16.00	$18.00	24.00	27.00
No. 112 Ice Tub................each	16.00	15.00	24.00	26.00	32.00	34.00
No. 242 Nut Bowl..............each	12.00	12.00	....	....	26.00	....
No. 242 Ice Bowl (Handled)...each	14.00	....	....	....	30.00	32.00

Where blank spaces occur, prices named on application.

Although American cut glass of the "brilliant period" flourished approximately during the same years that Art Nouveau enjoyed its vogue, the two fashions had little else in common. The forms of cut glass were regular and balanced, the patterns typically geometric. Migrant glass cutters worked from accustomed and patented designs as they wandered from factory to factory with hopes of improving their fortunes. At the Libbey Glass Company in Toledo, Ohio, one John Rufus Denman cut a large punch bowl with twenty-three matching cups (362) for display at the Louisiana Purchase Exposition held at St. Louis in 1904. It was described as "the largest and most elaborate ever produced, valued at $2,700," and it won a gold medal. Denman also cut the glass of a three-piece table (360) that was almost three feet tall. A kerosene floor lamp (361) produced and cut at Libbey's was more than two feet taller. As one page from its 1896 catalogue (363) indicates, the firm also produced a generous assortment of wares for ordinary household use, as did numerous other factories, until increased costs and changing taste gradually led to other fancies.

Common Denominators

During the years that saw the rise and decline of Art Nouveau, the abundant achievements of Louis Tiffany, and other sophisticated developments in design and craftsmanship, factories in the East and West were producing great quantities of furniture suited to conventional tastes and modest budgets. In 1893 it was reported that there were sixty-two such firms in Grand Rapids alone, employing nine thousand men and with an aggregate capital of over eight million dollars. The furniture made there for display at the Columbian Exposition, it was further reported, was on the whole "characterized by economy in the use of materials. . . and a characteristic devotion to the demands of the market and of the customer." "We can furnish the home of the Mechanic or the Millionaire," boasted one Grand Rapids firm in the 1890's, listing three-piece "Chamber Suits" (including a carved bedstead) at prices from $11.85 to $67.50. Although many different woods were used, some imported and relatively expensive, "golden" or "antique" oak enjoyed a lively vogue about the turn of the century.

364. *Opposite: detail of headboard of a child's bed*

365. *Above: so-called Morris chair of golden oak*

366. *Right: oak roll-top desk with carved details*

367. A golden oak desk-bookcase made in Grand Rapids; a prize winner at the Chicago world's fair

Our $24.50 Buffet.

No. 9194. We have had a growing demand for handsome dining room furniture in the way of well made and attractive buffets. We have been fortunate in making contracts with one of the leading manufacturers in this line of goods, and are offering the beautiful buffet in **quarter sawed oak**, as shown in illustration, at an unusually low price. This buffet stands 75 in. high and is 50 inches wide. It is, as stated above, made from choicest quarter sawed oak, decorated with beautiful hand carving. The extra **heavy bevel plate mirror** is fancy pattern shape and 18x22 inches in size. The door of cabinet is fitted with **double thick glass**, and has lock and key and fancy handle. The drawers are large and roomy, one drawer being lined with plush for silverware. Large cupboard at bottom with doors. Fancy pattern base. The buffet weighs about 175 lbs. when packed for shipment. Our Special Price.............. ....$24.50

368. Above: an advertisement by Sears, Roebuck for a buffet, 1897

369. Right: an oak davenport-bed, made by the Kindel Bed Co., 1900

Both local and outside manufacturers exhibited their wares at the semiannual markets held in Grand Rapids. More than two hundred firms were represented there in the 1908 presentations, and far more in the years immediately following. In 1913 more than twenty-seven hundred buyers attended the two markets. Among the designers who worked for Grand Rapids companies were men who had studied in France, Austria, England, and other European countries. (One of them is said to have designed a chair by having people of varying sizes and contours sit in snowbanks and transferring the resulting impressions onto his drawing board.) The term "Grand Rapids" has taken on some derogatory associations, but in public estimation the products of that city have enjoyed widespread appreciation over the years. Such, indeed, was the "reputation, popularity and good will" earned by the local products that early in this century some factories in other sections of the country incorporated the words "Grand Rapids" into their company names, and so labeled their furniture—an unethical practice that was later forbidden by the Federal Trade Commission.

271

Regardless of the descriptive trade names given to the wide assortment of designs that issued from Grand Rapids and other such centers of mass production, the actual furniture forms generally revealed only the slightest relation to the historic styles with which they were associated for promotion purposes. A rocking chair advertised by the Bishop Furniture Company (371) as being in the Art Nouveau style is just one case in point. The progressive modernization of factories and improvement of mechanical equipment, made necessary by intense competition, resulted in ever faster and more economical procedures— and in "styles" that bore the clear imprint of the machines that spawned them. At the time of the Chicago fair one reporter described the displays from Grand Rapids as "economic and artistic, rather than majestic or magnificent." In any case, they apparently appealed to buyers from Germany, who purchased "very heavily" from the exhibitors. Paris and Glasgow firms also bought many examples.

No. 965 L'Art Nouveau
Parlor Rocker.

GOLDEN OAK AND MAHOGANIZED BIRCH.

L'ART Nouveau designs in parlor rockers
are becoming very popular but on account of the expense of nice carvings and
select material retail dealers are unable to
handle them in large enough quantities to
make the price within the reach of the person of moderate means. By making large
quantities of this rocker as well as our
other designs the price is reduced to a
minimum and we can sell it at about the
same price as the retail dealer has to pay
for it. The material is selected for fine
grain effects, and the back and arms are
strongly mortised so it is just as strong as
a large massive rocker. The entire surface
is rubbed and polished. Retail value of
rockers of similar design and equal quality
$10.00.

Quartered golden oak
or mahoganized birch.
Price C. O. D........... $7.25
Price cash with order   6.89

370. *Opposite: rocking chair with upholstered seat*

371. *Above: "L'Art Nouveau Parlor Rocker"; from
a Grand Rapids advertisement of the early 1900's*

372. *Left: a late 19th-century serving board made
of oak, with carved decoration and paw feet*

373. *Above: an oak sideboard, late 19th century*

PARLOR TABLES.

In this extensive line of Parlor Tables, we offer our patrons only the latest styles, the best workmanship and finish at the lowest possible prices. We could furnish an inferior grade of parlor tables at lower prices, but we do not care to sacrifice the reputation which we have established, by handling a class of furniture which we could not honestly guarantee to be first-class in all respects. Kindly note that no cheap wood enters the construction of this line of goods, only the most select material being used. Every article on the following pages is beautifully finished, carefully rubbed down with pumice stone and oil and hand polished throughout.

HERE IS OUR LEADER.

PARLOR TABLE.

Hand polished. Oak, Antique or Birch, Mahogany finish.

No. 716.   Top 16 x 16........................Price $ .85
No. 716-1. Top 16 x 18........................Price 1.14
No. 716-2. Top 24 x 24........................Price 1.42
No. 716-3. Top 20 x 30........................Price 1.78

For Brass Feet add 50c. to above prices.

374. Top: an upholstered, cherry wood sofa from a Grand Rapids set made in the 1890's

375. Left: parlor chair of the same period

376. Above: advertisement of a table by the Grand Rapids Wholesale Furniture Co., 1890's

377. Top: a "democratic milieu," 1894

378. Above: a table matching the one
shown in the advertisement opposite

"Any one in doubt as to what is correct in taste need not lack information on such topics when such a journal as *The Decorator and Furnisher* is published," that periodical advised its readers in 1894. On the following page was illustrated an example of "middle class American decoration" (377). "Here," it was reported, "the home feeling is essentially preserved, and apart from any aesthetic purity of style, the principles of grace and economy are in the ascendant." This, the magazine added, constituted a democratic milieu without pretense to "society decoration and social ambition." Suites of furniture composed of elements in remote approximations (or caricatures) of the Chinese Chippendale (374) or Louis XV (375) styles, in cherry, mahogany, and other woods, were available from Grand Rapids manufacturers at modest prices. Five-piece, upholstered parlor suites appropriate to a "democratic milieu" could be had for less than twenty dollars.

In 1907 the Sligh Furniture Company of Grand Rapids produced a bedroom suite, from designs by John E. Brower, in which there was no apparent reference to any past style. Rather, in their design and construction these pieces anticipated a style of furniture that was to become widely popular in the 1920's—a relatively simple, restrained, and symmetric style that was perfectly accommodated to mass-production methods and machinery. In 1919 the Bauhaus, a celebrated and revolutionary art school in Germany, was founded to further the happy union of art and industry through strictly contemporary designs and with whatever materials, however unusual, that best suited the purpose. Earlier in the century, however, American mass-produced furnishings had made a strong impression on architects, designers, and manufacturers in Germany and Austria who sought means and styles to please a growing middle-class public.

*379, 380. Chair and bed of solid gumwood, stained green, from
a suite of bedroom furniture designed in 1907 by John Brower*

Around
the
House

*Inside
&
Out*

Late in the last century Dr. James Fullarton Muirhead, an English author and editor who knew this country much better than most Americans did, referred to it as a "Land of Contrasts"—a land of "stark, staring, and stimulating inconsistency." Here one could always confidently expect to meet the unexpected. Recalling a passage from one of William Dean Howells' novels, Muirhead pointed out that Americans were even proud of the size of their inconsistencies; as they also were, he could have added, of the continental scale of their nation and of the magnitude of their accomplishments as a people. European visitors were inevitably impressed by the diversity of the land itself. Except for extreme arctic and tropical conditions, almost every variety of climate and terrain could be found within the nation's boundaries. And within a relatively few generations, with explosive suddenness as history is reckoned, that entire varied expanse had been transformed from a raw wilderness into a settled, industrialized state. Never before had such a great part of the natural world been so quickly and so radically modified to accommodate the needs and purposes of human society. It almost lent credence to the old tall tales of Paul Bunyan's yanking crooked rivers straight and uprooting forests, and of Davy Crockett's riding a streak of lightning in pursuit of some heroic mission.

Only the most widely traveled and experienced reporters could safely generalize about the American scene. Reflecting on his travels in America, H. G. Wells confessed that he felt like an ant crawling over the carcass of an elephant. Other, less modest travelers, assuming that whatever aspect of American life they had witnessed was typical of the whole, often reached widely divergent conclusions. However, most foreigners who published accounts of their experiences in the United States agreed that, by and large, Americans—in the North, East, South, and West, regardless of climate and terrain—enjoyed a higher standard of material well-being than was known by the general population of their home countries. Yet here again, to some this revealed a rampant materialism that excluded any possibility of cultural attainments; others, more sympathetic, found nothing incompatible between the American's devotion to his creature comforts, his growing abundance of mechanical household gadgetry, and his spiritual welfare. One cultivated English journalist expressed his mixed feelings on leaving America for home with a rare combination of sardonic humor and genuine regret. "Good-bye, New York! I am going home. . . . Good-bye to central heating and radiators, fit symbols of the hearts they warm! Good-bye to frequent and well-appointed bath-rooms, glory of the plumber's art! . . . . Good-bye to . . . a land where wealth beyond the dreams of British profiteers dwells, dresses, gorges, and luxuriates, emulated and unashamed!"

Opposite and above: details from design for a living room by Will H. Bradley, 1902

279

The telephone habit; detail from a painting

Gaslit hydraulic elevator car, made in 1881

Although those observations were made a few years after World War I, they would have been relevant decades earlier. Throughout the second half of the nineteenth century the American home underwent a progressive "modernization," at least in urban areas—and the living facilities in those areas, like the fashions there promoted, became models for the hinterland. In 1869 Catharine E. Beecher and her sister Harriet Beecher Stowe issued a book, *The American Woman's Home*, devoted to the "principles of domestic science," in which the authors were seriously concerned with the practical organization of the "Christian house," as they termed their model dwelling, in the disposition of rooms and stairs to avoid unnecessary steps and climbing, the placement of facilities to avoid wasting time and movement, the design of space-saving furniture, and the essential matters of ventilation, heating, and lighting. The kitchen they proposed, arranged as it was with scrupulous regard for convenience and utility, was a triumph of household engineering.

Over the remaining years of the nineteenth century and into the twentieth the practice of the domestic sciences advanced rapidly and inexorably. Washing machines and sewing machines, refrigerators, sanitary plumbing, efficient lighting devices, canned foods (and can openers), gas stoves, central heating, and a host of other new and improved household contrivances and equipment played an increasingly important part in the management of the American home. It was no small part of their functions that they helped to alleviate America's chronic servant problem—what one contemporary authority referred to as "the great unsolved American Question." Beyond that they liberated the American woman from some of the age-old, tiresome chores of housekeeping and provided her with time to pursue other interests, such as continuing her education, taking an office job, bicycling, playing golf or tennis, or talking on the telephone.

As mechanical household operations became more commonplace they affected the actual structure of living arrangements. With central heating, for example, the interior of a house, even in regions where the winters were cold, could be opened up to provide a new sense of space, as it often was in the so-called Queen Anne house that for decades remained a popular type of domestic architecture (and as it emphatically was in the houses designed by Frank Lloyd Wright around the turn of the century). Central heating, along with passenger elevators, electrical services, more complicated and efficient plumbing, and the telephone, also made apartment-house living a more practical scheme for urbanites. An "enormous number" of apartment buildings were rising in New York and other large cities during the 1880's, as high as fourteen stories in at least one instance. In such structures, where gas, plumbing, and other utilities and facilities had to be economically engineered to serve numerous families, the dwelling units could not be tailored with the same freedom as in private houses. For one thing, as Clarence Cook pointed out in 1881, in apartments the traditional parlor had to be eliminated, "there being no provision made for it in the common plans." In any case, Cook thought, parlors—those decorously furnished, lugubrious chambers that for decades had generally been reserved for such formal occasions as the last rites of the deceased, the clergyman's visit, and proposals of marriage—those "ceremonial deserts," as he called them, were useless and out of place in "modern" life, even in individual dwellings. The best room in the house should be a "living-room," an open area, where general domestic activities could be enjoyed.

Still other inventions and improvements were reshaping the pattern of living in America in the decades on either side of the year 1900. Earlier in the nineteenth century the proliferating railroads had substantially encouraged the growth of cities. Wherever rails were laid old cities flourished with new vigor; new cities sprang into being at likely junctions. They provided unprecedentedly far-reaching and speedy lanes of distribution by which large masses of hungry people could tap the distant countryside for necessary foodstuffs in exchange for the products of growing urban industries. Then, the evolution of electric trolley cars late in the century provided simpler means for urban workers to get out of the city of an evening and in again of a morning than any other way yet made possible. And cities sprawled out in widening circles of suburban developments.

In those urban outskirts, throughout the land, bungalows took root and flourished alongside Queen Anne houses during the closing years of the last century and the early years of the present one. The bungalow was typically a small, one-story structure with wide overhanging eaves that extended over an ample porch and with an almost completely open plan within. (It was, in effect, the forerunner of today's popular ranch house, and in such inexpensive, informal dwellings Mission furniture found a fitting architectural setting.) The suburbs also found room for thousands of *Ladies' Home Journal* houses, dwellings of varied design that were built at small cost from plans and specifications prepared by professional architects and published by that magazine. Theodore Roosevelt expansively remarked that the architecture of the entire nation had been changed for the better by these features—"so quickly and yet so effectively that we didn't know it was begun before it was finished."

Whatever the style or pretension of the houses of those years, as their more purely functional features became modernized, problems of design and decoration arose that earlier had not existed. For one thing, industrially engineered equipment was transforming the kitchen and the bathroom into elements of the house whose style contrasted remarkably with that of other rooms furnished in traditional manner—a contrast that may quite possibly have spurred the quest for more up-to-date forms in those other areas. Central heating had its obvious conveniences but, as a writer in *The House Beautiful* complained in 1902, now people had to put up with the "hideous, necessary radiator." Benefits of a new order were also provided by electric lights, again not without attendant disadvantages. Unless lamps were carefully placed and shaded, wrote a contemporary critic, "the glow of the incandescent filament is dangerous for the eye"; beyond that, electric-lighting fixtures in the ordinary home were "brutally ugly." Illuminating engineers, he concluded, had yet to solve such vexing problems in a generally satisfactory way.

However, as *The House Beautiful* noted with interest, Frank Lloyd Wright (and some others) had an answer to most of those questions; he proposed to do away with "fixtures of every kind, and to incorporate into the architecture all means of lighting, heating, or ventilating." Except as ornamental and gracious accessories, the fireplace and the candle were heading the way of the parlor and the outhouse, toward obsolescence. With the advent of the automobile, so, too, went the horse and carriage. As wise men had predicted at the time of the Philadelphia Centennial, the circumstances surrounding daily life were changing more rapidly than ever before during the second century of our independence. Nowhere on earth was human society so richly benefited and so pitilessly tested by advances of technology as in America. With almost disconcerting speed the forms and artifacts of yesterday became the curiosities of today, fast on their way to the changing stocks of "antiques" dealers.

Early advertisement for a can opener, 1874

A trade card advertising canned baked beans

Time Will Tell

With the increasing industrialization of American society, time — and timing — took on new significance. In the early days of the railroad Henry Thoreau was surprised to note that even his most dilatory neighbors caught the train to Boston. Trains were then punctual; the timetable presented a schedule "as inexorable as fate"; and "getting left" (a colloquialism of the timetable era) was a privation few could endure. To do things "railroad fashion," on time, that is, became a byword of the period. Aside from that, in mass-production, assembly-line operations every fraction of a second was important. In the early 1880's, to improve factory performances, time studies of industrial procedures were instituted.

To enable the nation to meet its demanding schedules, clocks and watches of every description were produced in extraordinary quantities and at all price levels. "Ever since Sam Slick's day," wrote the indefatigable observer and critic, Clarence Cook, "America has been known as the land where cheap clocks abound. If we were a legend-making people, we should have our Henry IV, who would have said he wished every peasant might have a clock on his mantel-piece." In 1868 the New Haven Clock Company alone turned out one hundred fifty thousand timepieces, almost entirely by automatic machinery. A one-day brass clock could be made at a cost of less than fifty cents.

381. Opposite: a sign from a 19th-century railroad station

382. Above: clock in black iron case, made by Ingraham, 1890

383. Right: walnut 8-day clock made by E. N. Welch Co., 1880

Cook had a different attitude toward time and timepieces from that of the hard-headed industrialists. "A clock finds itself naturally at home on a mantel-piece," he wrote, "but it is a pity to give up so much space in what ought to be the central opportunity of the room, to anything that is not worth looking at for itself, apart from its merely utilitarian uses"; something "to make us forget the burden of time-and-tide in the occasional contemplation of art eternities." "We get this habit of clocks," he added, "with their flanking candlesticks or vases, on all our mantel-pieces, from the French," whose clocks, he observed, were "delightfully irresponsible." Cook also observed that a clock in the dining room was a rebuke to those who came down late for breakfast, and, in the drawing room, an ill-mannered reminder to visitors to go home.

Inexpensive American watches, meanwhile, were winning favor around the world. During the Civil War every soldier in the Union army apparently wanted a watch, and as that conflict ended, the American Watch Company of Waltham, Massachusetts, was producing three hundred of them a day. By the time of the Centennial, American watchmakers were exporting huge quantities abroad; they had created markets in the Indies and Australia and had opened branch offices in Russia. A Swiss expert at the Centennial reported: "I am terrified by the danger to which our industry is exposed."

384. *Opposite: a mantel set by Bailey Banks & Biddle*

385. *Left: an inexpensive alarm clock, made about 1890*

386. *Above: a page from a Sears, Roebuck catalogue, 1902*

285

New Lights on Things

The search for truly efficient and inexpensive artificial illumination led in all directions during the course of the nineteenth century. Late in the preceding century a Swiss, Aimé Argand, had developed an oil lamp with a tubular wick that consumed its own smoke. The Argand lamp and its derivatives burned vegetable and animal oils, as all lamps had for time out of mind. Whale oil, for a long while a most satisfactory illuminant, was expensive enough to discourage its universal use. In the 1830's a method of combining turpentine and alcohol was devised and a wide variety of new "burning fluids" was put on the market. They undersold whale oil and gave good results, but unfortunately they had a tendency to explode with careless handling and were commonly referred to as "liquid gunpowder." Oil pressed from lard

proved to be better than any of the others, but as the price per gallon rose to more than a day's pay for skilled labor, its popularity was accordingly limited. About at mid-century the qualities of "carbon oil," or kerosene, as an illuminant were recognized—the first mineral oil to be so used. It proved to be safer, better, and, as supplies became abundant, cheaper than anything that had earlier been tried. Among other advantages, kerosene was light and could climb a relatively long wick by capillary attraction, which made it possible to keep the oil container well below the burner and out of the way of the light. The first American kerosene lamp was patented in 1859, along with forty others that same year. For the next twenty years still others were patented at the rate of about eighty different models a year.

387. Opposite: a double student lamp

388. Left: student, or "Harvard," lamp

389. Above: a parlor, or reception, lamp
with painted decoration, made about 1890

390. *Above: lamp advertisement, 1886*

391. *Right: a blue overlay lamp with Amberina chimney, patented in 1876*

392. *Above: a painted kerosene lamp*

393. *Opposite: an extension hanging lamp with opaque shade, about 1875*

The first rich strike of petroleum, of which kerosene is a derivative, was made in western Pennsylvania in 1859, and it sent speculators and prospectors swarming to the area in search of other finds. Every conceivable strategem was used to locate new sources. Some relied on dreams for guidance, others used divining rods, and still others literally tried to smell their way to the right spot and to fortune. As a popular song of 1865 observed, addressing its lyrics "to the afflicted," everyone those days seemed to be troubled with "Oil on the Brain." However, as earlier stated, the oil industry very soon became a highly organized and well-financed enterprise, and kerosene thereafter rapidly became a commodity that was widely available at acceptable prices. The lamps that were made to accommodate its use were generally larger than earlier types, and they offered designers a wide range of novel possibilities; they also provided the metal and glass industries with an expanded market for their wares.

394. Above: gas chandelier made by Mitchell, Vance & Co., and displayed at the Philadelphia Centennial

395. Right: gaslight fixture in a morning-glory design

396. Below: bronze and Favrile Tiffany candlestick

As the century progressed, kerosene had increasingly to compete with gas and electric light. Gas had been put to practical use fairly early in the century, both in and out of doors, but it long remained an essentially urban convenience — and it was relatively costly. For some time even city folk with adequate means objected to gas on other grounds. It was, as Edgar Allan Poe complained in 1840, "totally inadmissible within doors. Its harsh and unsteady light is positively offensive." He added, "no man having both brains and eyes will use it." About forty years later that sharp and sometimes acerbic critic Clarence Cook wrote that he lived "in the blessed hope that gas will one day be superseded by something better. It is unhealthy, it is troublesome, it is expensive, it tarnishes our silver, our picture-frames and our wall-papers," he went on, "and how can it do this without injuring those who breathe it?" In 1884 *The Decorator and Furnisher* commented enthusiastically on the "surprising affluence of tasteful ingenuity" then shown in the design of gas fixtures. Almost predictably, Cook thought otherwise, as did Elsie de Wolfe thirty years later. "Gas lamps," she pronounced flatly, "are hideous." And, along with Cook and others, she preferred the dim but pleasant light of candles, especially for situations where graciousness prevailed. What was more, candlesticks continued to be made in pleasant designs.

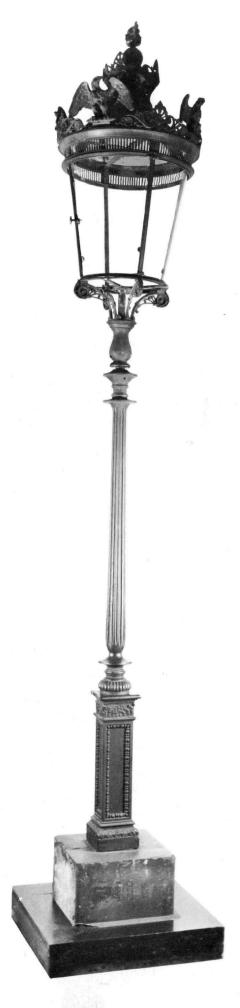

397. A gas streetlamp, designed by Stanford White, in the classical revival style

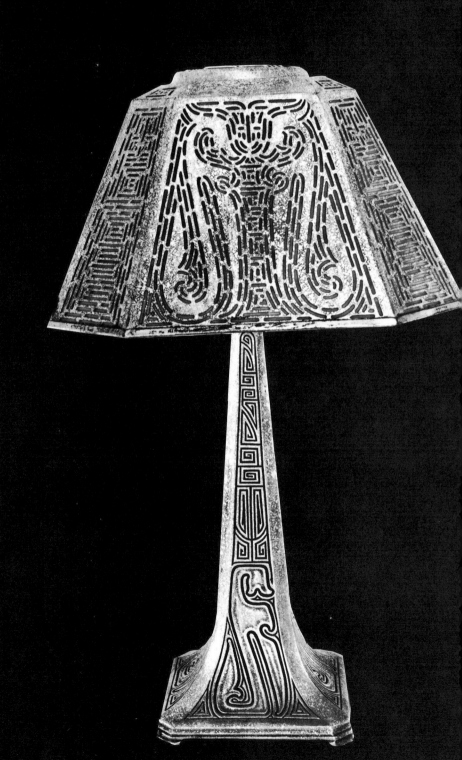

398. Above: converted cut-glass kerosene lamp

399. Right: a gilded bronze lamp, by Tiffany

400. Opposite: design for a group of electric
"shower lights," from Craftsman Homes, 1906

The design of lighting fixtures virtually started anew with the development of a practical electric-light bulb. Early in the nineteenth century the possibilities of using electricity in arc lights had already been realized in the laboratory. But it was not until 1880 that Thomas Alva Edison produced a sixteen-candle-power lamp with carbonized bamboo filaments in a pear-shaped bulb, much like the modern incandescent product. With this innovation, for the first time in history the source of light could be pointed downward, as well as up, opening new possibilities in the design of lamps and other fixtures. The relatively bright glare from such bulbs called fresh attention to the design of shades. And further, the unobtrusively thin and flexible wires through which current could be supplied — in contrast to the rigid, cumbersome gas pipes — opened up new possibilities in matters of installation. That also made it relatively simple to convert old oil lamps, candlesticks, and gas fixtures to electricity, which is still being done on a large scale with antique appliances.

As early as 1880, in the interior designs for the Madison Square Theatre, Louis C. Tiffany had been associated with Edison; Tiffany and his early associates provided a drop curtain (see page 235), and the electric lighting was installed under Edison's personal supervision. Five years later the two men worked together on the interior of the new Lyceum Theatre. Tiffany's concern with the problems and possibilities of designing handsome and effective electric lamps was evidenced by the great variety of original forms that issued from his studios. He was, to be sure, not the only one. Among others, the firm founded and incorporated by Philip J. Handel turned out lamps in a wide variety, some of which closely resembled Tiffany's work. One advantage of Handel's five-branch lily lamp (401) was that with its cluster of lights pointed in different directions (like similar Tiffany formations), the shadows cast by each bulb were neutralized.

401. Opposite: five-branch lily lamp by Handel

402. Top: design for a table lamp by Tiffany

403. Left: Tiffany lamp with adjustable shade

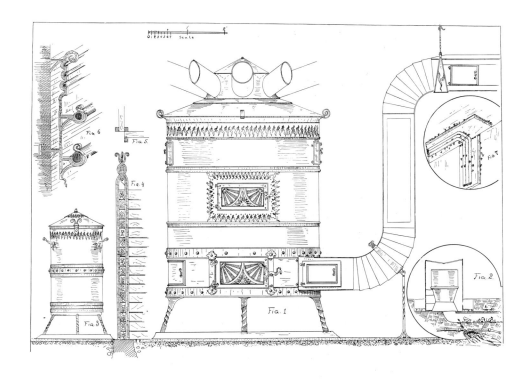

404. Top: a sanitary central heating system, 1885

405. Above: an "artistically" designed steam radiator

406. Left: a cast-iron cover for a heater, patented 1862

Radiators
& Firesides

In 1888 it was confidently reported that the best way to warm a house was with central steam heating. With it an even temperature could be maintained even in "the most remote parts of the house"; the fuel-burning apparatus could be hidden in the basement, thus saving the space that would be occupied by stoves in the several rooms of a house; and, among still other benefits, the system was economical. However, as it was pointed out a few years later, "the grim aggressiveness" of the steam radiator remained an obstacle to be overcome by the home decorator. Artistically designed radiators were beyond the budget of many people; and not everyone could afford to build such necessary elements unobtrusively into the architecture. In ordinary circumstances the best thing to do, advised *The Decorator and Furnisher*, was to hide them with an "apron curtain" of some handsome fabric.

407. *Wrought-iron fireplace equipment; photograph from a catalogue of the 1890's by A. Kimbel & Sons, New York City*

The advantages of warming houses from a central source of hot air, steam, or hot water were undeniable, but, as *The House Beautiful* observed in 1902, the "one beautiful, if inadequate, method of heating remains the open fire. . . . As an ornament it is so superior to all others that if forced to choose, everything else had better be sacrificed to it." The fireplace may have been reduced to a supplementary household appliance, but it continued to serve, as it always had, as "the warm heart of the house." It also served as a rudimentary ventilating device. Without it, and without other conduits from and to the outside air, problems of air stagnation and pollution became serious—especially in buildings of increasingly airtight construction. For such varied reasons the fireplace survived the introduction of the newer heating systems (although it has become something of a luxury these days) and, as ever, care was devoted to its design and to its accessories.

408. *Opposite, top: a water-color design by the Tiffany Studios for a hunt room mantel*

409. *Opposite, below: an embroidered fire screen in carved walnut frame, about 1880*

410. *Above: an andiron in the Gothic style*

411. *Left: an andiron in the form of a dog*

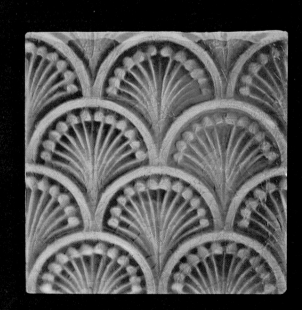

As the need of an open fire became less imperative for warmth, its charm and comfort became increasingly appreciated. In laying down her precepts for a fashionable home, Elsie de Wolfe counseled her readers that "an open fire is almost as great an attribute to a drawing-room as a tactful hostess." Gustav Stickley, who was closer to a popular level in such matters, suggested that a well-designed living room might have for its necessary central point of interest a fireplace, "either recessed or built in the ordinary manner, with fireside seats, bookcases, cupboards, shelves, or high casement windows" (413). Like other designers and architects of the period, Stickley recommended the use of decorative art tiles as a surround for the fireplace opening and as a facing for the chimney breast. One of the most eminent of the many producers of such tiles was John Gardner Low who, with his father, John, set up his works in Chelsea, Massachusetts, in 1877. Only one year after his kilns were operating, Low's tiles won a gold medal at a competition exhibit held in England, and other honors followed.

412, a-f. Opposite: glazed tiles made by J. & J. G. Low

413. Above: fireside with a chimney piece paneled with tiles and with flanking seats; a Stickley design, 1907

On Walls & Floors

By the 1870's, thanks to power looms perfected before the Civil War, the price of machine-made carpets had become so reasonable that they were not only found in private homes but "invaded schoolhouses, churches, counting-rooms, railroad-cars, court-houses, and public buildings." Centennial exhibits included a "brilliant display of rich, soft American carpets," not only the "opulent Axminster, laid down in the Old World only for the feet of emperors and noblemen," but also "the more humble but still agreeable ingrains, three-plies, Brussels, and tapestry carpets." Centennial judges, furthermore, were happy to report that rival English manufacturers had "generously admitted" American carpets to be the equal of European imports. While contemporary commentators hailed the progress "from the hand-made rag-carpet of the farmhouse, to the aristocratic Axminster," the hooked rug remained an artistic activity in many Victorian households. Among the popular patterns were floral designs, nautical motifs, welcome mats, dogs, stags, lions, or a cat with kittens, and patriotic themes such as the Centennial (414).

414. *Opposite: hooked rug celebrating the Centennial*

415. *Above: a family group in their Victorian parlor, water color by an unknown artist, painted about 1875*

416. *Left: Axminster carpet shown at the Centennial*

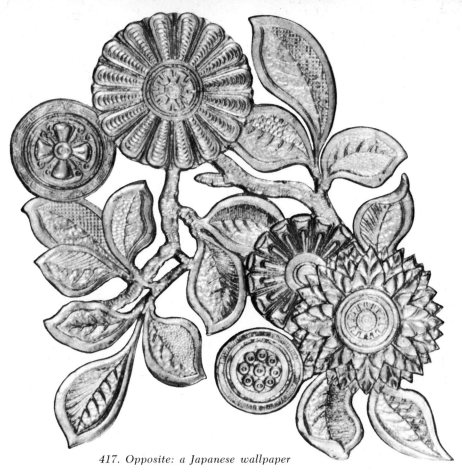

417. *Opposite: a Japanese wallpaper*

418. *Above: detail of embossed canvas*

419. *Below: wallpaper advertisement*

Among the rich mélange of wall decorations typifying high Victorian design, simulated leather was particularly popular, with Japanese imports generally viewed as the ultimate in "indefinable charm" and "exotic and artistic feeling." This example (417), imported between 1875 and 1885, was hand tooled and finished with lacquered "gold" foil. Among American firms, one Boston factory offered "reproductions of the rare old illuminated leathers of the Moors, the Spaniards and the Venetians." Even the mail-order customers of Sears, Roebuck and Company, in 1897, could enjoy the current vogue with "Embossed Leatherettes . . . for halls, dining rooms and libraries" at fifty cents per double roll. Lincrusta-Walton, named for its inventor Frederick Walton, could also simulate leather; the raised designs were stamped onto canvas treated with linseed oil. This example (418), gold on red, came from the Rockefeller house on West Fifty-Fourth Street in New York City.

For "those who [would] nobly take into their own hands the work of making home artistically beautiful," there was no apparent limit to the wall decorations that a dedicated Victorian housewife could create with needle or brush. Rather than ready-made wallpapers, for example, stenciled patterns achieved an effect at once "restful, harmonious, and certainly inexpensive." The amateur artist was not confined to water-color sketches. Pictures could be painted on velvet, sprinkled with glitter (423), and mounted in shadow boxes. Printed patterns on perforated paper were worked in brilliantly colored yarns and framed, as were wreathed arrangements of shells, feathers, or pressed flowers and ferns. Wall pockets (422), a decorative fad of the Victorian era, were lovingly fashioned by jig saw or needlework and held whisk brooms, combs and brushes, hairpins, letters or magazines. A tasseled wall pocket serving as a newspaper rack is shown in the painting on page 303.

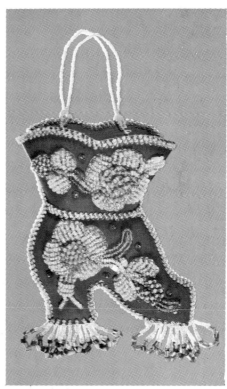

420. Opposite: wallpaper patterned on the nursery rhyme "Little Boy Blue," about 1890

421. Top: stenciled and embroidered motto

422. Above: wall pocket trimmed with beads

423. Left: detail of a painting on velvet

Some Tastemakers

Hand in hand with America's unprecedented expansion and subsequent building boom came the arbiters of good taste, delivering their dicta—even as they do today—in books, magazines, and newspaper articles. Questions of suitable architecture and attractive interior decoration no longer belonged to the rarefied province of the wealthy. They had become matters of concern to the average householder as well, and where the householder was *not* concerned, the arbiters of taste doggedly set out to teach, reform, and encourage. Curiously enough, the tastemakers—whether writing in the 1860's or the early 1900's—were in basic agreement on the rules of right and wrong in design. Their watchwords were simplicity, proportion, sincerity, and suitability. Away with clutter. Away with vulgar display. Away with stuffy, sunless rooms, unsanitary plumbing, dark and inefficient kitchens, dust-catching draperies, pretentious expenditures, and cheap gewgaws. Homemaking had become a craft, and beauty in home furnishings an aesthetic responsibility.

For Catharine E. Beecher (1800–1878) and her younger sister Harriet Beecher Stowe (1811–96), the coauthors of *The American Woman's Home*, reform and good works were their lifeblood—certainly not surprising occupations for the daughters of the Reverend Lyman Beecher, a vigorous and indomitable New England Calvinist. (All seven sons in the Beecher family ultimately became clergymen.) Catharine's plans for marriage had been shattered in 1823 by the accidental death of her fiancé, and she set about, from that time on, "to find happiness in living to do good." Female education became her particular field, and she devoted her energies to raising the academic level of the curriculum used in the training of young women. Mrs. Stowe was famed, of course, as the author of *Uncle Tom's Cabin*.

With *The American Woman's Home* in 1869 the Beecher sisters offered "A Guide to the Formation and Maintenance of Economical, Healthful, Beautiful, and Christian Homes." In the course of its thirty-eight chapters the book touched on virtually every circumstance the housewife might encounter during a lifetime. Its counsel ranged from the care and clothing of the body, morals and manners, and the health of the mind, to the care of domestic animals, "Suggestions to wealthy and unoccupied women," the beauty and tractability of ivy, and the prospect of "millennial glory." In a chapter entitled "Home Decoration" they eschewed Victorian fads and fancies and decried architectural "curlywurlies," the ugliness of Brussels carpets, and "narrow, cold, marble-topped" tables. They stressed "harmony of color" as a "great, simple principle of beauty." They recommended glazed English chintz—"at about twenty-five cents a yard"—for cushions, lambrequins, and "lounge" covers, with white muslin curtains for "an air of grace and elegance." Plants and flowers were invaluable in creating a "poetical and attractive" room, and reproductions of fine works of art were deemed inestimable in teaching children "correctness of taste and refinement of thought." Throughout, they offered inexpensive decorating hints. A charming room could be achieved with even the most limited of budgets.

Three decades later, when novelist Edith Wharton and architect Ogden Codman, Jr., collaborated on *The Decoration of Houses*, domestic moralizing such as that offered by the Beechers had become a quaint vestige of the mid-Victorian era. Edith Newbold Jones Wharton (1862–1937) and Ogden Codman, Jr., (1863–1951) were born to and traveled in the upper echelons of society, both at home and abroad. Their book, which evolved from the project of redecorating Mrs. Wharton's Newport house, was specifically aimed at reforming the lamentable levels of taste often found among the well to do. "When the rich man demands good architecture his neighbors will get it too. The vulgarity of current decoration has its source in the indifference of the wealthy to architectural fitness." They led off with an historical resumé of Italian, French, and English antiques, and then wended their urbane way through town house and country house, drawing room, boudoir, smoking room, ballroom, music room, and gallery—the milieu, in short, familiar to Mrs. Wharton and Mr. Codman, whether in Bar Harbor, Newport, Boston, or New York. They roundly denounced the "labyrinth of dubious eclecticism" into which architecture and decoration had wandered. They deplored the cheap showiness of current furniture designs, the "exquisite discomfort" of dreary drawing rooms, the "lingerie effects" of extravagantly curtained windows, harsh electric lighting "which makes the *salon* look like a railway-station." It was small wonder, they concluded, "that many houses are deserted by the men of the family for lack of those simple comforts which they find at their clubs." The remedies offered for this sorry state of affairs were impressive, including such touches as marble floors, mirrored ballrooms, Oriental rugs, candlelit chandeliers for dining, and the best of antique furniture—preferably European. But those with limited incomes had not been forgotten, and here Mrs. Wharton and Mr. Codman joined forces with the parsonage-bred Beecher sisters. *The Decoration of Houses* recommended the inexpensive and simple charm of willow armchairs with denim cushions, stained deal tables and painted deal bookcases, with a "cheerful drugget" on the floor. If one could not afford an old carved Italian chest for a woodbox, the best substitute was a "plain wicker basket." Furthermore, the harmonious use of color could create "pleasing and restful" rooms, and once again "good objects of art" were considered vital in awakening the "aesthetic sensibilities" of the children in the family.

Mrs. Wharton's professional excursion into decorating was limited to *The Decoration of Houses*, 1897. It was her first book; thereafter, her talents were directed to the witty and ironic novels upon which her fame now rests. Elsie de Wolfe, however, a contemporary of Mrs. Wharton's who was equally top drawer and cosmopolitan, made interior decoration a full-time career. She considered herself, in fact, to be the first woman interior decorator. Miss de Wolfe (1866–1950), later Lady Mendl upon her marriage to Sir Charles Mendl, a British diplomat, had originally taken to the stage as a means of supporting herself and her widowed mother—a bold venture for a young woman of breeding and position, who had been presented at court and whose family included Queen Victoria's chaplain at Balmoral Castle. In 1900 Elsie de Wolfe abandoned the theatre and gave her attention to the furnishing and decoration of houses—with such success that her name became a symbol of international chic. (*Vogue* cited the "magic elegance" of her clothes; a popular song included lyrics on "an apartment by Elsie de Wolfe.") Miss de Wolfe thoroughly disapproved of brownstone-front houses, "those hideous outcroppings of Victorian architecture at its worst." She declared that "the three most glaring errors we Americans make are rocking-chairs, lace curtains, and brass beds." Her architectural and decorative creed was firmly stated: "My business is . . . to preach to you the beauty of suitability. Suitability! *Suitability.* SUITABILITY!!" Despite glowing descriptions of exquisite and formidably expensive houses that she had decorated in America and France, Miss de Wolfe's book *The House in Good Taste*, 1913, was essentially practical. "The first considerations," she wrote, "must be light, air and sanitation." In a chapter devoted to the decoration of the small apartment, she suggested "a few good chairs of willow . . . less expensive and more decorative than the heavy, stuffy chairs usually chosen by inexperienced people." She was largely responsible for the nationwide appearance of chintz in upholstery, slip covers, and draperies, in town and country; its patterns were charming, its price modest. Her choice, wherever glass curtains were needed, was white muslin. She believed that a living room should be livable, big and restful "like an old shoe that goes on easily." And in a tone of heartfelt moralizing, so reminiscent of the Beecher sisters, Miss de Wolfe emphasized that tranquil, sunny surroundings created tranquil, sunny households.

In the field of domestic science, home furnishings, and architecture, possibly the greatest single influence of his time —a man whose pronouncements were read by millions of American women— was Edward William Bok (1863–1930). An immigrant Dutch boy, whose first job in America was window washing for a Brooklyn bakery at fifty cents a week, Bok edited *The Ladies' Home Journal* for thirty years, beginning in 1889. It was an interesting position for a man who wrote in his Pulitzer prize winning autobiography: "Edward Bok's instinctive attitude toward women was that of avoidance. He did not dislike women, but it could not be said that he liked them." Nonetheless, he set about with zeal to improve his readers' lives through the pages of his magazine. No aspect was left unattended—personal problems, child care, spiritual needs. He was appalled by the "wretched architecture of small houses . . . repellently ornate," and published a series of enormously successful and influential plans for low-cost, attractive housing. He next offered plans for landscaping the small gardens of his small houses. He ran picture pages of furniture designs in "Good Taste and Bad Taste" with suitable examples in each category. He offered reproductions of masterworks by such painters as Rembrandt, Raphael, Gainsborough, and Whistler. He happily waged a one-man war against the interior *décor* used by the Pullman's Palace Car Company, "the heavy decorative style of a decade ago . . . unintelligent carving . . . fearful gilt . . . unhealthy plushes and velvets, filled with dust and soot." Moreover, he attributed bad taste among the *nouveaux riches* to the "atrocious taste displayed in these cars." And he rejoiced mightily, in the editor's column of the *Journal*, when new cars appearing on western railways met his standards of comfort, simplicity, and artistic design. Bok was, in all things, an uncompromising reformer, whether fighting for the Pure Food and Drug Act, raising funds for the Philadelphia Orchestra Association, or agitating for the removal of billboards at Niagara Falls and elsewhere. He had followed his professed goal of making the world "a more beautiful place to live in." In sum, he wrote of himself: "Bok had begun with the exterior of the small American house and made an impression upon it; he had brought the love of flowers into the hearts of thousands . . . he had changed the lines of furniture, and he had put better art on the walls. . . . He had conceived a full-rounded scheme, and he had carried it out."

Reproductions of water-color designs by Bradley for a model house. 424. Above: the nursery. Opposite, top: the dining room; middle, left: the boudoir; middle, right: a chamber; bottom: the hall

Bradley's Model House

In 1901, after Edward Bok had commissioned Will H. Bradley to prepare designs for a model house (see page 224), he obviously planned to reproduce them in full color in *The Ladies' Home Journal*. As shown on these pages, the color plates were actually made, but apparently the cost of color printing proved prohibitive and the renderings appeared in the magazine only in black and white copies. Bradley's original drawings show a startling similarity to the work produced at about the same time by the celebrated Scottish designer Charles Rennie Mackintosh. Mackintosh's skillful combination of geometric forms, restrained curvilinear ornament, and color used with refined intensity strongly appealed to insurgent designers of the time, especially in Germany and Austria. Because of the influence of his work he is considered a "forerunner, if not an originator," of what we now call modern design.

Changing Silhouettes

As interior design and decoration went through successive changes during the half century following the Civil War, the silhouettes of up-to-date American houses changed apace. More was involved than just the shifting in architectural styles as such; the differences in outward appearance were to a degree also expressions of different interior arrangements and facilities, different structural materials and principles, and different social attitudes and conditions. To realize how vast the sum of all those differences of fashion and function could be, it is enough to compare the profile of such an architectural "whatnot" as the Carson house (425) in Eureka, California, with that of Frank Lloyd Wright's Robie house (431) in Chicago. The former was built in the years following the war; the latter, early in the present century. In the one the basic construction was concealed by or overlaid with a mixed confection of motifs borrowed from everywhere and nowhere. In the other the form and decoration of the building were both a direct result of construction and without any apparent reference to any preceding historical style. In concept they represent two totally different worlds of thought.

The Carson house was the wooden dream-palace of a successful lumber magnate. It was an especially exuberant reflection of that same eclectic spirit that gave rise to Samuel Colt's Armsmear (see page 16) and Frederick Church's Olana (see pages 42–43)—a spirit that had led Phineas T. Barnum to build Iranistan in an extravagant attempt to domesticate the Taj Mahal in Bridgeport, Connecticut. (In a subsequent moment of disenchantment, the Bohemia-born, Vienna-trained architect of Iranistan concluded that American architecture seemed to be "the art of covering one thing with another thing to imitate a third thing which, if genuine, would not be desirable.") Those architectural fantasies were, to be sure, isolated monu-

426. *House in the Queen Anne style, Friendly Island, N. Y.*

ments to the idiosyncrasies of their several wealthy owners, but they were landmarks of their times. And as a selected group they represent a culmination of the romanticism that had produced the Greek, Gothic, and other revival styles earlier in the century—an apotheosis or a *reductio ad absurdum*, according to one's point of view.

In such whimsical concoctions there was no trace of traditional American architecture. The eclectic builders in their most extreme examples borrowed from virtually every other source but the native vernacular. With the mushrooming popularity of what was called the Queen Anne style (426) in the final quarter of the last century there was a return, if not to early American precedents, at least to elements of the earlier English styles on which the colonial builders had based their practices and designs. Aside from this, "Queen Anne" was an almost indefinable

425. *The Carson house, Eureka, Calif.*

427. *The Dakota apartment house, New York City*

term. It was, wrote one highly critical author in 1883, a name "which has been made to cover a multitude of incongruities, including, indeed, the bulk of recent work which otherwise defies classification, and there is a convenient vagueness about the term which fits it for that use. But it is rather noteworthy that the effect of what is most specifically known as Queen Anne is to restrain the exuberances of design."

What Queen Anne houses may have lacked in the exuberance of their designs they made up for in the variety of their outlines. They were rarely symmetrical, typically featured a corner tower, and were generally considered "picturesque" and "quaint," qualities cherished by contemporaries who professed artistic sensibilities. With its many irregularities the Queen Anne house was, in the words of one appreciative critic, "a delightful insurrection" against monotony. Those outlines, with their bays and recesses, also hinted at the more free and open plan of the house within, a development that was becoming progressively more popular. That sense of spaciousness was extended to the inevitable porches covered by sloping eaves, which served, in effect, as outdoor living rooms.

The spread of the Queen Anne style across the nation coincided with a revived interest in early American architecture. In the minds of contemporaries the two were somehow allied. There was, in fact, an interplay of influences; the example of colonial architecture helped to modify and naturalize the Queen Anne, which had early been seen in America as an English import at the Philadelphia Centennial. However, the colonial revival had a separate development along more purely antiquarian

paths back to the Georgian modes of eighteenth-century America. This phase of revivalism, which the firm of McKim, Mead, and White did so much to foster (and which Edward Bok promoted in *The Ladies' Home Journal*), led far away from the eccentric, unbalanced designs of Queen Anne. Buildings in this manner were, rather, recommended for the "symmetry, restfulness, and good proportion" that had distinguished their prototypes—all qualities that ultimately derived from formal, classical principles of design. "The closer the adaptation, up to a certain point," observed one informed reporter, "the greater the success"—a success thus achieved by the architect Dudley Newton's own house (428) built in Newport in 1897, which is a direct copy "up to a point" of the eighteenth-century house in Cambridge, Massachusetts, where Longfellow lived for many years.

Architectural silhouettes that were without precedent appeared in major cities with the proliferation of apartment houses, or "French flats" as they were early called, in the last decades of the century. There were those who felt that no American in his right mind would choose to live in such hives. "The flat abolishes the family consciousness," complained William Dean Howells in *A Hazard of New Fortunes*. "It's confinement without coziness; it's cluttered without being snug. You couldn't keep a self-respecting cat in a flat; you couldn't go down cellar to get cider." Never-theless, such accommodations eased many difficulties of domestic life in the city, and even those with means to buy a house of their own joined the growing race of "cliff dwellers." The Dakota (427), and see page 107, built in New York City in 1884, was a har-

428. *Colonial Revival house, Newport, R. I.*

binger of the luxury apartments that in years to come would line the major avenues of the city. About the same time that the Dakota went up, one periodical complained that there were not enough apartments for people of modest incomes; people who could not afford a private house in the city and who could ill afford the costs of traveling morning and evening to a home in the suburbs. On a note familiar to modern ears, the article continued, "we often hear of specially desirable small apartments, but when we attempt to find them, they are like the will o' the wisp."

Beyond the congested city centers, in areas where land costs were not exorbitant, Americans continued to indulge their traditional preference for living in houses of their own. At the popular level they were guided in matters of selection or construction, style, and decoration by a continuing stream of publications, notably including *The Ladies' Home Journal, The House Beautiful,* and several other so-called "shelter" magazines. In 1894 *The Decorator and Furnisher* ran an article extolling the merits of the bungalow as an informal and inexpensive solution to the housing problem, a matter of ever increasing concern. (The term "bungalow," the magazine explained, was derived from the Bengalese word referring to certain low, thatch-roofed huts in India that were used as hostelries. Rudyard Kipling's father thought such structures were "about as handsome as a stack of hay . . . a purely utilitarian contrivance developed under hard and limiting conditions.") This type of dwelling, the article stated, was "a homely, cosy little country house with piazzas and balconies, and the plan so arranged as to ensure complete comfort with a feeling of rusticity and ease." Cheapness and economy were important factors, but not at the sacrifice of solidity and utility—characteristics that a few years later led one wag to remark that a bungalow should be defined as "a house that looks as if it had been built for less money than it actually cost."

429. *Design for a clapboard bungalow*

The big promotion of bungalows came early in the present century. In 1910 Henry L. Wilson, a Chicagoan who called himself "The Bungalow Man," published an inexpensive book in which he described "the Evolution of the Bungalow from its Primitive Crudeness to its Present State of Artistic Beauty and Cozy Convenience, Illustrated with Drawings of Exteriors, Floor Plans, Interiors, and Cozy Corners of Bungalows Which Have Been Built from Original Designs." This alluring tract quickly went through five editions. About the same time *Good Housekeeping Magazine* printed the "Bungal-Ode" by Burgess Johnson, which ended:

> Oh, a man that's bungalonging
>   For the dingle and the loam
> Is a very bungalobster
>   If he dangles on at home.

> Catch the bungalocomotive;
>   If you cannot face the fee,
> Why, a bungaloan 'll do it—
>   You can borrow it of me!

and which gave a fair indication of just how popular bungalows had become. Some were designed for summer retreats at the seashore or in the mountains, others as permanent quarters in the outskirts and suburbs of cities. They were made of shingles or clapboards, bricks or concrete, logs or cobblestones, and their floor plans varied with their size and purpose. There were, however, certain constants by which they could be recognized. "No bungalow is worthy of the name without at least one big fireplace for the living-room," wrote one authority. And if the building were to merit the title, it must be kept "low down on the ground." Essentially, the bungalow was the forerunner of the modern ranch house, horizontal in design, simple in outline, and free and open in its interior plan. In 1906 a report in *The Architectural Record* observed that the bungalow had "already become an extremely popular type in the temperate climate of California [the spawning ground of ranch houses], and it is there that [they] are being built more and better than anywhere else in the country."

The early decades of the present century also saw an

430. *Rendering of a* Ladies' Home Journal *concrete house*

enormous increase in the use of concrete in construction of all sorts, including houses of every description. "Some one in the cement business," reported *The House Beautiful* in 1908, "has said that this is the age of concrete, just as twenty or thirty years ago the electricians were saying that it was the age of electricity. . . . We hear a lot about deforestation; we need no longer worry, say these cement men, for future cities and future country buildings will be made of concrete, and concrete will never give out." Wilson and others included plans for concrete bungalows in their publications, and Edward Bok suggested concrete

431a. Interior of the Robie house

houses of more ample design (430) in the series of articles that appeared in *The Ladies' Home Journal* over these same years (see pages 224, 310). So did fashionable architects recommend concrete to their wealthy clients for still more pretentious dwellings in exclusive areas such as Tuxedo Park and Palm Beach. And, it was said, concrete was also an ideal material for cow barns, chicken houses, and icehouses, for garages, schools, and churches, for bridges, reservoirs, and embankments. One company contracted to supply the United States government with four and one half million barrels of cement for the Panama Canal, which caused a decided boom in the market.

Frank Lloyd Wright early recognized the design possibilities inherent in the nature of the new material. In the same year as the article quoted above, 1908, he used concrete (not for the first time, however), in the construction of the house he designed for Frederick Robie (431) on Chicago's South Side, an area that was then still related to the outlying open prairie. It was one of his most important achievements in domestic architecture. A scant generation separates it from the Carson house, yet it belongs to an entirely different age. To use a phrase of Henry James, it is a house "all beautified with omissions," and for that reason it is as trim in its outlines as a ship, to which indeed it has been compared because of its long, horizontal "decks," its topmost "bridge," and its stacklike chimney. The Robie house, like others of Wright's buildings, is still controversial, even years after his death. No one contests the man's originality, although without stretching the point too far his work could be viewed as a culmination of earlier American theories and practices. Some years before Wright was born, in 1851, the Yankee sculptor Horatio Greenough wrote to Emerson explaining his theory of structure, which he saw justified in the sailing ships of the time and which he thought offered a "*glorious* foretaste" of what could be accomplished elsewhere in the near future. "Here is my theory of structure," he wrote. "A scientific arrangement of spaces and forms to functions and to site—An emphasis of features proportioned to their *gradated* importance in function—Color

and ornament to be decided and arranged and varied by strictly organic laws—having a distinct reason for each decision—The entire and immediate banishment of all makeshift and make believe." In their different ways both H. H. Richardson and Wright's own *lieber Meister* Louis Sullivan had also anticipated some of the ideas to which Wright ultimately gave unique expression.

As Wright repeatedly explained, his houses looked the way they did on the outside chiefly because of what he did with them on the inside. He decried the box-within-box arrangement of rooms in earlier dwellings as a "cellular sequestration that implied ancestors familiar with penal institutions." His own plans were extreme extensions of the open-space interiors of the later Queen Anne houses. They were strongly influenced by Japanese precedents with which he was familiar through the exhibits he had seen at the Columbian Exposition and the Japanese prints he admired and collected. In his autobiography he wrote that he saw a house "primarily as liveable interior space under ample shelter. . . . So I declared the whole lower floor as one room, cutting off the kitchen as a laboratory. . . . Scores of unnecessary doors disappeared and no end of partition. . . . The house became more free as 'space' and more liveable too. Interior spaciousness began to dawn." And, at a time when Elsie de Wolfe was in the full glory of her career, Wright advised his clients to eliminate the decorator, who was, to his mind, "all 'applique', and all efflorescence, if not all 'period.' Inorganic." He wished to design at least some of the furniture as part of the architecture of a house, and did so when he could, although in later life he confessed he was "black and blue in some spot" almost all his life from too intimate contact with his early furniture. In general, he believed that about three fifths of the furnishings of every house was quite unnecessary.

431b. Exterior view of the Robie house, Chicago, Ill.

Household Harmonies

432. *Top: a Renaissance style upright piano*

433. *Above: pencil sketch by Winslow Homer*

The upright piano was developed early in the last century. Because of its compactness, compared with the grand piano, it became by far the more popular as a domestic instrument. However, in 1892 one critic complained that its "rigid uprightness" made it one of the "most perverse and uncompromising obstacles to woman's penchant for household decoration." Nevertheless, that same year America produced about forty thousand pianos (of all sorts), and the American instruments by Chickering and Steinway had been consistently winning awards at international exhibitions for the past thirty years. At the same time even more organs were produced here each year, some for export all about the globe. The cabinet organ, or American organ as it was sometimes called, was a type that produced tones by the vibrations of reeds of various lengths and shapes. The gentle and sympathetic tones of the "sweet-voiced cabinet-organ," it was claimed, were "far better adapted to the . . . repose of the family life than the more brilliant but less gracious piano."

434. Above: Sunday service on the railroad

435. Right: an Eastlake style cabinet organ

By 1889 the primitive talking machine, produced by Edison slightly more than a decade earlier, was showing promise of becoming a sophisticated instrument—a device, according to the *Atlantic Monthly*, that might yet "sing and play for us . . . at almost no cost, and become a constant source of amusement and instruction." The magazine reminded those who scoffed at such a probability that they had forgotten "the ridicule they heaped upon the rumor that an American inventor proposed to talk from New York to Chicago. . . . Just at present there is needed a funnel for so magnifying the sound that if the instrument is placed in the center of the table, all persons sitting around can hear." However, Edison prophesied that within a year the phonograph would be far less of a curiosity than the telephone. Barely a decade later, in the year 1900, more than one hundred fifty thousand machines and almost three million records were sold. The enduring trademark of the Victor Talking Machine Company was originally adapted from a painting in which the dog's master lies in his coffin.

436. *Opposite, top: jigsaw puzzle reproducing a painting that was copyrighted by Victor, 1913*

437. *Opposite: Edison phonograph, with an oak cabinet, similar to that shown in the puzzle*

438. *Right: an Edison phonograph, about 1908*

Homely Pursuits

While sewing machines relieved women "of the fatigue and wear of all general . . . sewing," it was fancywork—created by hand—that remained a source of artistic pride and delight. Magazine articles and sewing manuals offered myriad suggestions for "ingenious feminine fingers." Using basic needlecrafts, such as crocheting, needle point, embroidery, and appliqué, the ladies added decorative touches to every possible article in the household. Not only were pillowcases, pincushions, antimacassars, lambrequins, draperies, tablecloths, and other linens transformed by exquisite and lavish needlework, but penwipers were stitched in the form of pond lilies, thermometers were mounted in embroidered plush, and tennis rackets were covered in daisy-embroidered pongee. "There is really no excuse," wrote one author in 1889, "for anything that is not pretty and attractive."

439. Opposite: illustration, 1885, of "Ladies Work"

440. Left: a sewing bird, clamped to the table edge, held material in its beak for such tasks as hemming.

441. Below: a wicker sewing table, made around 1900

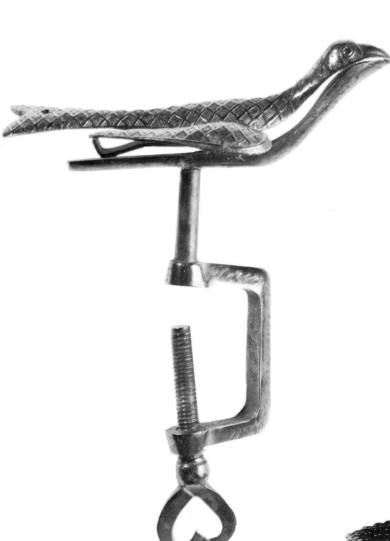

442. Detail, an embroidered Victorian crazy quilt

443. Above: a sewing machine pictured in Godey's, 1884

444. Opposite: a sewing machine and its cabinet, 1876

"The newspapers, the old board fences . . . the rocks of the field, the trees, and every other contrivance upon which a description of the merits of a sewing-machine can be printed, pasted, or hung, have been pressed into the service," wrote an economist in 1892 in his commentary on the advertising campaign launched by America's booming sewing-machine industry. These exports quickly became a world-wide business venture, and for those American customers "without capital," the sewing-machine companies were among the first in the country, at mid-century, to introduce the installment plan. Aesthetics, meanwhile, were not forgotten. "The best talents of the cabinet-maker have been employed in fitting the machines with a casing of handsome woods, for the purpose of making them beautiful objects . . . as well as blessings to the household."

445. Sewing machine made about 1863

446. Above: canisters, spice drawers, and flour bin combined in a painted tin "Home Economizer"

447. Left: small portable icebox, about 1875–85

448. Opposite: a lithograph of the kitchen, 1874

"The kitchen rules the house," *The Decorator and Furnisher* stated in 1884, "and on the details of the kitchen . . . rest the order, comfort, and glory of the mansion." Kitchen engineering had become a prime consideration in well-run households. And the kitchen itself, as had been so often the case, was no longer an architectural afterthought, tacked onto the house as an extra wing or hidden "below stairs" in the basement. ("An underground kitchen always seems unpleasantly associated with black beetles," wrote one reformer in home management in 1881.) Sunshine, ventilation, convenience, laborsaving devices, and properly installed drainage systems were prerequisites in kitchen planning, and the storage of perishable foods a vital concern. (Poor refrigeration "will sow the seeds of disease and death," warned an article on kitchen equipment in the 1880's.) Iceboxes were manufactured in numerous shapes and sizes to suit all budgets and space requirements—from a three-dollar model offered by Sears, Roebuck, to built-in units made to order to "match the surrounding wood-work." The kitchen range was fueled by coal or wood, with gas coming into general use toward the end of the century, and the kerosene stove an immediate success upon its appearance in the 1890's.

For a housewife facing the rigors of wash-day, Mrs. Partington's "machine," as advertised (452) during the 1860's, was little more than an elaborate scrub brush. But by the 1890's true washing machines were common on the market—all generally based on the principle of a large tub set on legs with some sort of hand-pumped agitator to churn the clothes through the soapsuds. And the housewife may well have mixed a home-brew laundry compound, such as that recommended by the manufacturers of the Anthony Wayne Washer: one pound of potash, one ounce of salts of tartar, and one ounce of ammonia dissolved in a gallon of water. Early flatirons usually came in sets of three, were heated on the stove, and used in rotation. An iron heated by its own gas burner (453) offered an improvement over the earlier type, as did the charcoal-heated iron equipped with its own small firebox and flue. Specially designed irons were made for fluting (454) or ruffles. Lace and similar delicate fabrics could be pressed with a lightweight flatiron, scarcely bigger than a toy. For hot irons—or hot dishes— trivets were imaginatively wrought in a variety of patterns (449-51).

452. Left: advertisement, a washday aid

453. Above: a gas iron, patented in 1903

454. Below: fluting iron, patented 1869

449, 450, 451. Opposite: three
examples of designs for trivets

"IMPERIAL" PORCELAIN AND PORCELAIN-LINED BATHS,

FOOT BATHS WATER CLOSETS ETC.

Possibly one of the most radical architectural innovations of the post Civil War years was the appearance of the completely equipped bathroom in "all modern houses." Concurrent with the bathroom came the development of dependable supplies of running water — hot and cold — and dependable sewage systems. Countless Americans continued, of course, to rely on such comparatively primitive arrangements as the commode and the hip bath (458), a type sold by Sears, Roebuck in 1897 for four dollars. However, as *The House Beautiful* explained in 1908, "In the best houses, as in the best hotels, every bedroom and suite must have its private bath." Furthermore, even "the little seven or eight room house must have at least one small room devoted to soap and water." And the author of this article was happy to report that America had entered "the age of comfortable and sanitary bath-rooms, and plenty of them, clean towels, and soap that floats."

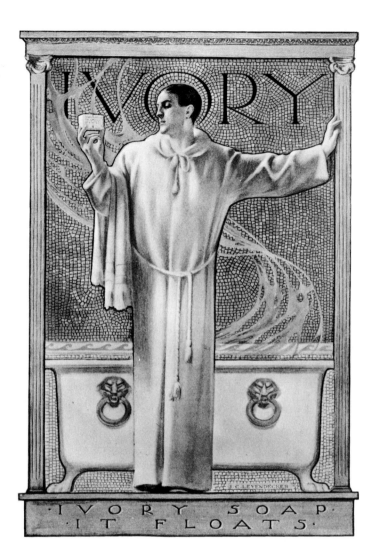

455. Opposite: bathroom fixtures, advertised 1883

456. Left: both Ivory Soap and the haloed bather were clearly 99 44/100% pure; advertised 1900

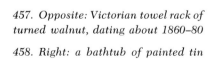

457. Opposite: Victorian towel rack of turned walnut, dating about 1860–80

458. Right: a bathtub of painted tin

By the 1890's American cutlery was deemed equal to European imports. The American scythe, for example, was cited as "the aristocrat of the harvest-field," and the American razor praised for the fine quality of its steel. This, of course, was the formidable hollow-ground straight razor. (The safety razor, a new device, was variously advertised during the nineties: "No practice required. Impossible to cut the face.") Shaving gear included such niceties as the shaving mug bearing its owner's name (461), to be kept at the local barbershop if the gentleman in question did not shave himself. The mustache cup (460) served to keep a gentleman's mustache from dipping into his morning coffee—said mustache possibly having been waxed and curled, or even touched up with "Old Reliable Hair and Whisker Dye. In use since 1860." And while well-groomed males slicked their hair with brilliantine or some such product comparable to Macassar oil, the ladies busily crocheted antimacassars (or "tidies") and pinned them, at head level, to the upholstery.

459. Left: shaving stand, adjustable mirror, the 1880's

460. Above: silver-plated mustache cup, made about 1895

461. Opposite: rack of shaving mugs with owners' names

330

After the Civil War, tobacco became a leading American industry. The price of the finished product declined and the quality rose — in snuff, cigars, pipe tobacco, chewing tobacco, and (after 1880) the newfangled cigarette. Antitobacco societies thundered in protest. "The deadly cigarette . . . converts the guileless boy into an assassin," the "nauseous cigar" led but to the asylum, chewing tobacco to "grave-robbing, incest, and perjury," and snuff drove its users to "swear, steal, and rob chicken-coops." But President Grant and Mark Twain were rarely seen without their cigars. President Cleveland and James Whitcomb Riley were tobacco chewers, an "unwholesome and obnoxious" habit that accounted for the ubiquitous spittoon and outraged comments on the ubiquitous spitter. By 1896 it was noted that "ladies in the smart sets" enjoyed smoking, their "gold cigarette-cases . . . always within the reach of the fair smoker's hand." Matches were often carried in ornamented matchboxes of gold, silver, or merely "solid nickel." Tobacconists provided a light for their customers with such devices as the one shown here (464), its "lighters" presoaked in kerosene (in the two cylinders) and ignited at the gas jet behind the miniature desk.

*462. A walnut box holding porcelain cuspidor;
the lid was lifted by depressing the rod, 1870's*

463. Above: ash tray, hammered brass, glass lining, made at Elbert Hubbard's handicraft shop about 1900

464. Right: cigar lighter for a tobacco shop, 1870's

465. Below: a device to cut plugs of chewing tobacco

PLUG CHEWING TOBACCO CUTTER

466. Above: a cast-iron jockey hitching post

467. Top: a lithograph by Currier & Ives of a fashionable turnout in Central Park in 1869

468. Right: section of horse-head hitching post

Drawn by Horse

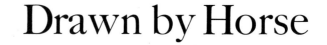

As early as the eighteenth century several American communities felt obliged to pass traffic regulations to control the clatter and congestion caused by horses and carriages "in great Numbers Crouding into Town." With the increasing and more broadly based affluence of the next century (and with the gradual improvement of streets and roads), the "carriage class" became a truly substantial sector of the population. Around mid-century it was estimated that there were nearly twenty thousand fashionable carriages in New York alone—not to mention all the carts, omnibuses, and other horse-drawn conveyances that added noise and confusion to the scene (a "tumultuous" noise that, in 1870, Walt Whitman likened to a "heavy, low, musical roar, hardly ever intermitted, even at night"). In city and country alike hitching posts and carriage steps, usually of cast iron, were as familiar as parking meters are today, although they appeared in more varied and agreeable designs.

469. Carriage steps made of cast iron

For most of the nineteenth century and the early years of the present one, the finest carriages in America, if not in the world, were produced by three successive generations of the Brewster family. The founder of this dynasty of craftsmen, James Brewster, a descendant of Elder William Brewster of the Plymouth Plantation, set up his first shop at New Haven in 1810. Twenty years later he was not only supplying the carriage trade along the eastern seaboard with a variety of handsomely designed, superbly constructed vehicles, but shipping others to Cuba, Mexico, and South America. Subsequently, under the direction of James's son Henry, the main headquarters of the firm was established in New York. At the great Paris Universal Exposition of 1878, in competition with carriage builders to the Queen of England and the Czar of Russia, among others, the Brewster entries were given the highest award. No one with serious social aspirations or of high station could afford not to have a Brewster carriage or sleigh of one sort or another. The firm's clients included John Jacob Astor, John Pierpont Morgan, William Rockefeller, Abraham Lincoln, Ulysses S. Grant, and others. Early in the present century, Henry's son, William Brewster, undertook to supply custom-made automobile bodies of impeccable quality. With changing times, in 1925 the Brewster company sold out to Rolls-Royce. In 1911 the interior appointments of one Brewster-built body for an automobile called for "a coat rail, memo book, cigarette case, scent bottle, mirror box, card cases, hat brush, vase and holder, watch, and rug."

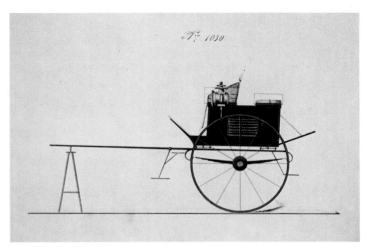

470. Dogcart, 1850–74

471. Small calèche, 1850–74

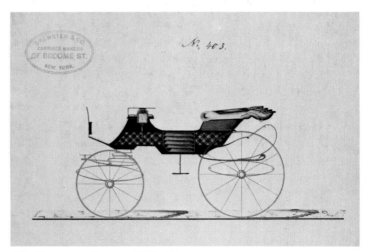

472. Four-seat phaeton, 1850–74

All illustrations are of water-color designs by Brewster & Co.

475. *Curtain coach, 1874*

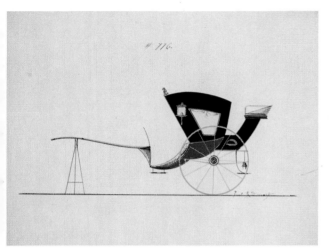

473. *Cab, 1850–74*

476. *Road wagon, 1876*

474. *Roof-seat omnibus, 1890*

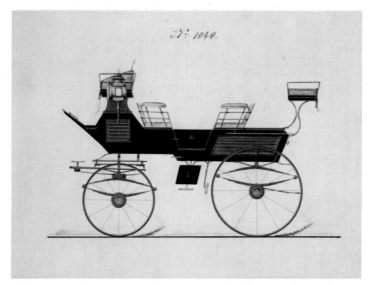

477. *Drag on four springs, about 1850*

Popular Patterns

Some Vanishing Americana

Over the years covered in this volume a succession of critics and reformers, designers and decorators, from John Ruskin to Elsie de Wolfe, produced a steady flow of advice on questions of good taste and sound practice in household and industrial arts. Although their individual pronouncements were usually issued with an air of finality and infallibility, they varied widely in their separate opinions. In general, however, what they had to say stemmed from one or the other of two major preoccupations of the age, industrialism and romanticism — two preoccupations that were giving shape to an evolving new culture. The one faced the future, the other looked to the past; the one hoped with the aid of the machine to increase the material benefits of life, the other clung to, or sought to revive, what seemed to have been good in years gone by, with or without assistance from the machine. Those were not necessarily discordant attitudes. They were often more complementary than antagonistic — two sides of a single coin.

Ruskin so deeply distrusted industrialization and mechanization that he had his books printed in a country-garden retreat and then, lest they be contaminated by the railroad, shipped them to their destinations by horse-drawn mail coaches. (Ultimately, he became resigned to the machine, but he never was at peace with it.) Miss de Wolfe trusted even her own elegant person to the railroad, always taking with her a tiny alarm clock designed by Cartier. But she would not accept the revolutionary modern designs in furniture and furnishings that her contemporaries were creating, particularly the strange new forms of Art Nouveau. For her the only safe formula for good and gracious living was to be found in the revival or adaptation of "period" styles, preferably the historic European styles that conveyed "the ever-present suggestion of permanence" that was so dear both to her and to her affluent clients.

Whether industrialism could assure a more welcome future remained a moot point in some circles. As Ruskin remarked, there was "thunder on the horizon, as well as dawn." However, once launched, industrialism established its own increasing momentum. Well before the end of the nineteenth century the railroad — the very symbol of the advancing machine age — had undeniably proved itself to be the most powerful consolidating force that civilization had yet known. "The nineteenth century," wrote H. G. Wells just after that century had passed, "when it takes its place with the other centuries in the chronological charts of the future, will, if it needs a symbol, almost inevitably have as that symbol a steam-engine

Opposite and above: a cigar-store Indian chief displaying a bunch of tobacco leaves

running upon a railway." And nowhere was this more importantly and more dramatically demonstrated than in the United States. Nowhere else was any "suggestion of permanence" more illusory than in this land of constant change. Even as early as the 1820's, James Fenimore Cooper noted that relatively few of the buildings then standing in New York City dated from before 1783. Much of the city had burned to the ground during the Revolution, to be sure, but what had survived was in good part systematically razed in the following years—and so it has been ever since. By the outbreak of World War I there was less left of Peter Stuyvesant's New Amsterdam, which had once covered the southern end of Manhattan Island, than there was of Pericles' Athens.

The experience of New York represents an extreme case, but it emphasizes a familiar trend in American history. To discard the past has been an act of faith in the future, an act ritually performed by so many immigrants who quit the certainties of the Old World for the promises of the New. Also, a pioneering people who labored against the wilderness could not accept the world about them as they found it; they had to visualize it as it one day would be when they had changed the face of the land, cleared their fields, and built their dreams about them. And, as Cooper had observed in passing, the buildings in cities were no less proof against the same transforming spirit. "He who at some future time," wrote Walt Whitman in 1845, "shall take upon himself the office of writing the early history of what is done in America, and of how the American character was started, formed, and finished . . . will surely have much cause to mention what may be called 'the pull-down-and-build-over-again spirit.'" The desire—indeed the need—for changing things was given a further, ironic twist when, in later years, to keep the machinery of mass production running at a paying rate, planned obsolescence was built into commodities to ensure a need for replacement.

In effect, the same was true of architecture. The trend to replace the old with the new, earlier recognized by Cooper and Whitman, was greatly accelerated by technological advances (and the rising value of real estate). Traditionally, houses and public structures alike had been built to serve successive generations (even if they did not last that long), but more modern materials and methods encouraged ever more rapid production and a quicker turnover. "The best we can do with all the data and facilities at our command," explained one writer in *The American Architect* about half a century ago, "is out of date almost before it shows signs of appreciable wear. So a building erected today is out-classed tomorrow." He recalled the remarks of one planner early in the present century who directed that a building about to be constructed must be "the cheapest thing that will hold together for fifteen years." In the context of such attitudes and practices, change and progress become hopelessly confused, one with the other, in all areas of life.

More and more different kinds of household gear and other accessories of living were probably produced in the half century between the Civil War and World War I than were turned out in all the earlier years of our history, and more were more quickly discarded than ever before. It would be pleasant to believe, as some people have since the publication of Darwin's *The Origin of Species*, that some law of natural selection governs the survival of objects from the past. But it would be hard to justify such a conclusion. In the haste to clear away the debris piled up by the advancing machine, much of what was once highly valued has been forever destroyed—and, by some chance or another, much of what was once considered trivia has been preserved. With time, however, even the latter

Carved and painted figure of Uncle Sam

assumes some special interest as a reminder of past experience. None of the guardians of styles and standards who wrote of taste, sincerity, suitability, and fashion in design had much to say about the sorts of things illustrated on the following pages of this chapter. Such evidence of the passing scene—the colorful advertising signs and figures that were gradually disappearing from the streets with different times and ways, the picturesque paraphernalia of the fire laddies that were giving way to more prosaic apparatus and equipment, the little whittled and painted forms that served as hunters' decoys, and the rest—these things were rather ignored by the critics of the day as having no relevance to significant issues. Yet, we find the examples that have survived attractive, suggestive, and even important souvenirs. Often, objects from the past can evoke intimate aspects of that earlier time that are beyond the reach of conventional history.

Above: a Christmas card, made around 1889

Below: signboard, reverse painting on glass

Much of what is shown here, as well, falls outside the range of formal histories of design. In large part the objects illustrated were commercial products, made for sale on the open market. Some, like the carved cigar-store Indians and circus figures, represent a lingering handicraft tradition that had its roots in the colonial period. Others, like some of the children's toys and the sheet-music covers, were turned out in quantity by modern machinery. And a few, like the jigsaw fretwork and the hand-painted china, could have been done by amateur enthusiasts, male or female, as well as by professional artisans. On the whole, they reflect little of the self-consciousness apparent in the design of stylish furniture and furnishings of the period. They were produced with small regard for esthetic theory, but with a keen awareness of their popular appeal and the purpose they served.

There is usually a gap of at least two generations before objects that have been put aside by our forebears as obsolete or out of style return to favor. (American colonial furniture did not begin to regain respectable status until almost a century after the Revolutionary War.) With the passage of those years the quantity of surviving material constantly diminishes through neglect, fire, or purposeful demolition. By the time some antiquarian or collector calls fresh attention to one or another category of relics, the relative rarity of what remains becomes an added factor to whatever other interest it holds; the discovery of more and scarcer examples tends to become an end in itself; and the uniquely different survival assumes more importance than that which was most representative of its time. Something is gained in that process, for as a consequence small pockets of the past are sometimes subjected to the closest, continued scrutiny. At times we may read into these objects more or different meanings than those who made and first used them cared about. However, we also may discover attitudes and assumptions on their part of which they were unaware. In any event, the more we learn about the relationship of antiques to the life of the times the more their intrinsic interest as attractive and colorful forms is enhanced.

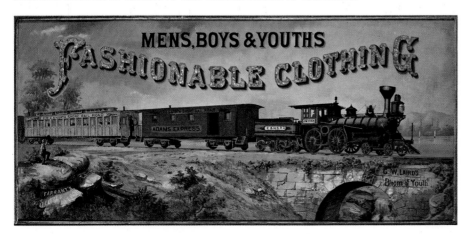

341

Signs of Another Day

At one point in a meeting of the Second Continental Congress, either to divert or comfort Thomas Jefferson as revisions of his draft of the Declaration of Independence were being proposed, Benjamin Franklin told him an anecdote that Jefferson remembered all his life. The story was of a young hatmaker who, considering a signboard for his new shop, asked several friends for suggestions. The sign was to have read, "John Thompson, hatter, makes and sells hats for ready money," with a figure of a hat added. One friend thought the word "hatter" unnecessary, since the sign said that Thompson made hats. Another thought the word "makes" could be omitted, since if the hats were good enough, they would sell whoever made them. A third thought "for ready money" was a useless phrase, because it was not then customary to sell on credit. The fourth critic questioned the word "sells," for it could hardly be expected that the hatter would give his wares away. And, since there was to be a picture of a hat, the word "hats" might also be eliminated. In the end the sign included only Thompson's name and the picture. Such trade signs, with a self-explanatory symbol and a minimum or absence of verbal copy, have an ancient history. Few remain on our streets, but the striped barber poles continue to remind us that barbers were once also surgeons of sorts whose symbol represented the ribbon used for bandaging the arm in bleeding an ill person. For no very good reason this uniformed stalwart puffing a cigarette (481) has been identified as Captain Jinks of the Horse Marines (who fed his horse "good corn and beans"), subject of a popular ballad written about 1868 (and later a play and a musical comedy).

480. *Left: 20th-century shop sign from Michigan*

481. *Below: a figure of a sergeant; one of several similar figures that served as shop signs*

478. *Opposite: barber pole, about 1875*

479. *Above: striped-razor barber's sign*

343

482. *Left: Natchez Indian squaw that stood in the dining room of the Mississippi steamboat* Natchez

483. *Above: a miniskirted squaw carrying cigars*

484. *Opposite, top: New York street scene, detail*

485. *Opposite, right: "Seneca John" in full panoply*

All sorts of modeled figures, from ladies of fashion to race-track touts and from kilted Scotsmen to turbaned Turks, have been used to identify tobacconists' shops. Among the most endearing are the cigar-store Indians, a diminishing tribe of colorful braves, squaws, and occasional papooses that, less than a century ago, numbered in the tens of thousands. Although tobacconists' figures in various forms appeared in England early in the seventeenth century and in America in the eighteenth, it was not until the nineteenth century that the wooden Indian was introduced in this country. In the 1820's the celebrated Philadelphia wood sculptor William Rush carved an early example for a local shopkeeper. In subsequent years the type proliferated in innumerable varieties, no two of them quite alike. They were not necessarily made to order. Thomas V. Brooks, who set up his own shop in 1847, later advertised that he had "From 75 to 100 figures always on hand." Carved effigies of red men also served as ship's figureheads and, on occasion, as decorative accessories (482) in steamboat saloons. With the passing of wooden ships some carvers turned from figureheads to shop figures.

The ideal trade sign was one that fixed attention with an image that needed no further explanation, as did this optometrist's sign (486). The eyes of painted glass were first probably lighted by gas from behind; later the device was converted to electricity, an indication that it continued to serve its purpose effectively over a span of years. With the advent of the horseless carriage, sign makers—and advertisers generally—had a fresh outlet for their skills. One appealing but understandably unsung artist, A. E. Martin, gave his message a suggestive form in the simplest possible terms (487). However, long before this there was mounting agitation over the unpleasant confusion of signs and other impedimenta that were cluttering city streets. "Indiscriminate street-advertising," editorialized *The Nation* in 1875, ". . . ought to be abolished as being unsightly, mentally disturbing, and a decided inconvenience to the eye, which is impelled by means of it to look where it does not want to look." At the same time increasing skeins of overhead telephone wires, with those for the telegraph and electric lights, were spreading an all but solid copper canopy over the main streets of big cities. In 1884 New York ordered them all put underground. Before long, ordinances in most cities also prohibited the use of standing figures and protruding signs as obstructions and hazards to passing pedestrians.

486. Top: illuminated optometrist's sign of painted glass, 1860–75

487. Above: automobile repairs sign, painted on wood, 20th century

488. Opposite: a lithograph of Broadway, New York, about 1880

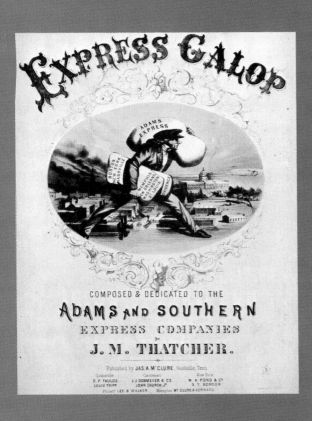

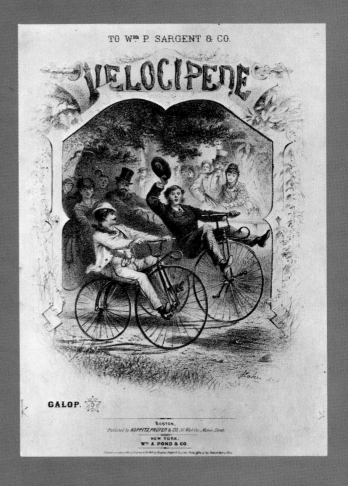

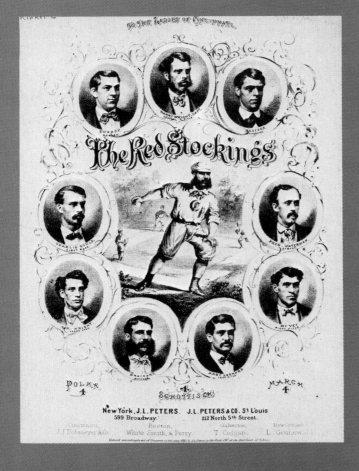

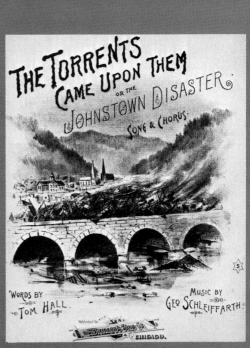

Lithographs from 19th-century sheet music depicting some contemporary events. 489. "Express Galop," 1867; 490. "Velocipede," 1869; 491. "The Red Stockings," 1869; 492. "The Johnstown Disaster," 1889; 493. Opposite: "Croquet," 1866

Some Musical Anecdotes

A singular and remarkably comprehensive graphic history of nineteenth- and early twentieth-century America could be compiled from the illustrated sheet-music covers of the time. Developments of all sorts, from passing fads to great events, were celebrated with published songs aimed at large audiences. "Of all the epidemics that have swept over our land," reported *The Nation* in 1866, "the swiftest and most infectious is croquet." And songs were promptly created as an aside to the excitement. At almost the same time the bone-shaking velocipede was introduced with even greater enthusiasm. This novelty, the successes of the Cincinnati Red Stockings (the first all-professional baseball team), the important continent-spanning services of the Adams Express Company, and the awful tragedy of the Johnstown flood, among scores of other episodes and accomplishments, were all promptly greeted with such musical accompaniments.

BROOKLYN BRIDGE

GRAND MARCH.

By E. MACK.

OLIVER DITSON COMPANY

Boston
453-463 Washington Street

London
192 High Holborn W. C.

New York	Chicago	Boston	Philadelphia
C. H. DITSON & CO.	LYON & HEALY	JOHN C. HAYNES & CO.	J. E. DITSON & CO.
867 Broadway	Cor. State and Monroe Sts.	33 Court and 453 Washington Sts.	1228 Chestnut St.

COPYRIGHT 1883 BY OLIVER DITSON & Co.

In 1883 the completion of the Brooklyn Bridge provided a gracefully arched exit from the cramped island
of Manhattan to the still independent city of Brooklyn,
across the East River, and beyond. However, it also
provided an easy entrance into New York for more and
more transients, and as soon as it opened it created
new traffic and transportation problems. So it was with
the first subways in Boston and New York about the
turn of the century. Every effort to relieve urban congestion succeeded only well enough to invite ever
larger crowds to the crowded city scene. The earlier
introduction of electric trolley cars had already served
to increase the throngs struggling for headway in down-
town streets, but on such conveyances it was at least
possible to get to "the beautiful sea" for a week-end
frolic. The early automobile offered more privacy on
an excursion, and more uncertainties. And for those
who went nowhere the crowded city could be a des-
perately lonely place.

494. *Opposite: the "Brooklyn Bridge . . . March"*

495. *"All Aboard, Squeeze Right In," issued 1911*

496. *"He'd Have to . . . Get Under," issued 1913*

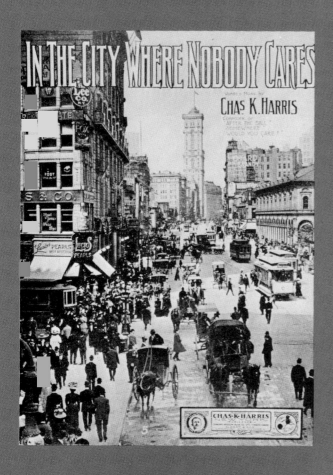

497. *"In the City Where Nobody Cares," 1910*

498. *"By the Beautiful Sea," published in 1914*

China Painting

"At first there were but a few outside of a factory who ventured to paint on china," stated an article in 1895, summarizing the fad for china painting that had swept the ranks of the artistically inclined. "By degrees others tried their hand at it. . . . Ever since then china painting has been on the crest of the wave. . . . Professionals were importuned for lessons; books were written on the subject . . . colors were prepared ready for the amateur's use; the demand for undecorated china increased, and new and fascinating shapes were constantly being placed on the market that were simply irresistible. . . . And as the amateurs progressed and were not satisfied to have someone else finish their work by gilding and firing, kilns were next supplied, then gold and silver and various-colored bronzes . . . in fact the American girl never ceased clamoring until she obtained every necessary accessory." Such accessories (499) included oil and mineral paints, mixing dishes, thinning oils, a porcelain palette, and a box of brushes and paint spreaders. Needles were useful to flick away dust—"and not injure the work." Many china painters achieved professional status, as did Mrs. Fanny Rowell, who had a Fifth Avenue studio from 1899 to 1908, where she decorated the oblong dish and the cup and saucer (500, 501).

499. A display of assorted materials used for china painting

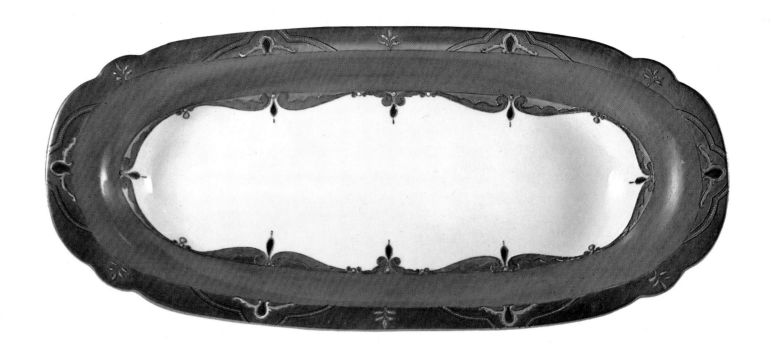

500, 501, 502. Oblong dish, a cup and saucer, and a plate, all imported French china, that were hand decorated around the turn of the century by the artful brushes of American women

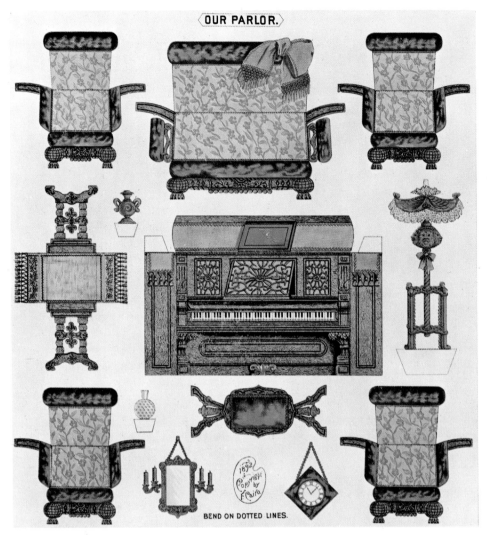

503. Cardboard cutouts, a set of parlor furnishings

504. Left: sideboard for a dollhouse

505. Above: a doll-size Mission sofa

506. Opposite: a mechanical toy, the carpenters set in motion with a crank

Minors' Arts & Crafts

In 1892, when economist Albert S. Bolles compiled a survey of American industries, he reported in a brief section devoted to toys: "playthings have become so necessary a part of American life that the trade in them has suffered the least of all by the hard times. Playthings are a luxury; but, even if there is retrenchment in the family, the children have to be amused just as much as ever." Children's amusements, as always, reflected the tastes and trends of the times. Dollhouse furniture, for example, duplicated household fashions of the moment. And this team of house-raisers (506) used balloon-frame construction, an up-to-the-minute technique that had replaced the use of heavy timbers joined by mortise and tenon. Further, as Bolles also noted, "One of the most important departments in the toy establishments is presided over by young men whose inventive minds are constantly engaged in producing new toys, and 'improvising amendments' upon those already in vogue."

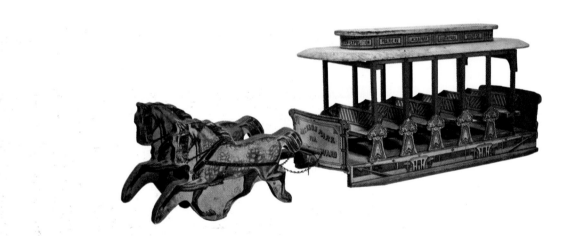

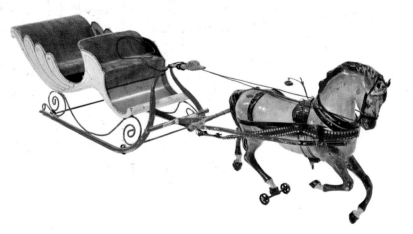

507. *Toy train, the "Little Wonder Railway"*

508. *Toy fire engine with galloping horses*

509. *Horse-drawn, open-air trolley car to*

510. *A trim rig, the one-horse open sleigh*

511. *Opposite: a windup, double-decker bus*

Trains, trolley cars, fire engines, covered wagons, circus wagons, farm wagons, express wagons, steamboats, sailboats — any form of transportation, in fact, served as a model for toymakers. Such playthings were perennial favorites with small boys, as indeed they are today. And before the appearance of the toy automobile, concurrent with that of the automobile itself, horse-drawn vehicles and horses of every shape and size were among the most popular toys of all. Here a matched pair of spruce dapple-grays pulls a trolley car (509) to the Columbian Exposition at Jackson Park, the destination gaily printed on the dashboard. This toy is made of wood covered with lithographed paper, as is the train (507) with its "U.S. Grant" locomotive. The sleigh (510), elegantly decorated with a swan's head and wings, and again with a dapple-gray in harness, is made of tin. Tin plate was extensively utilized by the toy industry. "It is lighter than wood or papier-maché," reported Bolles, "is cheap, and can be easily fashioned by the use of dies and stamps." The dashing fire engine and its spanking team (508) are cast iron, another widely used material for toys that made them, happily, all but indestructible. The tin autobus (511) with its windup works had an English patent and was imported. Numerous toys also came from Germany. America, however, easily competed with the foreign market, and there was a growing demand for American toys both in Europe and South America.

512. *Above: assemblage of 19th-century toys*

513. *Top: Master Ralph E. Finch, a mother's darling, brushed and curled and turned out in his Sunday best; Cooperstown, N.Y., dated 1903*

When Master Finch posed for his photograph (513), over five hundred factories were making toys for the nation's children. The beanshooter was declared to be the all-time best seller, with millions of "these infernal machines" sold each year: "One of the simplest playthings made . . . known to every school-teacher in the country." Toy timepieces were also childhood treasures. "Every urchin has had the little gilt toy-watch that is always at half past seven o'clock," it was noted in 1864, and a similar toy watch was very likely tucked into young Finch's vest pocket. Toy firearms, soldiers, and drums were continuously in demand—a demand that had increased sharply after the Civil War. Early in the 1900's, for example, one Massachusetts firm alone was geared to produce seven thousand drums per day, a number reflecting the nostalgic popularity of romantic tales of little drummer boys who marched with the Union and Confederate troops.

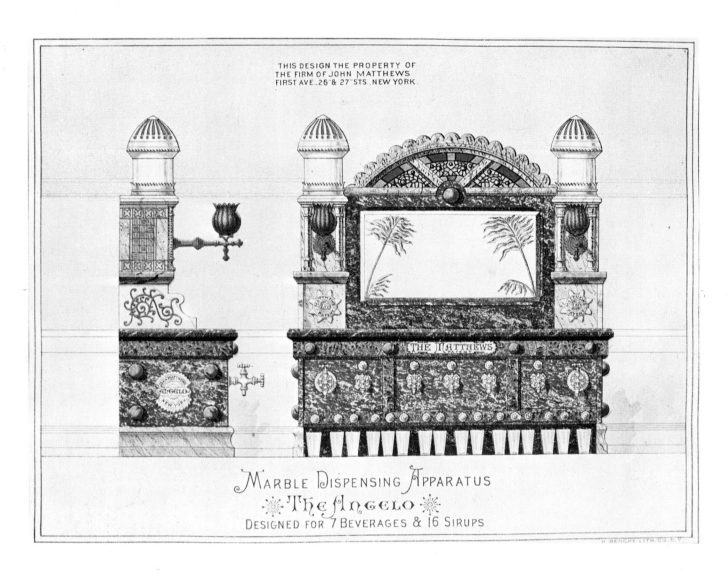

MARBLE DISPENSING APPARATUS
The Angelo
DESIGNED FOR 7 BEVERAGES & 16 SIRUPS

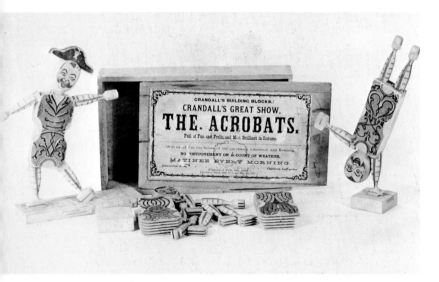

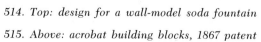

514. Top: design for a wall-model soda fountain

515. Above: acrobat building blocks, 1867 patent

516. Right: anagram game, made about 1875–95

For home entertainment Americans, both young and old, enjoyed a host of parlor games—jackstraws, parchesi, pigs in clover, checkers, dominoes, jigsaw puzzles, and tiddlywinks, to name but a few. And there was the magic of a magic lantern show (517), with sets of slides to suit every taste. For an evening of culture, illustrations of Bible stories, European scenery, famous historic events, statuary, or astronomy were suitably edifying. For comic relief, "The Dancing Skeleton" was sure to amuse. For stark tragedy, the evils of drink were succinctly depicted in such views as "Joe Morgan with Delirium Tremens" and "Frank Slade Kills His Father." By the turn of the century the motion picture offered its dazzling fare of vivid, visual entertainment. ("No, It Is Not A Magic Lantern Show," announced one early advertisement.) The movie palace would become America's home away from home, second only to the soda fountain, which had become a fact of American life in the 1870's. Like the ice-cream soda, the soda fountain was purely an American inspiration, the splendor of its varicolored marble, polished onyx, and shining fixtures (514) glistening—from sea to sea—in the nation's drugstores and ice-cream parlors.

517. A tin magic lantern, or slide projector, made in the form of a portly, benign mandarin

Every feasible material was used for dolls: paper, wood, muslin, china, bisque, wax, celluloid, rubber, metal, and papier-mâché. In the 1870's a Kentucky firm made dolls' heads from a composition of flour, glue, and pulp — kneaded in large tubs by barefoot employees, and a Connecticut firm briefly marketed dolls of rawhide, an unfortunate choice that proved far too tempting to rats and mice. A talking doll (518), with china head, composition limbs, and steel body (here in clothes of a later era), was developed by Edison about 1890, a few years after he invented the phonograph. The doll's hand-cranked miniature phonograph played such melodies as "Twinkle, Twinkle, Little Star." The plush-covered, excelsior-stuffed Teddy bear was inspired by a bear cub that Theodore Roosevelt refused to shoot on a hunting trip in 1902. The craze for these snuggly toys reached such heights by 1906 that one alarmed Michigan clergyman solemnly declared that little girls, in abandoning their dolls for Teddy bears, were losing all instinct for motherhood — and race suicide would inevitably follow.

518, 518a. Edison Talking Doll, her mechanism shown on the opposite page

519. Above: a Teddy bear of the early 1900's

520. Left: maple doll, its joints patented, 1873, by Joel Ellis, a toymaker in Vermont

"In the line of iron toys are . . . the iron banks," wrote a reporter for *The Chicago Daily Tribune* in 1898, "that decoy poor, defenseless little children into dropping their hard-begged-for pennies therein to see them work." The whimsical automatons of mechanical banks were indeed enticing to watch. The mechanism was primed with a penny—or a button, if one were hard pressed—a lever pushed, and the show began. There were close to two hundred and fifty intriguing designs from which to choose. This trick dog (523), a coin in his teeth, leaped through the hoop and deposited the coin in the barrel. The eagle (521) dropped coins from her beak into the nest, her iron wings flapped, and the eaglets opened their mouths to chirp—an actual chirp made by a bellows in the works. And when the stubborn mule (522) kicked over the old man seated on the bench, the coin—set under the bench—dropped into the bank below.

521. Opposite: "Eagle and Eaglets" mechanical bank

522. Above: a bank titled "Always Did 'Spise a Mule"

523. Below: bank featuring a clown and his trick dog

524. Bottom: a yawning whale "banked" Jonah's coins.

A foreign exporting agent reportedly commented in the 1850's that toy banks always sold in the United States, "for it accords well with the grasping character of the race." Whatever the merits of this caustic judgment, toy banks—whether of pottery, glass, tin, wood, or cast iron—were a leading item among American toy manufacturers in the years following the Civil War. (Significantly, those were also the years when savings and loan associations sprang up in towns and cities throughout the nation.) The native ingenuity that animated the mechanical banks, shown on the preceding page, took an architectural turn of mind with "still" banks, such as the examples shown here. A penny saved was a penny earned, and these cast-iron turrets, towers, and colonnades offered beguiling inducements to thrift. The birdhouse (526), again an architectural fantasy in cast iron, surely proved equally beguiling to its feathered tenants.

525. *Above: "Tower Bank" secured with a combination lock*

526. *Right: birdhouse, a Victorian caprice patented 1868*

Opposite: 527. a domed "Columbia Bank," late 19th century

528. *The church and steeple, a toy "Bank and Letter Box"*

529. *"Independence Hall Tower Bank," patented 1875*

367

530. Ornamental designs from a jigsaw manual

531. Above: a cutout hanging shelf, 1860–80

532. Below: treadle scroll-sawing machine, 1878

533. Right: a jig-sawed hanging corner shelf

THE SAWING-MACHINE.

Jig-sawed Gingerbread

"Within the past four years," it was reported in 1876, "aided much by the invention of treadle machines of great simplicity and beauty, a scroll-sawing fever has swept over the country." Demonstrations of jig-sawing at the Philadelphia Centennial that same year carried the fever to new heights. Within the next two years, according to *Harper's Monthly*, the sale of jigsaw blades had soared to a half million a month. Manuals were published with illustrated models for cutout ornamental designs to guide enthusiasts. (Even William Morris in England seems to have experimented with such treadle machines.) Ladies were advised that with small saws and some other tools they might "fashion all the lighter articles of household decoration and light fretwork panels for even heavy furniture." Men, women, as well as adept youngsters, it was said in 1878, were earning "large sums of pocket-money by cutting . . . beautiful household ornaments, and selling [them] among friends or acquaintances, or at the art stores."

534. Top: a wall clock with overlaid patterns

535. *Left: memorial to volunteer firemen, 1884*

536. *Top: trumpet of the "Big Six" fire wagon*

537. *Above: carved emblem of the Tiger Hose Co.*

538. *Opposite: fireman's hat, Citizens Hose Co.*

Art for Fire Laddies

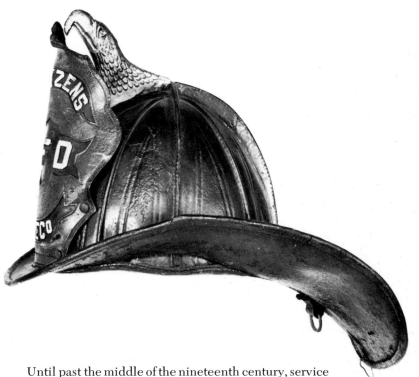

Until past the middle of the nineteenth century, service in American fire companies was voluntary and without pay. Membership was a distinction, and company rosters included the names of a community's most prominent citizens. There were also volunteer aides to the volunteers, young men who "ran with the machine" for excitement—toughs, mostly, who enjoyed fighting the men of rival companies for the use of a fire "plug" or hydrant (while the fire blazed merrily on). In either case, association with a company was a matter of great and sometimes fierce pride. The artistry that was lavished on equipment was usually paid for by the firemen themselves, and their friends. Decoratively painted or carved engines frequently were further embellished with nickel-, silver-, or gold-plated mountings. Special trumpets made of silver were presented to the worthy as gifts of honor and appreciation. The fire hat, handsomely designed and decorated, protected the head, obviously, and it shed water away from the back of the neck; reversed, it formed a face shield.

In America the fireman's axe had by the time of the Revolution already developed into an especially handsome and well-balanced tool. Leather fire buckets, usually painted with the name or initials of the owner and some other ornamental device, in some places remained in use into the second half of the last century. (Many early cities required householders to keep such buckets in the halls of their houses for use by the owners or by passing volunteers on the way to a fire.) Elsewhere new equipment gradually changed the nature of fire-fighting practices. With the replacement of manually operated pumping engines by steam apparatus, fewer firemen were needed. As cities grew larger, however, they were needed all the time; and paid professionals succeeded the volunteers. The horse-drawn steam engine, which perpetuated the old traditions of bright colors and polished metals of earlier machines, was the last stage in the evolution of fire engines before motorized equipment was introduced in the early years of the present century.

539. Above: painted leather fire bucket, inscribed "John Tyler-Prompt In Danger"

540. Right: a brass and copper weather vane, made by Cushman & White, 1875–85

541. *Top: fireman's axe from the Niagara Hose Co. No. 15*

542. *Above: fireman's belt, inscribed "rescue," made 1885*

Art of Deception

Whether the game was wild fowl or buffalo, passenger pigeons or grizzly bears, America was long a wide-open paradise for hunters. Although laws proclaiming closed seasons were passed as early as 1795 to control the growing scarcity of game in some sections, in this large land one usually did not have to go far to find the quarry in season. Here, recalled one happily surprised Englishman who had visited America early in the nineteenth century, "You could take your rod or gun, jump over a gate and wing or hook your victim . . . without the trouble of inquiring to whom it belonged. Here was no eternal 'Trespassers beware,' or 'Spring guns' to warn the reader that a rabbit's legs were of more value than a man's." Carving and painting wooden likenesses of ducks, geese, and other waterfowl to serve as decoys to lure living birds within gun range was a minor art that was developed from primitive, Indian precedents in colonial days. In the last century it reached a high level of accomplishment, which continues to this day. Some decoys are realistically enough fashioned to fool ornithologists as well as the fowl.

543. Left: a wooden heron decoy

544. *Left: sign for shop selling decoys*

545. *Top: a red-breasted merganser drake*

546. *Above: a painted sleeping black duck*

547. *Below: model of sickle-billed curlew*

548. *Above: "A Token of Love," valentine of 1880*

549. *Below: Christmas greeting card, about 1888*

550-55. *Opposite: Christmas and valentine cards*

Special Greetings

> Without you, life is dull and gray.
> With you, all things are bright and gay.

This wistful valentine message was carried in 1900 by the pantalets-clad little girl on the opposite page. The commercial production of such ready-made, brightly colored greeting cards was yet another American industry that arose after the Civil War, although there was strong competition from European imports until shortly before World War II. But American firms, meanwhile, were marketing cards for all occasions—birthdays, Easter, Halloween (1908), Thanksgiving (1909), Saint Patrick's Day (1912), and Mother's Day (1914). The now world-popular Christmas card had been introduced in England during the 1840's. The exchange of valentine sentiments, however, was an ancient custom, its origins found in a Roman festival held on February fourteenth, in honor of the goddess Juno Regina and associated with love. In the Christian calendar February fourteenth was designated as the feast day of Saint Valentine, martyred in Rome about 270 A.D. Thus, the pagan Juno was forgotten, and Valentine became the patron saint of lovers.

Circuses & Carrousels

"The Avenues Ablaze with Prismatic Hues. Eyes Dazzled and Heads Set Whirling. A Veritable Cyclone of Wonders and Tornado of Magnificent Objects." Thus ran an advertisement, in 1891, heralding Barnum & Bailey's "Free Street Parade and Pageant." This was the era that has been called the golden age of the circus, and the grand procession through a town or village was a wondrous cavalcade of clowns, animals, performers, and "floods of music." The brilliant circus wagons were extravagantly decorated with wood carvings—birds, beasts, mythical creatures, allegorical figures, leaves, flowers, and rococo curlicues. These carvings were exotica in themselves, a vivid expression of the American craftsman's art and imagination.

556. *Above: carved lion's head*

557. *Right: a circus procession*

GRAND PROCESS
DRAWN BY A T
NOW ATTACHED

LITH. OF SARONY, MAJOR & KNAPP 449 BROADWAY. N.Y.

OF THE STEAM CALLIOPE

SIX ELEPHANTS IN THE CITY OF NEW YORK.

ND'S, NATHAN'S & Cᵒˢ AMERICAN & ENGLISH CIRCUS.

The carrousel is an ancient device. A Byzantine bas-relief dating from the first century A.D., for example, shows carrousel riders in baskets spinning around a center pole. Over the centuries roundabouts in varying designs were found at fairs and festivals throughout the world. In nineteenth-century America the merry-go-round, aglow with lights and music, became a star attraction at the myriad amusement parks built across the nation—never more than a trolley-ride's distance from any fair-sized city. Like circus wagons, the merry-go-rounds were resplendent with carving—from the fanciful trappings of the animals to the lavish details of overhead woodwork and cornices. The giraffe (558), tiger (559), and horse (561) were carved at Gustav Augustus Dentzel's carrousel factory in Germantown, Pennsylvania, during the 1890's. The peacock (560) was a German import of the same era.

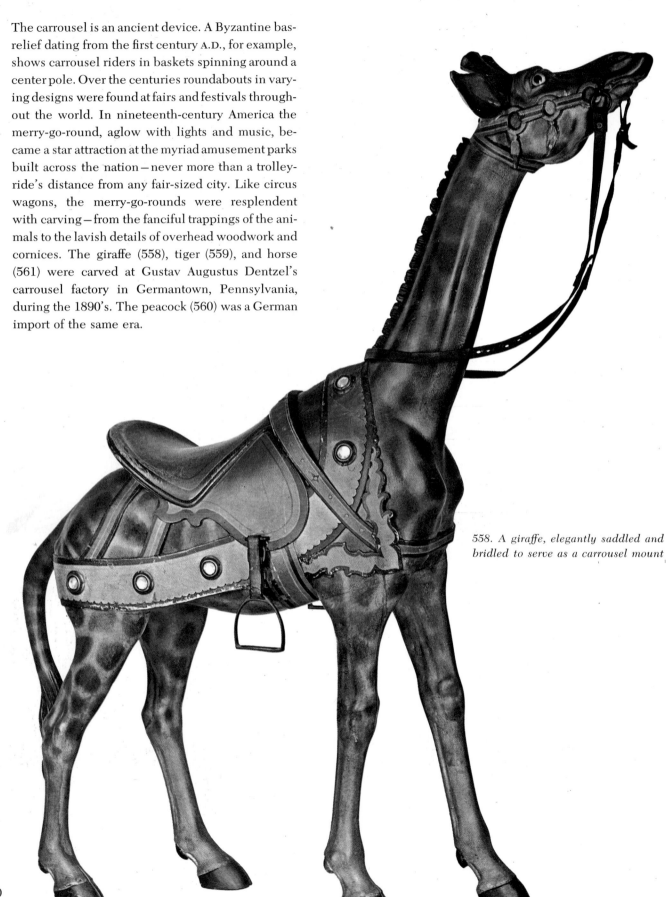

558. A giraffe, elegantly saddled and bridled to serve as a carrousel mount

559, 560, 561. Three carrousel animals, the tiger, the peacock, and the prancing horse

562. *Left: a dancing girl carved around 1900, in Milwaukee, as decoration on a Sparks circus wagon*

563. *Above: carrousel ornament, a smiling dragon*

564. *Opposite: a Barnum & Bailey poster for 1900*

A wagonmaker in Baraboo, Wisconsin, from whom the Ringlings ordered their first band wagon in 1884, later recalled his initial efforts at creating circus glamour: "I hacked out the eagles as best I could, as woodcarvers were too high priced. We painted the body red with the eagles and moldings yellow, so as to look like gold leaf." Sumptuous carvings did indeed raise the price of a circus wagon into the thousands of dollars, as did the application of gold leaf. Gold leaf was also used to highlight the carvings on carrousels, the animals themselves a virtual Noah's ark of whales, elk, kangaroos, bison, cats, rabbits, cows, pigs, as well as dragons rampant. This winged, flower-bedecked dragon (563) was originally appliquéd to a carrousel chariot. It was discovered, however, that bizarre or unfamiliar creatures did not appeal to most children. Their first choice on a merry-go-round was the traditional steed—a galloping horse, and preferably a dapple-gray.

565. OVERLEAF: A metal weather vane representing Columbia, made about 1870

383

Glossary
of
Terms

The numbers in parentheses refer to illustrations in the text.

ACANTHUS A carved ornamentation patterned after acanthus leaves, used decoratively on furniture; used in architecture principally on Corinthian and Composite capitals

AGATA A type of art glass with mottled decoration formed from mineral or metallic stains, patented in 1887 (170)

AMBERINA A type of art glass, patented in 1883, which is typically shaded in colors ranging from yellowish-amber to ruby (167)

AMBOINA A light reddish-brown curly-grained wood from the East Indies used mainly for veneers and inlay (24)

AMERICAN ORGAN See **CABINET ORGAN**

ANGLO-JAPANESE STYLE A style of decoration, developed in England during

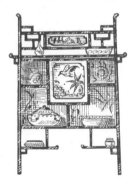

the 1860's and adapted in America, in which elements of Gothic and Japanese design, freely treated, were incorporated in lightly framed furniture forms and ornamental schemes. The style in America was strongly influenced by the Japanese exhibits at the Philadelphia Centennial International Exhibition of 1876.

ANTIMACASSAR A name, derived from Macassar hair oil, for the doily used to protect the back or arms of upholstered furniture; also called a tidy

ARGUS A pressed-glass pattern made up of regularly spaced indentations resembling thumbprints (95)

Bentwood chair

ART GLASS A general term applied to decorative glassware, often of vivid colors and extravagant form, widely produced in the last several decades of the 19th century

ART NOUVEAU An international style of design, variously interpreted in different countries in the decades just before and after 1900, based largely on curvilinear, organic forms and motifs

ARTS AND CRAFTS MOVEMENT The activities undertaken by various groups in the late 19th century in England, and to some extent in America, to improve the quality of industrial art and design, largely through a return to the principles and methods of hand craftsmanship. William Morris was the major prophet of the movement. In this country, the Art Workers' Guild in Providence, the Rookwood Pottery in Cincinnati, and the Roycrofters in East Aurora, New York, were manifestations of the movement.

BALLOON-BACK CHAIR A chair with an open back and transverse splat, the top rail rounded so as to be continuous with incurved uprights and thus assuming a roughly balloon-shaped outline (12)

BAUHAUS A revolutionary school of art and architecture, founded in Germany in 1919, that approached problems of design by considering all the arts and crafts in terms of modern materials and industrial methods

BENTWOOD FURNITURE Wooden furniture bent into extravagant curves by steam and pressure; developed in the 1830's by the German cabinetmaker Michael Thonet; first manufactured in Austria around 1840; shortly imported into and then copied in America

BERGERE A French term for an upholstered and commodious chair, with closed arms and a loose seat cushion; commonly designed in the Louis XV style (268)

BIBELOT A small decorative object or one of novel interest

BOUDOIR A woman's small sitting or retiring room; a woman's bedroom

BUNGALOW A typically small, open-plan, one-story house with eaves roofing over an ample porch; popular in decades around 1900 (429)

BURMESE A type of opaque art glass resembling porcelain in its shaded color and glossy surface (168)

BUTTERFLY WEDGE A butterfly-shaped wedge of wood or metal used to join two pieces of wood or stone (283)

CABINET ORGAN A musical instrument, also known as the American organ and

very popular in the late 19th century, that produced tones by the vibration of differently shaped and sized reeds (435)

CABRIOLE A reverse-curved leg ending in a shaped foot that was extremely popular during the Queen Anne and Chippendale periods and in the 19th-century revival of past styles (249)

CANDELABRUM A candleholder with several arms or branches (3)

CANE See RATTAN

CANTERBURY A low stand, usually on casters, consisting of a drawer surmounted by vertical openwork partitions, for holding music and papers (60)

CARPENTER GOTHIC Architecture that translated the Gothic Revival style from stone into wood, the "gingerbread" trim consisting of jig-sawed cusps, crockets, trefoils, and related motifs

CASED GLASS See OVERLAY GLASS

CASEMENT WINDOW A framed window hinged at the side to swing in or out

CASTER A small roller or wheel set into the feet or base of furniture to facilitate moving; also, a small stand with cruets and containers for condiments

Caster

CHASING A decoration on metal surfaces produced by a relatively blunt instrument that indents but does not cut into the surface

CHIBOUK See HOOKAH

CHIMNEY PIECE The decorative area above a fireplace (413)

CHROMOLITHOGRAPH A colored picture printed from a series of lithographic stones or plates, one for each of several colors (202)

CLAW-AND-BALL A carved foot resembling a bird's claw holding a ball, commonly used as the termination of a cabriole leg in the Chippendale period and in 19th-century revivals of colonial styles (249)

COLONIAL REVIVAL STYLE A style in late 19th-century architecture, furniture, and decoration that imitated or freely adapted designs of the colonial and subsequent early American periods

COMET See HORN OF PLENTY

CONVERSATIONAL See TETE-A-TETE

CORAL GLASS See PEACHBLOW

COZY CORNER See TURKISH CORNER

CRAFTSMAN FURNITURE Furniture in the Mission style made and marketed by Gustav Stickley from 1901 to his bankruptcy in 1915 (286)

CREST RAIL The top rail of a chair, settee, or any other seating form

CROCKET A carved, projecting ornament, of curved and bent foliage, used on the sloping edge of spires and gables in Gothic and Gothic Revival architecture; sometimes used to decorate furniture in those styles (18)

CROWN MILANO A type of art glass, white opal in color, with raised enamel decoration (165)

CUSP A Gothic ornamental detail, consisting of a point or knob, frequently carved, projecting from the intersection of two curves (18)

CUT GLASS Glass ornamented by grinding and polishing to produce more or less elaborate designs, principally geometric (358)

DADO The separately decorated lower portion of the wall of a room

DAMASCUS TABLE A small, low, side table, usually inlaid, in the Moorish style

DIAPER PATTERN A repeating design of lozenges, squares, diamonds, and related shapes in a diagonal pattern

DIVAN An upholstered sofa usually without a back and arms (the form and term are of Turkish origin); also a smoking room, often decorated in the Moorish style (230)

EASTLAKE STYLE A term loosely applied to furniture design that actually or

allegedly followed principles stressing "sincerity" of purpose and simplicity of form, first presented in book form by Charles L. Eastlake in England in 1868

EBONIZE To simulate ebony by staining black

EGG AND DART A convex molding with a design resembling alternating eggs and darts

EGYPTIAN REVIVAL STYLE A style, mainly architectural and in vogue during the first half of the 19th century, featuring such elements as Egyptian columns, and pyramidal shapes; also, then and later, a related style in furniture and decoration

ELECTROPLATED WARE See **PLATED WARE**

EMBOSS To raise decorations in relief from a surface

EMPIRE STYLE A style in furniture and furnishings, developed during the reign of Napoleon Bonaparte, in which ancient Greek, Roman, and Egyptian models were more or less closely followed. The style was adopted and adapted in other western countries. The American version was popular, roughly, from 1815 to 1830, and was again revived late in the nineteenth century.

ENCAUSTIC TILE A decorative tile whose painted design is fixed to the surface by heat. Used as ornament on furniture in the Eastlake style and as architectural trim (136)

ENGAGED COLUMNS Half columns, divided vertically, applied as decoration to furniture and architecture

ENGRAVE To produce a pattern on a hard surface by incising with a graver or burin

ETAGERE See WHATNOT

EWER A form of pitcher or jug, often with a wide mouth, used for pouring water or wine (175)

EXTENSION HANGING LAMP A lamp hung on chains with pulleys for raising and lowering it (393)

FAÏENCE Earthenware with ornamental designs applied in opaque, colored glazes (177)

FAVRILE GLASS The name given to a large variety of decorative, colored glassware developed by Louis Comfort Tiffany in which the designs, colors, and textures emanate from within the glass itself (307)

FINIAL A device used as a terminal ornament

FIRE SCREEN A screen, often decorative, mounted on or within a supporting

frame, to shield against the glare and heat of a fire (409)

FLUX In glassmaking, a substance used to promote fusion when melting a batch of ingredients

FONT The oil container of a lamp (15)

FRESCO Colored design applied to wet plaster so that it becomes an integral part of the wall

FRETWORK An ornamental design resembling latticework, either applied, freestanding, or cut in low relief; popular in the Chippendale and Federal periods and in the 19th-century revival of past styles (248)

GALLERY Open fretwork or small balustrade forming a railing around the top of a form (248)

GILT Overlay made of or resembling gold leaf, used to decorate furniture, silver, and ceramics

GOTHIC REVIVAL STYLE A term used to refer to architecture and furnishings featuring pointed arches, cusps, crockets, and other design elements associated with the medieval past; popular in America largely in the several decades after 1840

GRANDFATHER CLOCK See TALL CASE CLOCK

GRANDMOTHER CLOCK A modern term for a miniature tall case clock

"GRAND RAPIDS" FURNITURE A loosely used term referring to such inexpensive, mass-produced furniture as was manufactured in Grand Rapids, Michigan, from the 1850's (61). Similar furniture was made in many other places; also, furniture of excellent quality has long been made at Grand Rapids.

GREEK REVIVAL STYLE A term referring to architecture and furnishings, especially from about 1820 to about 1850, in which ancient Greek forms and ornamental details were used in more or less free interpretations

Harvard lamp

HARVARD LAMP An adjustable desk lamp with one or two arms and a colored shade (388)

HIGHBOY A modern term for a high chest of drawers comprised of two sections: an upper case, with drawers of varied depth and length, set upon a lower case, also with drawers, supported by legs (249)

HONEYCOMB The popular name of a pressed-glass pattern designed to look like a bee's comb (94)

HOOKAH Elaborate Oriental pipe with a long flexible stem designed to cool the smoke by drawing it through water (232)

HOOKED RUG A rug made of strips of cloth or yarn drawn through a burlap backing; often with elaborate designs (414)

HORN FURNITURE Furnishings made of steer, buffalo, or elk horn, popular in Europe as well as in America between 1860 and 1920 (289)

HORN OF PLENTY A pressed-glass pattern resembling repeated cornucopias; also called Comet (91)

INLAY Decoration formed by contrasting materials set into the surface of a piece (2a)

JAPANESE STYLE See ANGLO-JAPANESE STYLE

JAPANNING The process of simulating Oriental lacquer by the use of varnish or paint with decoration in low relief, usually with gilded *chinoiserie* designs

JARDINIERE A decorative pot or stand for plants and flowers (182)

JIG SAW A saw with a thin, vertical, reciprocating blade, used for cutting openwork patterns in wood (532)

LAMBREQUIN A short ornamental drapery on a shelf or mantelpiece or over a door or window

LINCOLN DRAPE A pressed-glass pattern, presumably inspired by Lincoln's funeral trappings (92)

LITHOGRAPH A print made by offsetting onto paper an image drawn with grease on a flat stone or metal surface; when the surface is wetted it rejects the printer's ink except for the greased areas

LOUIS XIV REVIVAL STYLE A 19th-century style of furnishings imitating or recalling the large-scale, ornate, baroque forms that had been favored under the monarchy of Louis XIV

LOUIS XV REVIVAL STYLE A 19th-century style in the manner of the curvilinear, rococo fashions that characterized the Louis XV period. See also Rococo; Rococo Revival Style

LOUIS XVI REVIVAL STYLE A 19th-century style that favored the straight lines and classical details common to furnishings originally designed during the reign of Louis XVI

MAGNET AND GRAPE One of several pressed-glass patterns featuring grape and grapeleaf motifs (96)

MAJOLICA A type of earthenware with tin-enamel glaze in rich colors (176)

MARQUETRY Decorative inlay in which a pattern is formed of various woods or other materials before being glued to a groundwork (23)

MARTELE A special line of silverware of higher than sterling quality, handmade at the Gorham Manufacturing Company; characterized by Art Nouveau design and the unplanished hammer marks of its surfaces (330)

MEDALLION BACK An oval-shaped back of a chair or settee, resembling a medallion (13)

MERIDIENNE A French term for a sofa or day bed having one arm lower than the other

MISSION STYLE A style of furniture, popular in the early 20th century, made generally of oak in simple rectilinear designs, and associated by some with the rude furnishings of early Spanish missions in California. See also Craftsman Furniture

MORRIS CHAIR An easy chair with adjustable back first produced by William

Morris and his associates in England in the 1860's (page 102)

MORTISE AND TENON The method of joining two pieces of wood by inserting a tenon, or extension of one piece, into the mortise, or socket, of another; usually further secured by a pin piercing both pieces

MOSAIC A picture or design made by inlaying bits of colored glass, stone, or other material in mortar

MOUNT A piece of decorative hardware or metal ornament on a piece of furniture (2b)

MURAL A wall painting

NIELLO Decoration made of designs incised in metal and filled with a black metallic alloy

OLEOGRAPH A kind of chromolithograph in imitation of an oil painting (118)

ORMOLU Gilded brass or bronze used for furniture mounts and other purposes; also called gilt-bronze

OVERLAY See SILVER DEPOSIT

OVERLAY GLASS Glass with one or more casings of differently colored glass ground away in decorative patterns revealing the underlying glass (391)

PATERAE Flat, circular ornaments resembling the classical saucers used for wine in libations; usually in low relief, ornamenting a frieze or other element of architecture or furniture (19)

PATINA The color or finish of bronze, copper, or wood surfaces resulting from age or use

PATINATE To produce an artificial patina on wood or metal

PATTERN GLASS Mechanically pressed glass usually produced in sets, the different pieces of which carry the same pattern (93)

PEACHBLOW A type of art glass colored and shaded to simulate Chinese porcelain with a "peach bloom" glaze (172)

PEACOCK MOTIF An element of design resembling a peacock or its feathers used by Art Nouveau artists, especially Tiffany

PIONEER See WESTWARD HO

PLATE Term used for forms made of solid silver or gold of sterling or standard quality (188)

PLATED WARE Forms made of a thin layer of silver over a heavier base of copper, either manually fused (as in old Sheffield plate) or, later, chemically electroplated (189)

POMONA A type of art glass with etched decoration resembling ice crystals on a stippled or frosted ground (169)

PORPHYRY A dark-red or purple rock embedded with feldspar crystals of different colors

Peacock mirror

PRE-RAPHAELITES A group of 19th-century English artists who sought to emulate the simplicity and spirit of Italian art before Raphael. Some of them collaborated with William Morris in his revival of the handicrafts, setting a precedent for similar American accomplishments in the arts and crafts.

PRESSED GLASS Glass whose shape and decoration are formed by being mechanically pressed in a mold

QUEEN ANNE STYLE A term used in the second half of the 19th century to refer to architecture vaguely and variously recalling aspects of 17th-century and earlier English structures (426)

QUEEN'S BURMESE WARE See BURMESE

RATTAN A type of palm whose stem (either the outer casing or the inner pith called "cane") was used to make furniture often of intricate design (212)

RENAISSANCE REVIVAL STYLE A fashion, largely in furniture, influenced by the revival in France of 16th-century

forms and motifs; popular in America in the 1860's and 1870's

REPOUSSE Designs in metal raised on a surface by hammering from the back (3)

REREDOS An ornamental screen behind a church altar

RIBBON A striped motif used in many variations in pattern glass (98)

ROCOCO A style of art and decoration developed in the 18th century in France, characterized by designs curvilinear in form and imitative of shellwork, scrolls, and foliage asymmetrically arranged

ROCOCO REVIVAL STYLE A style popular in the middle decades of the 19th century, which freely interpreted French designs of the first half of the 18th century and was characterized by S- and C- curves, scrolls, and shell and floral carvings

ROMANESQUE REVIVAL STYLE A type of architecture inspired by the rounded arches and massive masonry of the Romanesque period; the greatest American exponent of the style was Henry Hobson Richardson who treated it with originality and imagination

ROYAL FLEMISH A type of art glass in which panels or segments, delineated by heavy raised enamel lines, are colored to look like stained glass (166)

ROYCROFTERS A name for those who practiced the crafts under the direction of Elbert Hubbard in East Aurora, N. Y.

RUSSIAN A glass pattern consisting of a spoked geometric shape surrounded by circles used in many variations (359)

SANDWICH GLASS Glass made at the Boston and Sandwich Glass Company. The term is sometimes erroneously used to refer to any American pressed glass, especially of the lacy variety.

SCARAB A stone or jewel carved to look like a beetle in imitation of ancient Egyptian charms (343)

SCROLLWORK Ornament with scrolls cut in wood with a jig saw

SECRETARY A desk, usually slant-topped, surmounted by a bookcase (65)

SERVING BOARD A type of sideboard

SETTEE A small sofa

SETTLE A long seat or bench with arms and high, solid-wood back (238)

SHADOW BOX A glass-covered case or frame for displaying and protecting a picture (423)

SHEFFIELD PLATE See PLATED WARE

SIDEBOARD A dining-room piece for storage and serving, consisting of a wide chest, generally with cupboard space beneath one or more drawers (373)

SILVER DEPOSIT An overlay of silver electrochemically deposited on glass, pottery, and other materials in ornamental, openwork designs (322)

STAINED GLASS Decorative arrangements of colored glass or of clear glass cased with color, with applied painted details, secured together by lead framing. Louis Comfort Tiffany substituted designs formed by the nature and the manipulation of the glass itself for such painted details (309).

STERLING A term applied to a standard of silverware indicating a proportion of 925 parts fine silver and 75 parts fine copper in each 1000 parts

STRETCHER A horizontal support bracing the legs of chairs, tables, stools, or connecting furniture legs to strengthen case pieces

STUDENT LAMP See HARVARD LAMP

TALL CASE CLOCK A clock incorporated within a tall, standing case to protect the works and accommodate the pendulum; also called long case clock and grandfather clock

TETE-A-TETE S-shaped love seat designed so that two people may sit face to face; also called a conversational

THONET FURNITURE See BENTWOOD FURNITURE

THUMBPRINT See ARGUS

TREE OF LIFE Popular name for a pressed-glass pattern consisting of vine-like tracerïes on a reticulated ground (195)

TREFOIL A stylized, three-lobed design, often used in Gothic and Gothic Revival patterns (15)

TRIVET A decorative stand with three short legs used on the hearth or table to support hot objects, such as a kettle, plate, or flatiron (449)

TULIP A pressed-glass pattern featuring a three-lobed motif resembling a flower (99)

TURKISH CORNER An informal alcove or corner of a room for lolling and smoking, heavily upholstered and furnished in a manner to evoke Near Eastern *décor*; also called a cozy corner

VENEER Thin layers of wood or other materials glued to a solid ground

WALL POCKET A Victorian device, consisting of a rack or flap attached to a wall, for holding small items (422)

WESTWARD HO A pressed-glass pattern, originally called Pioneer, decorated with scenes of life on the western frontier (100)

WHATNOT An open stand of shelves, sometimes with drawers underneath, for displaying bric-a-brac; also called an *étagère* (14)

WICKERWORK Furniture and other forms made of strong, pliant twigs of willow (213)

WINDSOR CHAIRS Chairs constructed with a solid wooden seat and turned, splayed legs. The variously shaped backs of Windsors are made of spindles joined to the back rail (254).

The illustrations on these and the following pages, arranged roughly chronologically, represent a broad cross section of the furniture and furnishings that were offered for sale over the years covered in this volume. To a large degree they summarize through advertising and similar promotional literature the progression of styles and the varieties of equipment that have been pictured and discussed in earlier pages. The precise dates and the original sources of these notices cannot always be determined, since in those instances they reproduce clippings long ago separated from the magazine or catalogue in which they were originally published. For the most part, however, the year and the place where they first appeared have been ascertained, and this information is recorded in the credits listed serially on page 405. (In some cases, the same illustration with the same copy was printed over and over again, even for several running years.) In every case, they provide visual evidence of how such varied objects were intended to appeal to the contemporary eye and purse. Where the prices are included, and can be read in this necessarily reduced scale, they tend to evoke a shock of nostalgia—as in the case of number 578 on the opposite page, for example, in which a suite of six chairs and a sofa (in a style currently popular among collectors) is offered for just twenty-four dollars. In some cases, these notices illustrate forms the likes of which have not survived. The convertible sofa and bathtub (600) may have been "the common sense invention of the age" when it was produced in 1886, but nothing of the kind remains to tempt the dealers and collectors of today.

566

569

567

570

568

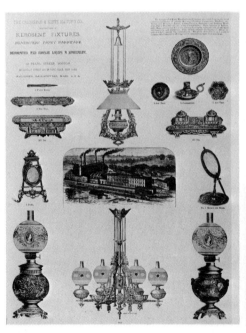

571

Advertisements: 1860's–1870's

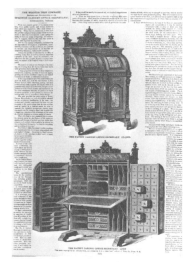

572

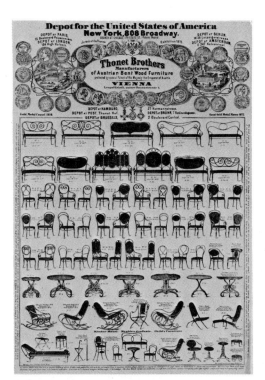

576

579

573

577

581

580

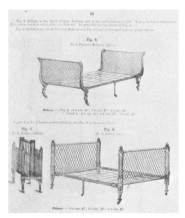

574

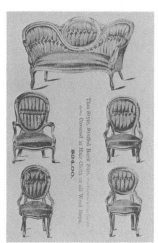

578

582

Universal Wood Worker.

PATENTED April 3, 1883.
THREE MORE PATENTS APPLIED FOR.

The simplest and best Router or Mortising Machine, Boring Machine, Straight Sticker or Variety Moulder, Engraving and Rosette Machine, Wagon Hub and Window Pulley Mortiser ever invented.

THE MOST USEFUL MACHINE
IN A
Furniture or Cabinet Makers' Shop in the World.

Don't fail to send for illustrated catalogue and full particulars. Every Machine warranted and sample work sent to any address in the United States, express on samples paid by me.

R. T. WHITE,
40 Oliver Street, BOSTON, Mass.

583

TELEPHONES SOLD.

Don't pay exorbitant rental fees to the Bell Telephone Monopoly to use their Telephones on lines less than two miles in length. A few months' rental buys a first-class Telephone that is no infringement, and works splendid on lines for private use on any kind of wire, and works good in stormy weather. It makes homes pleasant; annihilates time; prevents burglaries; saves many steps, and is just what every business man and farmer should have to connect stores, houses, depots, factories, colleges, etc., etc. The only practicable and reliable Telephone that is sold outright and warranted to work. Chance for agents. No previous experience required. Circulars free. WM. L. NORTON, Buffalo, N. Y.

584

THE PATENT EXPANSION LAMP SHADE

WITH WHITE'S IMPROVEMENTS,
MANUFACTURED BY
WOODSUM & CO., BOSTON, MASS.

585

DESIGNERS AND MANUFACTURERS OF

ARTISTIC FURNITURE

IN ROSEWOOD, MAHOGANY, AMARANTH AND EBONY
ALSO
Importers of Antique Oak and French Furniture.

DESIGNS AND ESTIMATES FURNISHED WHEN REQUIRED.

GEORGE W. SMITH & CO.,
1216 CHESTNUT ST., PHILADELPHIA.
FACTORY: POWELTON AVE., ABOVE THIRTY-NINTH ST.

We have on hand for the Holiday Trade an Unusually Large and Attractive Line of ARTISTIC GOODS.

586

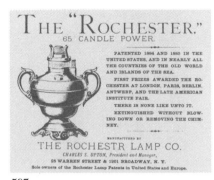

THE "ROCHESTER."
65 CANDLE POWER.

PATENTED 1884 AND 1885 IN THE UNITED STATES, AND IN NEARLY ALL THE COUNTRIES OF THE OLD WORLD AND ISLANDS OF THE SEA.

FIRST PRIZES AWARDED THE ROCHESTER AT LONDON, PARIS, BERLIN, ANTWERP, AND THE LATE AMERICAN INSTITUTE FAIR.

THERE IS NONE LIKE UNTO IT.

EXTINGUISHED WITHOUT BLOWING DOWN OR REMOVING THE CHIMNEY.

MANUFACTURED BY
THE ROCHESTR LAMP CO.
CHARLES S. UPTON, President and Manager.
25 WARREN STREET & 1901 BROADWAY, N. Y.
Sole owners of the Rochester Lamp Patents in United States and Europe.

587

ADJUSTABLE RECLINING AND READING CHAIR, MANUFACTURED BY THE
SARGENT MANUFACTURING CO., NEW YORK.

588

W. H. HARRISON & BRO
MANUFACTURERS OF

Plain & Artistic **GRATES**
AND **FIREPLACES**,
FURNACES & RANGES.
Agents for **LOW'S**
ART TILES.

Importers and Dealers in Tiles for Hearths, Facings, &c. Send for Illustrated Catalogue.
1435 CHESTNUT ST., Philadelphia

589

Brains vs Muscle!

BRAINS HAVE WON!

MUSCLE AT A DISCOUNT!

A Desperate Race for Life of over One Hundred Years. At last a Washer is made that women can use.

IT IS CALLED
"THE LITTLE JOKER."

MOTHERS, WIVES, DAUGHTERS,
and all the great army of Washers, take courage. There is a NEW washer made, and it will wash clean. It will wash QUICK. It will wash EASY. It is CHEAP, SIMPLE, DURABLE. TRY IT. A trial will convince the most skeptical.

590

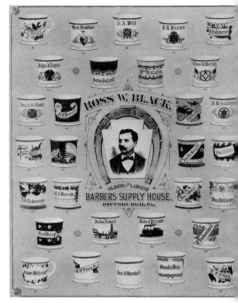

591

JONAS SMITH,
Willow and Rattan Furniture
MANUFACTURER,
CHAIRS, TABLES, SETTEES, ETC.,
No. 301 East Twenty-sixth Street
BETWEEN FIRST AND SECOND AVENUES,
NEW YORK.

592

CORNISH'S GREAT INSTALLMENT OFFER
$100 Organs Reduced to Only $65.00
Warranted for 6 YEARS. and sold for $35.00 Cash after 10 days' test trial, the balance of price $30.00 to be paid in Monthly Installments of $5.00 per month until all is paid.

STOOL, INSTRUCTION BOOK and delivery on board cars here F'R'E.

$65.00 ONLY
READ DESCRIPTION GIVEN BELOW.
STYLE "CRIMSON" No. 8,000.
5 Octaves, 14 Stops, Sub. Bass, 2 Octave Couplers
and 2 Knee Swells.
CONTAINS 8 SETS OF REEDS, VIZ.:

HOW TO ORDER.

REMEMBER

CORNISH & CO., NEW JERSEY, U.S.A.

593

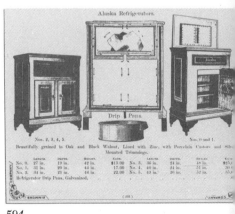

Alaska Refrigerators.

Drip Pans.

Nos. 2, 3, 4, 5.
Beautifully grained in Oak and Black Walnut, Lined with Zinc, with Porcelain Casters and Silver Mounted Trimmings.

Refrigerator Drip Pans, Galvanized.

594

Advertisements: 1880's

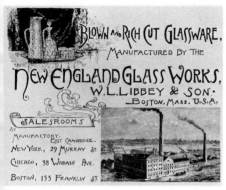

595

599

603

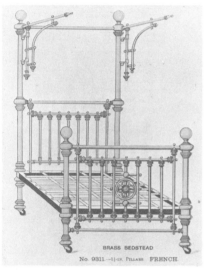

596

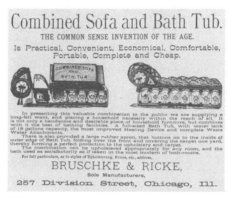

600

604

J. E. WALL,
Manufacturer of
BAMBOO FURNITURE

Bamboo Easels, Fire Screens, Folding Screens, Curtain Poles and other Novelties made from Japanese, Chinese and India Bamboo.

SEND FOR CATALOGUE.
73 CORNHILL, Boston, Mass.

597

601

605

A. H. ANDREWS & CO.

ANDREWS'
Improved Parlor
FOLDING BEDS,

8

602

606

Just Opened for the Summer Season of 1879.

W. S. HEDENBERG'S ICE CREAM GARDEN,
No. 639 Broad Street, Newark, N. J.

607

BE CAREFUL AND LOOK AT THE SIGN OF JORDAN & MORIARTY, 157 167, 167½, 169, 171, 172 CHATHAM STREET, or 207, 207½, 209, 211, 213 PARK ROW, BEFORE ENTERING.

WE MANUFACTURE THE BEST

PATENT LOUNGE

IN THE MARKET.

OPEN.

Covered in Plush, Rep, Raw Silk, Hair Cloth, etc.

CLOSED.

CALL AND EXAMINE OUR LATEST DESIGNS IN LOUNGES, TOO NUMEROUS TO MENTION IN THIS CATALOGUE.
One door from James Street.

608

Electric Light Radiator.
Made of Rich Cut Flint Glass.

J. HOARE & CO.,
CORNING, N. Y.

Manufacturers of

RICH CUT AND ENGRAVED

TABLE GLASSWARE

Of Every Description.

MANUFACTURED BY
J. HOARE & CO., Corning, N. Y.

609

BOSTON BRASS ANDIRON
AND POLISHING COMPANY.

Andirons, Fenders, Fire Setts and all kinds of House Brass Work Polished and Repaired.

11 Hawkins Street, BOSTON.
Orders by Mail or Express promptly attended to.

610

CHURCH STREET
BOARDING AND SALE
STABLES
19 & 21 CHURCH STREET,
Opposite Steamboat Landing
Rear Girard House,
ALBANY, N.Y.

Good accommodations for Shipping. Careful attention given to Horses consigned to our stables.

MATTHEW ELIFF,
Proprietor.

611

THE CELEBRATED PHILADELPHIA
Venetian Blinds,

Of all sizes, kinds and qualities, Upholstered in the best manner and furnished at short notice. In various shades of

GREEN, BROWN, DRAB, BLUE, STONE COLOR, LAVENDER, TAN COLOR, OLIVE, SAGE OR BOTTLE GREENS,

In Light, Medium, or Dark Tints, or made of Natural Woods, such as Black Walnut, Chestnut, Cherry, Spanish Cedar, Mahogany, Maple, Cypress, Ash or Poplar, in either Varnish or Oil Finish.

Made of Slats, 1¼, 1½, 1¾, 2 or 2½ inches wide, with Linen, Worsted or Silk Trimmings.

These Blinds will fit any window, without alteration to window frames, and are much better and cheaper for Bay Windows than inside shutters.

Used and recommended by the leading Architects of the country.

When estimates are desired, please give exact size of sash (or sash openings).
Illustrated Circular on application. Please mention this paper.

MANUFACTURED BY
EDWIN LOUDERBACK & CO.,
Nos. 413 & 415 South Fifth Street, Philadelphia, Pa., U. S. A.

612

STEPHEN A. MORSE.   CARLTON H. WILLIAMS.   EDWIN F. MORSE.

Clem & Morse,
MANUFACTURERS AND BUILDERS OF
Patent Hydraulic, Steam, Belt and Hand-Power
Passenger & Freight
ELEVATORS
WITH MOST APPROVED
SAFETY DEVICES

MAIN OFFICE & WORKS
411 & 413 CHERRY ST.
PHILADELPHIA.

BRANCH OFFICE, 108 LIBERTY STREET, NEW YORK.

613

English Hall Clocks
OF DIFFERENT STYLES,
With Very Fine Mahogany and Oak Cases inlaid in Brass.

The Movements are English, and imported by WALTER H. DURFEE, and are the Finest English make, with Dead Beat Escapement, Maintaining Power and Cathedral

FURTHER PARTICULARS GIVEN BY
WALTER H. DURFEE,
Manufacturer and Dealer,
295 HIGH ST., PROVIDENCE, R.I.

614

J. & R. LA[MB]
59 CARMINE ST.,

Sixth Avenue Cars pass th[e]

ARTISTIC
Stained Gl[ass]

NEW DESIGNS IN PROGRESS

MEMORIAL WIN[DOWS]

Door Lights, Window
Screens, &c.

FIRE SCREENS, &[c.]

Send for Hand-Book by

615

New American
AUTOMATIC STEAM HEATER.
NO GAS NO DUST   LOWEST PRICES
LEAST COST IN FUEL
LEAST ATTENTION
SELF FEEDING
GREATEST SATISFACTION

NEWELL UNIVERSAL MILL

616

398

617

620

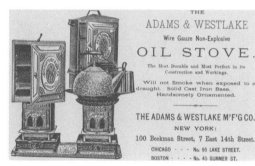

621

624

CHAS. WILLIAMS' SONS,

Manufacturers of

Heaters, Ranges, Grates, Slate
Wood and Marble
Mantels.

IMPORTED & DOMESTIC TILES.

Iron and Slate Work of all
descriptions.

Iron and Soap-Stone Backs and Jambs.

☞ GOODS NOT TO BE USED AS
PATTERNS. ☜

No. 906 FILBERT ST.

Factory, Nos. 402, 404, 406 & 408
Twelfth Street.

PHILADELPHIA.

...articular attention to our New and Improved Portable
...with Boiler and Attachments combined with Warming
all complete, doing away with all brickwork.

18

625

Holmes & Coutts
FAMOUS
SEA FOAM
WAFERS
NEW YORK

19

623

626

630

633

627

631

No. 656 (Clock)

Golden Oak

634

Bishop Furnitur

BISHOP FURNITURE COMPAN

635

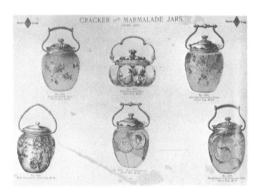

628

629

632

636

400

Advertisements: 1890–1917

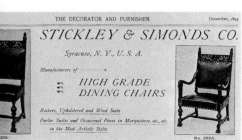

637

640

643

638

641

644   645

639

642

646

Acknowledgments

The editors wish to express their deep gratitude to the institutions and individuals mentioned below for their generous help in providing pictorial material from the collections in their custody and for supplying information and advice.

Antiques Magazine
  Ruth B. Davidson
  Edith Gaines
  Eileen Birk

Sheldon Barr

Brooklyn Museum
  J. Stewart Johnson
  Robert Hendrick
  Tina Ucciferri

Joseph T. Butler

Cincinnati Art Museum
  Carol Macht

Cooper-Hewitt Museum of Design, Smithsonian Institution
    Christian Rohlfing
    Catherine Lynn Frangiamore

Corning Museum of Glass
  Paul N. Perrot
  Kenneth M. Wilson
  Jane S. Shadel

Mr. and Mrs. Benjamin Ginsburg

Gorham Silver Company
  J. Russell Price
  Kathy Hynes

Grand Rapids Public Museum
  W. D. Frankforter
  Dorothy Jaqua

Henry Ford Museum and Greenfield Village
  Donald A. Shelley
  George O. Bird
  Katharine Hagler
  Walter E. Simmons, II
  Carlton Brown
  Charles Miller

International Silver Company
  E. P. Hogan

Samuel Kirk & Son
  Emanuel Levine

Lockwood-Mathews Mansion Museum
  Mimi Adams

Lyndhurst, National Trust for Historic Preservation
  John N. Pearce
  Gerald L. Fiedler
  Adelaide Smith

Metropolitan Museum of Art
  Berry B. Tracy
  Mary C. Glaze
  Janet S. Byrne
  Margaret Nolan
  Lynn Johnson
  Jay Cantor
  Dianne Hauserman

Museum of the City of New York
  Ralph Miller
  Margaret Stearns
  Sam Pearce
  A. K. Baragwanath
  Edna K. Spiess

Lillian Nassau, Ltd.

Newark Public Library
  William J. Dane

Newark Museum
  Tom Kyle
  Helen G. Olsson

New-York Historical Society
  James J. Heslin
  Martin Leifer
  William DuPrey
  Caroline Scoon

New York Public Library
  Elizabeth Roth

Old Print Shop
  Kenneth M. Newman, Jr.
  Robert Harley

Philadelphia Museum of Art
  Calvin Hathaway
  Alfred J. Wyatt

Rhode Island School of Design, Museum of Art
  Mrs. Kenneth Colt

Sagamore Hill National Historic Site
  Jessica E. Kraft

Seamen's Bank for Savings
  George Wintress

Shelburne Museum
  Bradley Smith
  Einars J. Mengis

Smithsonian Institution
  Rodris Roth
  Richard E. Ahlborn

Theodore Roosevelt Birthplace
  Helen MacLachlan

Toledo Museum of Art
  John Keefe
  Helen Popp

Picture Credits

The following individuals and studios have supplied special photography for this book: Adams Studio, Victor Amato, Armen Photographers, Edmund Barrett, Richard Benson, Jay Cantor, Chicago Architectural Photographing Company, Geoffrey Clements, Henri Dauman, Alan Fontaine, Wolfgang Hartmann, Helga Photo Studio, Harry Hess, Herbert Loebel, Einars J. Mengis, Charles Miller, Robert Rapelye, Robinson Studio, Thurman Rotan, Sleepy Hollow Studios, John Swanberg, Taylor & Dull, Inc., Vincent Photographers

The drawings on pages 385 to 401 were executed by Joseph Papin.

Front jacket: Renaissance Revival armchair, figure 68. HFM—Lamp by Tiffany Studios, figure 312. Courtesy of Lillian Nassau, Ltd.—Silver teapot. ISC—Elaborately carved and inlaid cabinet, figure 2. LM

Back jacket: Interior view of Olana, figure 32b. Photograph courtesy of Henri Dauman

Endsheets: Printed wallpaper, simulating stamped leather; American, about 1880. CHM

Front matter. Half-title page: Pediment from a desk attributed to L. Marcotte and Company. Theodore Roosevelt Birthplace. Title page: Still life with Art Nouveau objects. Courtesy of Lillian Nassau, Ltd. Table of contents page: Architect's drawing of a lamppost for Central Park. MCNY. Preface: Paperweight, made in America. NYHS. Index: Paperweight, made in America. Photograph courtesy *Antiques Magazine*

The location of each of the objects illustrated in this volume is listed below. Unnumbered illustrations are described after the page number; numbered illustrations follow the figure number. Both page and figure numbers are in boldface type. Where two or more illustrations appear on one page, the references are separated by dashes. To simplify the listings the following abbreviations are used:

AAS: American Antiquarian Society
BM: Brooklyn Museum
CHM: Cooper-Hewitt Museum of Design, Smithsonian Institution
CMG: Corning Museum of Glass
GRPM: Grand Rapids Public Museum
GSC: Gorham Silver Company
HFM: Henry Ford Museum and Greenfield Village
ISC: International Silver Company
LC: Library of Congress
LM: Lockwood-Mathews Mansion Museum
MCNY: Museum of the City of New York
MFA: Museum of Fine Arts, Boston
MMA: Metropolitan Museum of Art

NM: Newark Museum
NYHS: New-York Historical Society
NYPL: New York Public Library
PM: Philadelphia Museum of Art
SI: Smithsonian Institution
SM: Shelburne Museum

An Abundance of Styles
The Post-Bellum Years (1865-1876)

UNNUMBERED ILLUSTRATIONS LISTED BY PAGE:

8, 9 Painting of *The Hatch Family*. MMA, Gift of Frederick H. Hatch, 1926 10 Lithograph of grain elevators from *Chicago Illustrated*, 1866. LC—Ruins of Catholic cathedral, Charleston. The National Archives 11 Poster. The Union Pacific Railroad 12 Engraving of steam-powered threshing from *La Illustracion Española y Americana*. LC—Broadside, 1865. NYHS 13 Cover from the "Petroleum Galop" by Oily Gammon, Esq. AAS 14, 15 Advertisements from *Kimball's Book of Designs* by J. Wayland Kimball, Boston, 1876. MMA 16 Photograph of Armsmear, about 1885. Connecticut Historical Society 17 Engraving from *The Art Journal*, 1867. NYPL 52 Curtain tieback said to have been made by L. Marcotte. Theodore Roosevelt Birthplace—Label. SI—Detail of cabinet, figure 54. MMA, Rogers Fund, 1964 53 Detail of table, figure 23. MCNY

FIGURE NUMBERS:

1, a, b, 2, a, b LM 3-5 Furber Collection, GSC 6 Collection of Mrs. Vincent Astor 7 Courtesy of R. Esmerian Inc. 8 MCNY 9 SM 10 Sagamore Hill National Historic Site, National Park Service, U.S. Department of Interior 11 LM 12 HFM 13 From *Harper's Weekly*, January 1, 1876, page 14 14, 15 HFM 16 Lyndhurst 17 MMA, Harris Brisbane Dick Fund, 1924 18 Lyndhurst 19 BM 20 LM 21 MMA, Gift of Mrs. D. Chester Noyes, 1968 22-26 MCNY 27, a, b Lyndhurst 28 PM 29 Lyndhurst 30 MMA 31 Lyndhurst 32a Courtesy of Bankers Trust Company 32b Photograph courtesy of Henri Dauman 33a, b MMA, Gift of a friend of the Museum, 1897 34, 35 GSC 36 Samuel Kirk & Son 37, 37a MCNY 38 GSC 39, 40 ISC 41 SI 42, 43 ISC 44 HFM 45 ISC 46 NM 47 BM, Gift of Dr. Dorothea Curnow 48 From Plate 41, *Treasures of Art, Industry and Manufacture Represented in the American Centennial Exhibition at Philadelphia, 1876*, edited by C. B. Norton, 1877. MMA 49-51 Theodore Roosevelt Birthplace 52, 53 GRPM 54 MMA, Rogers Fund, 1964 55, 55a Lyndhurst 56 NYHS 57 Theodore Roosevelt Birthplace 58, 59 GRPM 60-64 HFM 65 GRPM 66 NYPL

67 GRPM 68 HFM 69 GRPM 70, 71 NM 72 HFM 73 Sagamore Hill 74, 75 HFM 76 GRPM 77, 78 HFM 79-82 MCNY 83 Lyndhurst 84 Collection of Marshall B. Davidson 85 HFM 86 From *A New Phase in the Iron Manufacture*, 1857. MMA 87 HFM 88 Rensselaer County Historical Society (photograph, *Antiques Magazine*) 89 From *AIA Guide to New York City*, by the New York Chapter, American Institute of Architects, 1967, page 83 90 Lyndhurst 91-93 CMG 94 HFM 95-97 CMG 98, 99 HFM 100, 101 CMG 102-108 NYHS, Bequest of Mrs. F. MacDonald Sinclair 109 NYHS 110 From *The Century*, April, 1886 111-113 NYHS 114 MCNY, Byron Collection 115 NYHS 116 MCNY 117 SM 118 LC 119 SI 120 CHM 121 GRPM 122 SI 123 ISC 124 From Plate 1, *Treasures . . . in the Centennial*. MMA

Matters of Taste and Sincerity
Styles Between Fairs (1876–1893)

UNNUMBERED ILLUSTRATIONS LISTED BY PAGE:

100, 101 Chromolithograph of the Pearl Room in the William H. Vanderbilt house. MMA, Print Department 102 Chromolithograph of the Corliss Engine from *Treasures . . . in the Centennial*. MMA—Morris chair. Victoria and Albert Museum 103 Cabinet designed by William Morris and painted by Burne-Jones, 1861. MMA, Rogers Fund, 1926—Drawing of table by H. W. Brewer. From *Hints on Household Taste* by Charles L. Eastlake, London, 1868 104 Engraving of a Drawing room from *Gothic Forms Applied to Furniture* by B. J. Talbert, 1867. CHM 105 Engraving of Japanese workmen. From *Frank Leslie's Illustrated Weekly Newspaper*, 1876 106 Design of flower stand by A. Jonquet. CHM 107 Engraving of Artistic Craze. From *Punch* 108 Design for a hall from *Modern Dwellings in Town and Country* by Henry Hudson Holly, 1878 109 Photograph of the Columbian Exposition at night. From *The White City*, Chicago, 1893. MMA 134 From an advertisement of Fr. Beck & Company, *The Decorator and Furnisher*, February, 1886—Lithograph of "Rustic Terra-Cotta Pedestal and Jardiniere." *The Decorator and Furnisher*, July, 1886 135 Engraving of "The Artistic Young Lady," from *Harper's Magazine*, October, 1882—Illustration from an article, "Fashionable Table Ware," *The Decorator and Furnisher*, September, 1886, page 172 182 Photograph of H. H. Richardson by George Collins Cox. History of Photography Collection, SI 183 Design for Trinity Church, Boston, by H. H. Richardson. From *Henry Hobson Richardson and His Works* by Marianna Griswold Van Rensselaer, Houghton, Mifflin & Co., Boston, 1888—Sketch of W. Watts

403

About the Turn of the Century
Styles of a New Order (1893–1917)

UNNUMBERED ILLUSTRATIONS LISTED BY PAGE:

About the House
Inside & Out

UNNUMBERED ILLUSTRATIONS LISTED BY PAGE:

Popular Patterns

Some Vanishing Americana

Contemporary Notices & Advertisements

Index

The figures in parentheses refer to the numbered illustrations and in each case precede the number of the page on which the illustration appears. Matter appearing in the glossary and notices and advertisements is not indexed.

BEECHER, CATHARINE E., 161, 280; quoted, 308

BEECHER, LYMAN, 308

BELL, ALEXANDER GRAHAM, 101

BENCHES, Art Nouveau, (357) 263; by H. H. Richardson, (238) 184, 185, (241) 186; Jacobean, (247) 202

BENNETT, ARNOLD, quoted, 101

BENTWOOD FURNITURE, 166–67

BERKEY & GAY FURNITURE COMPANY, 52; furniture by, 62–63, 65, 69

BERKSHIRE SILVER PATTERN, (193 a) 154

BESSEMER PROCESS, 10

BIERSTADT, ALBERT, 161; chromolithograph after painting by, 161, (204) 162–63

BING, SAMUEL, 226, 235, 257, 258; quoted, 240, 244

BIRDCAGE, rococo revival, (9) 28

BIRDS OF AMERICA, 161

BISHOP FURNITURE COMPANY, 208, 272

BLOCKS, toy, (515) 360

BOK, EDWARD WILLIAM, 224, 310, 313, 314; quoted, 309

BOLLES, ALBERT S., quoted, 355, 357

BONAPARTE, ELIZABETH PATTERSON, 203

BONAPARTE, JEROME, 203

BONAPARTE, NAPOLEON, 30, 203

BONNARD, PIERRE, 200, 226

BOOK COVER, (233) 179

BOOKRACK, Eastlake, 122, (147) 123

BOSTON, MASS., 16, 193, 207

BOSTON AND SANDWICH GLASS COMPANY, paperweights by, 87

BOSTWICK, JABEZ A., 52

BOUGHTON, GEORGE H., painting by, (260) 206, 207

BOURGET, CHARLES JOSEPH PAUL, quoted, 195, 196, 210

BOWLS, blown-glass, (163) 136, 138, (167) 139, 140, (170, 171) 141, (173) 143; gold, (336) 252; lotus ware, (178) 146, 147; pressed-glass, (93) 80, 84, (101) 85, (195) 156; silver-plated, (190) 152, 153. See also Punch Bowls

BOXWOOD, 18, 262

BRADLEY, WILL H., 200, 261; advertisement by, 229; furniture designs by, 224–25; model house designs by, 278, 279, 310–11; posters by, 200, 226, 227, 229, 230, 231

BRASS, on clocks, 180, 282; on furniture, 113; on weather vanes, 372

BRAZILWOOD, 18

BREAKERS, THE, interior (265) 210

BREVOORT HOUSE, 9

BREWSTER, ELDER WILLIAM, 336

BREWSTER, HENRY, 336

BREWSTER, JAMES, 336

BREWSTER, WILLIAM, 336

BREWSTER & COMPANY, carriages by, 336–37

BRIDGEPORT, CONN., 312

"BRILLIANT PERIOD," cut glass, 264, 267

BRONZE, on furniture, 261; and glass objects, 239, 241–44, 290; on lamps, 32, 130, 239, 292; objects, 235

BROOCHES, gold, (7) 26, 27; gold and enamel, (344) 255; jewels and enamel, (342) 255; silver, (328) 248, 249

BROOKLYN BRIDGE, 350

BROOKS, THOMAS V., 345

BROOKS HOUSEHOLD ART COMPANY, THE, furniture by, 212

BROWER, JOHN E., furniture designed by, 276–77

BROWN, FORD MADOX, 102

BRYCE, JAMES, quoted, 195

BUFFALO HUNT, statuette, (123) 98

BULL DURHAM, 11

"BUNGAL-ODE," 314

BUNGALOWS, 281, (429) 314

BUREAUS. See BEDROOM SUITES

BURGES, WILLIAM, quoted, 105

BURLEIGH, SYDNEY R., furniture by, 214–15

BURMESE ART GLASS, 136, 140, 143

BURNE-JONES, SIR EDWARD, 102; painted panel by, 103

BURNHAM, DANIEL, quoted, 197

C

CAB, carriage, (473) 337

CABINET MAKING AND UPHOLSTERY, quoted, 203

CABINET ORGAN. See ORGAN

CABINETS, Arts and Crafts, (272) 214; eclectic, (2, a, b) 20, (8) 27; Gothic, 102, (illus.) 103; Louis XVI Revival, (21) 35; Moorish, (231) 178; Renaissance Revival, 38, (28) 39, 54, (48) 55, (54) 58–59

CALECHE, carriage, (471) 336

CALIFORNIA, 10

CAMBRIDGE, MASS., 313

CANADIAN PACIFIC RAILWAY, 258

CANDLEHOLDERS, French silver and Favrile glass, 246, (323) 247; silver, (3) 22; Tiffany bronze and glass, (318–19) 244

CANDLESTICKS, pattern-molded art glass, (168) 140, 143; Tiffany bronze and Favrile glass, (396) 290, 291

CANISTERS, (446) 324

CANNED FOODS, 280, 281

CAN OPENERS, 280, 281

CANTERBURY, Renaissance Revival, (60) 64

CAPITOL, THE, 77

CAPRICE IN PURPLE AND GOLD, NO. 2: THE GOLDEN SCREEN, painting by Whistler, (151) 126–27

"CAPTAIN JINKS OF THE HORSE MARINES," 342

CARD RECEIVERS, electroplated, (201) 159; silver-plated and glass, (197) 156–57

CARDS. See GREETING CARDS

CARLYLE, THOMAS, 11

CARNEGIE, ANDREW, quoted, 13

CARPENTER GOTHIC, 32

CARPETS, Axminster, (416) 303; machine-made, 302

CARRIAGES, 334–337

CARRIAGE STEPS, (469) 335

CARRINGTON, DE ZOUCHE & COMPANY, upholstered furnishings by, (160) 132, 133

CARROUSELS, mounts and ornaments, 380, 381, 382, 383

CARSON HOUSE, (425) 312, 315

CARTER, WILLIAM T., furniture of, 118, 119

CARTIER, INC., 339

CARVING, on furniture, 20–21, 34, 35, 38–39, 54, 58, 60, 61, 258, 268, 273, 299; incised, 124; of interiors, 18–19; by machine, 64, 67, 68, 70, 73

CASTERS, (42) 50, (45) 51, (196) 156

CASTER STAND, silver-plated, (196) 156

CAST-IRON, architecture, 77, 79; furniture—advertisement for, (86) 77; garden bench, (85) 77; stool, (88) 79; objects—birdhouse, (526) 366; carriage steps, (469) 335; doorstop, (83) 76; hitching post, (466) 334; matchsafe, (84) 76; radiator covers, (90) 79, (406) 296; toy banks, (525) 366, (527–29) 367

CEDAR OF LEBANON, 18

CENTENNIAL INTERNATIONAL EXHIBITION, 1876, 17, 92–99, 101–3; and colonial revival, 108, 203, 313; as motif, 94–95, 302, 303; commemorative objects at, (116–17) 92, 93, (119–21) 96; exhibits at—art glass, 144; carpets, 302, 303; ceramics, 147; chandelier, 290; Corliss steam engine, 92, 101, (illus.) 102; furniture, 52, 53, 54, 55, 62, 66, 97, 132, 133; Japanese, 105, 106; tea-

house and bazaar, (152) 127, 130, 131; jig-sawing, 369; New England Kitchen, 203; silver and plated ware, 45, 98, 99, 150; telephone, 101; tiles, 123; Turkish Bazaar and Café, 175; watches, 101, 284—*passim*, 106, 129, 154, 179, 281

CENTERPIECES, Martelé silver, (334) 251, 250; silver-plated, (41) 49

CENTRAL HEATING, 280, 281, 296, 297, 298; design for system, (404) 296

CENTRAL PARK, N.Y., design for Ladies Pavilion in, 74, (80) 75; drawing for flower garden in, (82) 75; lithograph of outing in, (467) 334; statue in, 207

CENTURY, THE, 88

CENTURY COMPANY, THE, 229

CENTURY VASE, 98, (124) 99

CERAMICS, 144–49, 235. See also specific forms, types, and makers

CHAIRS, ARM-, Colonial Revival, (253, 254, 256) 205, advertisement for, (263) 209; Gothic Revival, 32, (18) 33; horn, (289) 222; Hunzinger, G., (31) 41, advertisement for, (30) 41; inlaid, (125) 110, (126) 110, 111, (365) 269; Louis XV Revival, 212, (271) 213, *bergère*, (268) 212; Louis XVI Revival, (267) 211; Mission, 216, (280) 217; Morris, (illus.) 102; rattan, advertisement for, (214) 169; Renaissance Revival, (19) 34, 35, (47) 54, (64) 67, (68) 70, (71–75) 71, advertisement for, 15; Richardson, H. H., (237) 184, (240) 185, (242) 186, (243) 187; rococo revival, (11) 29; upholstered, (162) 133, (227, 228) 176, (290) 223; Washington elm, (122) 97

CHAIRS, ROCKING, bentwood, (208) 166, (210) 167; Colonial Revival, (257) 205, (261) 208; Eastlake platform, (137) 117; Grand Rapids, advertisement for, (371) 273; upholstered, (370) 272, 273; wicker, 168, (213) 169

CHAIRS, SIDE, Art Nouveau, (351) 259, 262, (356) 263; Arts and Crafts, (274) 214; balloon-back, (12) 30; bamboo, (220) 172; bentwood, (209, 211) 167; Colonial Revival, (251, 252) 204, advertisement for, (255) 205; Hunzinger, G., (29) 40, (30) 41; imitation bamboo, design for, (223) 172, 173; inlaid, (128, 129, 130) 112, (133) 114; Louis XV Revival, 212, (271) 213, (375) 274; Louis

E

EARRINGS, gold, (7) 26, 27; jewels and enamel, (340) 254
EASEL, Neo-Gothic, (148) 124
EAST AURORA, N.Y., 219
EASTLAKE, CHARLES LOCKE, 104–5, 116, 119, 121, 123, 124
EASTLAKE STYLE, 15, 105, 106, 107, 116–25, 167, 317. See also specific forms
EAST LIVERPOOL, OHIO, Lotus ware made in, 147
EBONIZED WOOD, 35, 110, 116, 119
EBONY, 18
ECHO, magazine, poster of cover from, (301) 231
ECLECTICISM, 14, 27, 29, 30, 35, 38, 41, 42
ECOLE DES BEAUX ARTS, Paris, 53, 109, 183, 189
EDISON, THOMAS ALVA, 293, 318, 319; talking doll by, 362, 363
EGG-AND-DART MOLDING, 28
EGYPT, furniture from, 113
EGYPTIAN REVIVAL STYLE, 38
ELECTRICITY, 109, 189, 239, 280, 281, 291, 293, 294
ELECTRICITY BUILDING. See WORLD'S COLUMBIAN EXPOSITION
ELECTROPLATING, 49, 50, 158
ELEVATORS, (illus.) 280
ELIZABETHAN REVIVAL STYLE, 15. See also specific forms
ELLIN, ROBERT, & COMPANY, 53
ELLIS, JOEL, doll by, 363
EMBOSSED SILVER PATTERN, 154, (193 q) 155
EMBROIDERY, on crazy quilt, 321; on fire screen, 298, 299; on motto, 307; on theater drop curtain, 235, 294
EMERSON, RALPH WALDO, 315
EMPIRE STYLE, 30
ENAMEL, on art glass, 139; on jewelry, 254–55; objects, 235, 242; on silver, 246, 247
ENGLAND, 119; "arts and crafts" movement in, 197–98, 215, 216, 257; design influences from, 102–6, 116–25, 129; furniture imported from, 15; and the Industrial Revolution, 102
ENGLISH DESIGN, influence on American decorative arts, 103, 104; and Japanese influence on, 106; and morality, 102, 103, 104
ESSAY ON BROOM-CORN, 258
ETAGERES, eclectic, 30, (41) 31; Japanese style, 128, (156) 129

ETRUSCAN MAJOLICA, 147
ETRUSCAN SILVER PATTERN, 154, (193 k) 155
EUGENIE, EMPRESS, 36
EUREKA, CALIF., 312
EUROPEAN CRAFTSMEN, in America, 52–53, 70
EWERS, porcelain, 144, (175) 145; silver, (191) 152, 153
EXHIBITIONS. See specific titles
EXPORTS, American, 10, 11, 17
EXPOSITIONS. See specific titles
EXPRESSIONISM, 201

F

FACTORIES. See INDUSTRY
FAÏENCE MANUFACTURING COMPANY, porcelain by, 144, 147
FAIRMOUNT PARK, Philadelphia, 92
FAUVISM, 201
FEDERAL TRADE COMMISSION, 271
FEMALE FIGURE MOTIF, on silver, 248, 249, 250, 251, 262
FERRARI, GIUSEPPE, furniture by, 54, 55, 62
FIFTH AVENUE, N.Y., 52, 53, 107, 111
FINCH, RALPH E., (513) 359
FIRE COMPANIES, 371, 372; "Big Six," 370; Citizens Hose Company, 370; Niagara Hose Company, 373; Tiger Hose Company, 370
FIREMEN'S EQUIPMENT, 370–73; axe, 372, (541) 373; belt, (542) 373; bucket, (539) 372; engines, 371, 372; hat, 370, (538) 371; trumpet, (536) 370, 371
FIREPLACES, 297, 298, 301
FIRE SCREEN, (409) 298
FLATIRONS. See IRONS
FLATWARE, cake slicer, 252, (337) 253; serving fork, 252, (338) 253; spoons, (193 a–z) 154–55, (273) 214
FLEUR-DE-LIS MOTIF, 35
FLOOD, JAMES L., 52
FLOWER STAND. See PLANT STAND
FLUTING IRON. See IRONS
FORKS. See FLATWARE
FORT SUMTER, S.C., 10
"FRA HUBBARD." See HUBBARD, ELBERT
FRANCE, furniture exhibited in, (illus.) 17; furniture exported to, 17; furniture imported from, 15; influences of architecture of, in America, 16; influences of styles of, on

American furniture, 15, 21, 30, 35, 36, 52–53, 57, 59, 60, 210–13
FRANKLIN, BENJAMIN, 17, 342
FRENCH, DANIEL CHESTER, 207
FRENCH FLATS. See APARTMENT HOUSES
FRENCH STYLES, 34–37, 210–13
FRESHEL, MRS. CURTIS, designs by, 260, 261
FRIENDLY ISLAND, N.Y., 312
FRUIT BOWLS. See BOWLS
FUNCTIONALISM, 104
FURBER, HENRY JEWETT, 22, 23

G

GALLAND, PIERRE V., 53
GALLE, EMILE, 237
GAMES, 360, 361
GARDEN FURNITURE, cast-iron bench, (85) 77; iron-and-wire chair, (87) 78
GARLAND, HAMLIN, quoted, 189
GAS, uses of, 280, 291, 293, 326. See also Lamps and Streetlamps
GAUTIER, THEOPHILE, 183
GEMS, 235, 246, 254. See also Jewelry
GERMANTOWN, PA., 380
GIBSON, CHARLES DANA, 201
GIBSON GIRL, (illus.) 200, 201
GILBERT AND SULLIVAN, 106, 130
GILDED AGE, 111
GILLINDER & SONS, glass by, 84
GILT AND GILDING, on circus wagons and carrousels, 383; on furniture, 20, 21, 54, 58, 59, 62, 112, 171, 172, 178, 212; of interiors, 18
GINGERBREAD STYLE. See CARPENTER GOTHIC
GLASGOW, SCOTLAND, furniture design in, 257
GLASGOW SCHOOL. See ART NOUVEAU STYLE
GLASS, art, 136–43; cut, 264–67, 292; Favrile—jewelry of, 254–55; manufacture of, 235, 237, 240, 244; objects of, 235–45, 246, 247, 290—frosted, 32, 83, 84; mosaics of, 235, 237; painted, 139, 287, 288, 341, 346; paperweights, 6, 86–87; pressed and patterned, 80–85, 156, 157; stained, 193, 200, 201, 234, 235, 237, 239
GOBLET, pressed-glass, (96) 82
GODEY'S LADY'S BOOK AND MAGAZINE, quoted, 98, 102, 196; sewing machine from, 322

GODKIN, EDWIN LAWRENCE, 13
GODWIN, EDWARD W., 129
GOING TO CHURCH, chromolithograph, (203) 161
GOLD, discovery of, 22; jewelry, 26, 27
"GOLDEN DOOR." See WORLD'S COLUMBIAN EXPOSITION
GOLDEN OAK, 268–73
GOOD HOUSEKEEPING MAGAZINE, quoted, 314
GORHAM MANUFACTURING COMPANY, THE, furniture by, 262, 263; jewelry by, 248, 249; Martelé ware by, 250–51; silver by, 22–23, 44, 45, 46, 47, 98, 158–59; silver-deposit on glass and ceramics by, 247, 249
GOTHIC FORMS APPLIED TO FURNITURE, engraving from, 104
GOTHIC REVIVAL STYLE, 15, 32, 185, 299. See also Carpenter Gothic, Neo-Gothic
GOTHIC STYLE, MODERN ENGLISH. See NEO-GOTHIC STYLE
GOULD, JAY, 38
GOULD & COMPANY, advertisement of, (66) 69
GRAIN ELEVATORS, (illus.) 10
GRAND RAPIDS, MICH., 52, 199, 219; furniture made in, 59, 62, 64–73, 208, 268–77
GRAND RAPIDS FURNITURE RECORD, advertisement from, 205
GRAND RAPIDS WHOLESALE COMPANY, 274
GRANT, ULYSSES S., 92, 332, 336
GRANT ADMINISTRATION, 17, 27
GRECIAN CROSS LEGS. See CURULE LEGS
GREEK KEY MOTIF, 35
GREENOUGH, HORATIO, quoted, 315
GREENPOINT, N.Y., ceramics made in, 144, 147
GREENWOOD POTTERY COMPANY, porcelain by, 144
GREETING CARDS, 165; Christmas, advertisement for, (205) 164, 165; (illus.) 341, (549) 376, (550, 551) 377; Valentine, (548) 376, (552–55) 377
GRIFFEN, SMITH & HILL, majolica by, 146, 147

H

HAIRBRUSH, Art Nouveau silver, 252, (339) 253
HALE, EDWARD EVERETT, 165
HALL OF MANUFACTURES AND

409